OS/2 2.0 Control Program Programming Guide

> **Note**
>
> Before using this information and the product it supports, be sure to read the general information under "Notices" on page xvii.

First Edition (March 1992)

The following paragraph does not apply to the United Kingdom or any country where such provisions are inconsistent with local law: INTERNATIONAL BUSINESS MACHINES CORPORATION PROVIDES THIS PUBLICATION "AS IS" WITHOUT WARRANTY OF ANY KIND, EITHER EXPRESS OR IMPLIED, INCLUDING, BUT NOT LIMITED TO, THE IMPLIED WARRANTIES OF MERCHANTABILITY OR FITNESS FOR A PARTICULAR PURPOSE. Some states do not allow disclaimer of express or implied warranties in certain transactions; therefore, this statement may not apply to you.

This publication could include technical inaccuracies or typographical errors. Changes are made periodically to the information herein; these changes will be incorporated in new editions of the publication. IBM may make improvements and/or changes in the product(s) and/or the program(s) described in this publication at any time. It is possible that this publication may contain reference to, or information about, IBM products (machines and programs), programming, or services that are not announced in your country. Such references or information must not be construed to mean that IBM intends to announce such IBM products, programming, or services in your country.

Requests for copies of this publication and for technical information about IBM products should be made to your IBM Authorized Dealer or your IBM Marketing Representative.

Library of Congress Catalog Card Number: 92-62419
ISBN: 1-56529-154-9
95 94 93 92   8 7 6 5 4 3 2 1

Interpretation of the printing code: the rightmost double-digit number is the *year* of the book's printing; the rightmost single-digit number is the *number* of the book's printing. For example, a printing code of 92-1 shows that the first printing of the book occurred in 1992.

Contents

Control Program Programming Guide

Figures

Tables

Notices

References in this publication to IBM products, programs, or services do not imply that IBM intends to make these available in all countries in which IBM operates. Any reference to an IBM product, program, or service is not intended to state or imply that only IBM's product, program, or service may be used. Any functionally equivalent product, program, or service that does not infringe on any of IBM's intellectual property rights or other legally protectable rights may be used instead of the IBM product, program, or service. Evaluation and verification of operation in conjunction with other products, programs, or services, except those expressly designated by IBM, are the user's responsibility.

IBM may have patents or pending patent applications covering subject matter in this document. The furnishing of this document does not give you any license to these patents. You can send license inquiries, in writing, to the IBM Director of Commercial Relations, IBM Corporation, Purchase, NY 10577.

Trademarks and Service Marks

The following terms, denoted by an asterisk (*) in this publication, are trademarks of the IBM Corporation in the United States and/or other countries:

IBM	Presentation Manager
Operating System/2	OS/2
Systems Application Architecture	SAA
Personal System/2	PS/2

Double-Byte Character Set (DBCS)

Throughout this publication, you will see reference to specific values for character strings. The values are for single-byte character set (SBCS). If you use the double-byte character set (DBCS), note that one DBCS character equals two SBCS characters.

About This Book

The three volumes of the *OS/2 2.0 Programming Guide* provide information and code examples to enable you to start writing source code, using the functions in the application programming interface (API) of the OS/2* 2.0 operating system (OS/2). Each volume covers a different facet of the operating system, as follows:

Programming Guide: Volume I—Control Program Programming Interface (this book)
> Introduces you to the Control Program Programming Interface which describes the functionality provided by the base operating system.

Programming Guide: Volume II—Presentation Manager Window Programming Interface
> Describes the Presentation Manager* (PM) window programming interface. This volume will familiarize you with the windowed, message-based, PM user interface.

Programming Guide: Volume III—Graphics Programming Interface
> Describes the Graphics Programming Interface. This volume provides information on how to prepare graphical output for display and printing.

For complete and comprehensive information about the API, refer to the *OS/2 2.0 Control Program Programming Reference* and the *OS/2 2.0 Presentation Manager Programming Reference—Volumes I, II, and III*.

For information on how to compile and link your programs, refer to the compiler publications for the programming language you are using.

The OS/2 2.0 operating system is a 32-bit system, and this guide is about programming 32-bit applications. (Sixteen-bit applications are still supported by the operating system).

To illustrate programming with the API, this guide makes extensive use of code fragments. Also, there are sample applications available with the *Developer's Toolkit for OS/2 2.0* (Toolkit). You should familiarize yourself with the operation of each sample from a user's viewpoint. That will help you understand the code in the samples.

---

* Trademark of the IBM Corporation

xix

Structure of the Book

This book describes the different components of the OS/2 Control Program API. The file system and file management information is divided into four chapters, the rest of the components are covered in a single chapter each.

Each chapter of these books is divided into two sections: *about* the topic and *using* the functions related to that topic. The first section of each chapter provides concepts, terms, and background material; the second section is divided into subsections, each providing information about accomplishing a specific task. Code fragments are included for most of the functions.

Prerequisite Knowledge

These books are for application designers and programmers who are familiar with the following:

- Information contained in the Application Design Guide

- Information contained in the Control Program and Presentation Manager reference materials

- C Programming Language.

Programming experience on a multitasking operating system also would be helpful.

Control Program Programming Guide

Chapter 1. Introduction to the Control Program

The OS/2 operating system is an advanced, multitasking, single-user, operating system for personal computers. The operating system has a rich application programming interface (API) that supports:

- Multitasking
- Interprocess communication
- Error and exception handling
- Dynamic (run-time) linking
- Graphical user interface (GUI).

The operating system also provides advanced file system features such as installable file systems, extended file attributes, and long file names.

The OS/2 operating system runs on and takes full advantage of the 80386 microprocessor. Features based on the 80386 microprocessor include:

- 32-bit operands and operations
- Flat (non-segmented) 4 gigabyte address space
- 32-bit memory pointers
- Hardware-based memory protection and task management.

The OS/2 operating system provides a windowed, graphical user interface called the *Presentation Manager* (PM).

Control Program Functionality

The lowest-level functions supplied by the OS/2 operating system are those provided by the kernel and the kernel's subsystems—the control programs of the operating system. The Control Program functions involve the most basic aspects of program execution, such as memory management, file handling, and process, thread, and session management. They also involve more sophisticated programming tasks, such as exception handling and interprocess communications. The names of all the system functions in the Control Program API are prefixed with the letters "Dos", as in DosAllocMem.

The book describes the following topics from the operating system's Control Program API:

- File and disk management
- Memory management
- Program execution control (Process and session management)
- Semaphores
- Pipes
- Queues
- Timing functions
- Error handling
- Exception handling
- Device I/O support

- Message management
- National language support and code page management
- Debugging.

The Presentation Manager windowed GUI is covered in the *Programming Guide: Volume II*. The graphics programming interface is described in the *Programming Guide: Volume III*.

File Systems and File Management

The file system is the component of the operating system that supports storing information on mass storage devices, such as hard disks and floppy disks. Applications view a file as a logical sequence of data; the file system manages the physical locations of data on the storage device for the application and specifies how the device and the stored information are formatted.

The file system also manages file I/O operations. Applications use file system functions to open, read, write, and close disk files. File system functions enable an application to maintain the disk that holds the files—volumes, directories, and files on the disks of the computer. Applications also use OS/2 file system functions to perform I/O operations to pipes and peripheral devices connected to the computer, like the printer.

The file system also supports redirection of input and output, for example redirecting output from the monitor to a disk file or to the printer.

There are two types of file systems supported by the OS/2 operating system. The first is the File Allocation Table (FAT) file system. The FAT file system is the file system used by DOS. The second type of file system supported by the operating system is the installable file system (IFS). Installable file systems are external to the base operating system and are loaded by the operating system when the computer is started. The High Performance File System (HPFS) included with the OS/2 operating system is an installable file system.

Memory Management

The key features of OS/2 memory management are paged virtual memory and a 32-bit linear (flat) address space that is mapped through page tables to physical memory. This is in contrast to the segmented memory model used in previous versions of the operating system.

An application can allocate memory for its own use, or to be shared with other applications.

Program Execution and Control

Multitasking is the ability of the operating system to manage the execution of more than one application at a time. For the programmer, this includes the ability to multitask your own programs.

The OS/2 operating system supports two forms of multitasking for programs. An application can start other programs that will execute concurrently with the application. These programs can be a new copy of the application, a related program that is designed to work with the application, or an unrelated program. The operating system provides functions to communicate with and control the programs started by the application.

The OS/2 operating system also enables applications to run multiple threads of execution within the same application; separate activities can be multitasked within the application. An example of this is dispatching a separate subroutine to load a file and having the subroutine execute at the same time the main routine continues to monitor and respond to user input.

Semaphores

Semaphores signal the beginning and ending of an operation and provide mutually exclusive ownership of resources. Typically, semaphores are used to prevent more than one process or thread within a process from accessing a resource, such as shared memory, at the same time.

Semaphores are defined by the system and reside in an internal memory buffer. They are divided into three types, according to the functionality they provide:

- Event semaphores enable a thread to notify waiting threads that an event has occurred.

- Mutual exclusion (mutex) semaphores enable threads to serialize their access to shared resources.

- Multiple Wait (muxwait) semaphores enable threads to wait either for multiple events to occur, or for multiple resources to become available.

Pipes

A pipe is a named or unnamed buffer used to pass data between processes. A process writes to or reads from a pipe as though the pipe were standard input or standard output. A parent process can use pipes to control the input that a child process receives and to receive the output that the child process produces. There are two types of pipes—named and unnamed.

Queues

A queue is a named, ordered list of elements that is used to pass information between related or unrelated processes. The owner of the queue (the server process) can choose the order in which to read incoming information and can examine queue elements without removing them from the queue. Queue elements can be added and accessed in First-In-First-Out (FIFO), Last-In-First-Out (LIFO), or priority-based order.

Timers

Timers enable an application to suspend operation for a specific length of time, to block a thread of execution until an interval has elapsed, or to post an event semaphore at repeated intervals.

Error Management

The OS/2 operating system provides functions to facilitate error processing. DosErrClass returns a classification of the error and a recommended action. DosError enables an application to prevent the operating system from displaying the default error message in a pop-up window when either a hard error or a software exception occurs.

Exception Management

A multitasking operating system must manage applications carefully. A serious error (such as an attempt to access protected memory) occurring in one application cannot be permitted to damage any other application in the system. To manage errors that might damage other applications, the OS/2 operating system defines a class of error conditions called *exceptions* and defines default actions for those errors.

An exception is an abnormal condition that can occur during program execution. Common causes of exceptions include I/O errors and access protection violations. When an exception is caused by the user pressing Ctrl+Break or Ctrl+C, the exception is called a signal exception.

When an exception occurs, the default action usually taken by the operating system is to terminate the application that caused the exception. An application can register its own exception handling routine and try to handle the exception itself. It might be possible for the application to correct the condition that caused the exception and continue execution.

Device I/O

The OS/2 operating system uses devices to communicate with the real world. A device is a piece of hardware used for input and output. Devices used with computers include the keyboard, video display, mouse, floppy and fixed disk drives, and external systems, such as modems and printers. The operating system supplies functions that can be used to access and control such devices.

Message Management

For full-screen applications, text messages—used by an application to display information to the user—can be held in a *message file*. Keeping an application's messages in a message file simplifies changing those messages, which, for example, can facilitate marketing an application in several countries simultaneously.

National Language Support and Code Page Management

Many applications must support more than one national language, for example, French and German. This requirement is simplified through the use of such resources as string tables, menu templates, dialog templates, and accelerator tables.

A *code page* is a table that defines how characters are encoded. Code page management enables a user to select a code page for keyboard input, and screen and printer output before starting an application, a system command, or a utility program in the OS/2 multitasking environment.

Debugging

Debugging is the process of detecting, diagnosing, and eliminating errors in programs. A debugger program is designed to interact with the application that it is debugging. Because of the protected mode architecture of the OS/2 operating system, special steps must be taken to allow a debugging program to perform its functions in the program being debugged. DosDebug enables one application to control the execution of another application for debugging purposes.

Chapter 2. File Systems

An application views a file as a logical sequence of data; OS/2 file systems manage the physical locations of that data on the storage device for the application. The file systems also manage file I/O operations and control the format of the stored information.

Applications use the OS/2 file system functions to open, read, write, and close disk files. File system functions also enable an application to use and maintain the disk that contains the files—the volumes, the directories, and the files on the disks of the computer. Applications also use OS/2 file system functions to perform I/O operations to pipes and to peripheral devices connected to the computer, like the printer.

The following topics are related to the information in this chapter:

- File Names
- File Management
- Extended Attributes
- Device I/O.

About File Systems

A file system is the combination of software and hardware that supports storing information on a storage device. In the OS/2 operating system, the file system specifies how data is organized on the mass storage devices of the computer, such as hard disks and floppy disks.

Each drive is assigned a unique letter to distinguish it from other drives. A single hard disk can also be divided into two or more *logical drives*. A logical drive represents a portion of the hard disk and, like a physical drive, is assigned a unique letter to distinguish it from other physical and logical drives.

The file system organizes disks into volumes, directories, and files. A volume is the largest file system unit. It represents all the available storage on the logical drive. An optional volume name identifies the volume.

Volumes are subdivided into directories, which contain files and other subdirectories. Each volume has a root directory, which contains file and directory entries. All other subdirectories trace their ancestry back to the root directory. Each directory entry identifies the name, location, and size of a specific file or subdirectory on the disk. A file is one or more bytes of data stored on the disk. Subdirectories provide an additional level of organization and, like the root directory, can contain files and directory entries.

The file system also enables users and applications to access certain non-disk devices as if they were files. An example of such a device would be the printer, which can be accessed through the file system by using the printer's logical name, PRN, as a file name.

Types of File Systems

The OS/2 operating system has two file systems: the *file allocation table (FAT) file system* and the *High Performance File System* (HPFS). These file systems define how information is organized on the storage devices.

A user can choose to install either or both file systems. An application must be able to work with any file system. The OS/2 operating system provides a common set of file system functions that are not dependent on a particular file system.

Both of these file systems support:

- Existing logical file and directory structure
- Existing naming conventions
- Multiple logical volumes (partitions)
- Multiple and different storage devices
- Redirection or connection to remote file systems
- Extended attributes
- Metacharacter file-name processing.

Additionally, HPFS supports:

- Long file names
- An extendable application interface.

The High Performance File System is an example of a class of file systems called *installable file systems*. Installable file systems are installed by the user (by changing CONFIG.SYS) and are loaded by the operating system during system initialization.

The OS/2 operating system permits users to have multiple file systems active at the same time; for example a FAT file system for one hard disk and HPFS for another.

FAT File System

The OS/2 FAT file system is based on the DOS FAT file system. This file system, also used in previous releases of the OS/2 operating system and in PC-DOS, controls storage of data files for hard and floppy disks.

The FAT file system is hierarchical, supporting multiple directories on the disk. Each directory can contain one or more files or subdirectories.

The FAT file system uses the 8.3 file name convention. Under this convention, the file name consists of a file name of up to eight characters, a separating period (.), and a file name extension of up to three characters.

Installable File Systems

An installable file system is a file system in which software is installed when the operating system is started. The OS/2 operating system supports installable file systems and permits users to have multiple file systems active at the same time.

Users install a file system by specifying the file system components in the CONFIG.SYS file. The file system software consists of device drivers and dynamic link libraries. The device drivers access storage devices; the dynamic link libraries control the format of information on a device and manage the flow of data to and from the device. The user must use the DEVICE= command to specify the device driver and the IFS= command to specify the dynamic link library.

Installable file system drivers are loaded during system initialization when an IFS= statement is encountered in the CONFIG.SYS file. The operating system loads the device driver and dynamic link library and initializes a specific device for use with a file system.

These file systems can support file and directory structures different from the FAT file system.

An example of an installable file system might be a file system designed specifically for use on a network server. Another example of an installable file system is the High Performance File System (HPFS), which is included with the OS/2 operating system.

High Performance File System

The High Performance File System (HPFS) is an installable file system. It is a hierarchical system and supports multiple directories. In many cases, accessing files under HPFS is faster than accessing similar files under the FAT file system. During installation of the OS/2 operating system, users can install the HPFS on the hard disk they use to start their computer.

Features of HPFS include:

- Caching of directories, data, and file system data structures
- Multi-threaded I/O operations
- Write-behind logic
- Optional write-through
- Strategic allocation of directory structures
- Highly contiguous file allocation
- Enhanced recoverability
- Extended attribute support
- Long file name support
- Starting the OS/2 operating system from an HPFS disk.

File names under HPFS can contain 255 characters (one must be the terminating NULL, "\0") and can contain characters that are not valid for the FAT file system—for example, spaces. Each element of a path name residing on an HPFS disk can also have up to 255 characters. The total path including drive, directories, and file name cannot exceed 260 characters (259 with the terminating NULL). For more information on long file name support by installable file systems see "Long File Names" on page 3-4.

HPFS provides extremely fast access to very large disk volumes. HPFS uses a memory cache divided into blocks of 2KB. Data that is read from and written to the disk is transferred through this cache. Frequently-used data will often be found in the cache, thereby saving the time that a disk-read operation would require. When a user request specifies data that is not present in the cache, HPFS selects the least-recently-used block, writes the data within that block to disk, if necessary, and then fills the block with the requested data.

When a write-data request is received, it usually is not necessary that the data be immediately written to the disk. HPFS will copy such data into the block cache without actually performing the disk-write operation. When the data is in the cache, it is written to disk as a background activity (referred to as lazy writing) which enables the typical user-write operation to occur much faster than in file systems where all write operations are synchronous. Figure 2-1 shows the operation of the memory cache.

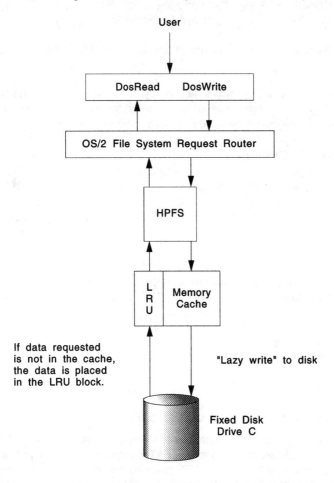

Figure   2-1. High Performance File System Data Caching

The High Performance File System consists of:

- The High Performance File System driver, HPFS.IFS
- The High Performance File System lazy-write utility, CACHE.EXE
- The High Performance File System lazy-write startup program, STARTLW.DLL
- The High Performance File System utilities, UHPFS.DLL.

The user determines the amount of lazy-write support by setting the following parameters on the command line that calls CACHE.EXE:

- MaxAge:

  When the data in a cache block exceeds the specified time the block is queued for writing to the disk. This reduces the amount of data lost due to inopportune system shutdowns.

- DiskIdle and BufferIdle

  When no user I/O request (non-lazy-write) has been made for *DiskIdle* number of milliseconds, all cache blocks (in oldest-first order) that have not been touched for *BufferIdle* number of milliseconds are queued for writing to disk. This enables HPFS to write out user data during times of relative disk inactivity and to reduce the need for rewriting heavily used cached blocks.

STARTLW.DLL contains the code that starts the lazy-write thread.

Local and Remote File Systems

Installable file systems work with a variety of storage devices. A file system on a local device such as a disk drive or virtual drive is called a local file system. A file system on a remote device, such as a disk drive on another computer, is called a remote file system. An application can establish a connection to a local or a remote file system by using DosFSAttach.

For a local file system, the operating system uses a block device driver, which accesses disk hardware, to handle input and output to the device. The operating system automatically connects most (if not all) local file systems when it starts. However, an application can attach and detach additional file systems as needed.

For a remote file system, the operating system uses a device driver that typically accesses a communications or network device. Usually, the actual storage device is located on another computer, and the two computers communicate requests and data through a network connection. An application can associate a remote file system with a drive letter by using DosFSAttach. Once the connection is made, the application can access directories and files on the remote device simply by using the assigned drive letter, treating the remote device as if it were on the same computer.

Recognizing DOS and OS/2 File Objects

The OS/2 FAT file system recognizes file objects created by the DOS FAT file system. This means that applications running under the OS/2 operating system (these include both OS/2 applications and DOS applications running in a DOS Session) can access file objects created by applications running under DOS.

Because the OS/2 FAT file system supports the same directory structure as the DOS FAT file system, applications running under DOS can access files and directories created by the OS/2 FAT file system.

However, the High Performance File System (HPFS) does not support the same directory structure as the DOS FAT file system. Therefore, the DOS FAT file system will not recognize file objects created by HPFS. This means that if you start the computer with DOS, applications running under DOS cannot access files and directories on HPFS disks.

DOS applications running in a DOS Session under the OS/2 operating system *can* recognize files and directories on both FAT and HPFS disks. A request from a DOS Session to read a file on a FAT disk is handled by the OS/2 FAT file system. Similarly, a request from a DOS Session to read a file on an HPFS disk is handled by the OS/2 High Performance File System.

Storage Devices and File Systems

OS/2 file systems store information on mass storage devices. These devices are usually hard disks or floppy diskettes, but can be other media, such as CD-ROM.

Each drive (or device) is assigned a unique letter to distinguish it from other drives. On most personal computers, drive A is the first floppy disk drive, drive B is the second floppy disk drive, drive C is the first hard disk drive, and drive D is the second hard disk drive.

A single hard disk can be divided into two or more partitions, each of which are then viewed as a separate logical drive. A logical drive, like a physical drive, is assigned a unique letter to distinguish it from other physical and logical drives. FDISK is the OS/2 utility used to partition physical storage devices; see the description of the FDISK utility in the online *OS/2 Command Reference*.

A personal computer running the OS/2 operating system can have up to 26 logical disk drives.

Each logical storage device can be managed by a different file system. The file system attached to a storage device manages that device. A user attaches a file system to a storage device by:

- Loading the file system driver during system initialization (by including an IFS= statement in CONFIG.SYS).

- Formatting the storage device by using the format options for the file system.

During installation of the OS/2 operating system, users have the option of formatting hard disks with the FAT file system or with the High Performance File System (HPFS). If the user chooses to use the HPFS, an IFS= statement is added to the CONFIG.SYS file so that HPFS is loaded automatically during each system startup. During formatting, the file system driver is associated with the logical storage device or drive letter of the hard disk.

When an application calls a file system function, the operating system directs the request to:

- The installable file system managing the storage device, or
- The FAT file system, if no installable file system is loaded and attached to the storage device.

The file system used to format the storage media manages that media each time the system is started, as long as the file system is loaded during system start-up. The operating system directs file system requests for a storage media to the file system that formatted the media. If no file system recognizes the format of the media, the OS/2 FAT file system attempts to manage that media. This might occur when the file system used to format the storage media is not loaded during system startup (the IFS= statement was removed from the CONFIG.SYS file after OS/2 installation). If the OS/2 FAT file system cannot recognize the media format (the media might have a different directory structure), the user receives an error when attempting to access the media.

For example, assume a system is configured with diskette drive A and hard disk drives C and D. During OS/2 installation, the user elects to format drive C using HPFS. Drive C is, then, managed by HPFS. Drive D was formatted with the FAT file system, so it is managed by the OS/2 FAT file system, as is diskette drive A (removable media cannot be formatted using HPFS). Figure 2-2 shows this relationship.

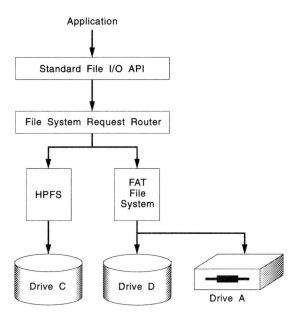

Figure   2-2. Routing of File System Requests

When an application calls DosOpen to open a file on drive C, the operating system directs the request to HPFS. When an application calls DosOpen to open a file on drive A, the operating system directs the request to the OS/2 FAT file system.

If HPFS is not loaded during system startup, the FAT file system will receive file system requests made for drive C. However, because HPFS supports a different directory structure than the FAT file system does, the OS/2 FAT file system cannot recognize file objects on the disk. The user will receive an error when attempting to gain access to the disk.

Users can determine which file system was used to format a storage device by using the CHKDSK utility. CHKDSK displays a message indicating which file system manages the specified drive. For more information on FORMAT and CHKDSK, see the online *OS/2 Command Reference*.

File System Utilities

Utilities for each file system are in a single dynamic link library. The utilities that the operating system calls are based on the file system that recognizes the volume on which the utility is to be run. The dynamic link library for each file system has the following utilities:

FORMAT   Disk formatter
CHKDSK   File system validation and repair
RECOVER   File recovery
SYS   System installation.

OS/2 Boot Manager

The OS/2 *Boot Manager* enables different operating systems to co-reside on the same computer. The user selects the operating system to boot when the computer is turned on. For example, DOS, AIX, and the OS/2 operating system can co-reside on the same machine. There can also be a previous version of the OS/2 operating system on the machine co-existing with the current version of the operating system.

Each operating system has its own partition and each partition is managed by the appropriate file system for the operating system that owns it. A DOS partition has a FAT file system. An OS/2 partition can have either a FAT file system or HPFS. An AIX partition will use the AIX file system to manage its partition.

Note: FAT partitions that follow HPFS partitions on the same physical disk cannot be accessed when using DOS because DOS stops at the first partition it does not recognize.

For information on installing and using the Boot Manager see the *OS/2 2.0 Installation Guide*.

Using File Systems

In order to take advantage of the capabilities of OS/2 file systems, application developers must be able to manage the file systems.

Most of the file system functions work with either the FAT file system or the High Performance File System (HPFS). If you have questions about a specific function, see the reference information for that function in the *Control Program Programming Reference*.

Note: In the example code fragments that follow, error checking was left out to conserve space. Applications should always check the return code that the functions return. Control Program functions return an APIRET value. A return code of 0 indicates success. If a non-zero value is returned, an error occurred.

Attaching and Detaching File Systems

A file system driver that uses a block device driver for I/O operations to a local or remote (virtual disk) device is called a local file system. A file system driver that accesses a remote system without a block device driver is called a remote file system.

An application, typically a network application, can call DosFSAttach to:

- Attach a drive to a remote file system
- Detach a drive from a remote file system
- Attach a pseudocharacter device name to a local or remote file system
- Detach a pseudocharacter device name from a local or remote file system.

DosFSAttach establishes or breaks the connection between a drive or device and a file system. If an attachment is successful, all requests to that drive or name are routed to the specified file system. If a detachment is successful, the operating system will no longer recognize the drive or name in a file system call.

DosFSAttach does not support:

- Redirection of drive letters representing local drives
- Attachment to drives or devices that are not in the system's name space. (DosFSCtl can be used to attach to drives or devices not in the system's name space.)

  A name space is a set of names that are known to the file system. For example, CON and PRN are always in the OS/2 file system's name space.

The following code fragment attaches a drive to a remote file system driver (FSD). Assume that the FSD does not require any user-supplied data arguments.

```
#define INCL_DOSFILEMGR   /* File System values */
#include <os2.h>
#include <stdio.h>

UCHAR  DeviceName[8]; /* Device name or drive letter string */
UCHAR  FSDName[40];   /* FSD name                           */
PVOID  DataBuffer;    /* Attach argument data               */
ULONG  DataBufferLen; /* Buffer length                      */
ULONG  OpFlag;        /* Attach or detach                   */
APIRET rc;            /* Return code                        */

strcpy(DeviceName,"Y:");
                 /* Drive letter with which to attach the */
                 /* file system driver                    */

strcpy(FSDName,"\\lan03\\src");

DataBuffer = 0;    /* Assume that no user-supplied data  */
                   /* arguments are required             */

DataBufferLen = 0; /* No data buffer supplied            */

OpFlag = 0;        /* Indicate Attach request            */

rc = DosFSAttach(DeviceName, FSDName, DataBuffer, DataBufferLen, OpFlag);

if (rc != 0) {
    printf("DosFSAttach error: return code = %ld", rc);
    return;
}
```

Figure   2-3. Attaching a Drive to a Remote File System Driver

Obtaining Information about an Attached File System

To obtain information about block devices, and all character and pseudocharacter devices, including the type of device and the name of the file system driver the device is attached to, use DosQueryFSAttach.

The information can be used to determine if the operating system recognizes that a particular file system is attached to a storage device. This is important to an application that must guarantee such a state. An application of this type must handle the situation where the file system driver that formatted a certain disk was not loaded during system startup. (The user might have omitted the IFS= statement in the CONFIG.SYS. file). In such a situation, the data on the disk could be destroyed because the wrong file system was attached to the disk by default.

The following code fragment returns information about an attached file system.

```
#define INCL_DOSFILEMGR    /* File System values */
#include <os2.h>
#include <stdio.h>

UCHAR       DeviceName[8];    /* Device name or drive letter string */
ULONG       Ordinal;          /* Ordinal of entry in name list      */
ULONG       FSAInfoLevel;     /* Type of attached FSD data required */
FSQBUFFER2  DataBuffer;       /* Returned data buffer               */
ULONG       DataBufferLen;    /* Buffer length                      */
APIRET      rc;               /* Return code                        */

strcpy(DeviceName,"Y:");      /* Logical drive of the attached file system */

FSAInfoLevel = 1;

DataBufferLen = sizeof(FSQBUFFER2);    /* Length of data buffer */

rc = DosQueryFSAttach(DeviceName, Ordinal, FSAInfoLevel,
                      &DataBuffer, &DataBufferLen);

if (rc != 0) {
    printf("DosQueryFSAttach error: return code = %ld", rc);
    return;
}
```

Figure   2-4. Obtaining Information about an Attached File System

In this example, information was requested about the drive whose name was specified within the *DeviceName* variable. After the DosQueryFSAttach call, the *DataBuffer* structure contained a set of information describing the specified attached file system, and the *DataBufferLen* variable contained the size of information within the structure.

Obtaining Information about a File System

An application can retrieve information about the file system on a given drive by using DosQueryFSInfo. The file system information includes information on the amount of free storage space on the disk. The storage space is given in number of allocation units (clusters) on the disk. Each cluster has an associated number of sectors; each sector contains a given number of bytes. A typical disk has 512 bytes for each sector and 4 sectors for each cluster. DosSetFSInfo enables an application to change the volume identifier for the disk in the given drive.

The following code fragment obtains information about the file system that is associated with a particular logical drive.

```
#define INCL_DOSFILEMGR    /* File System values */
#include <os2.h>
#include <stdio.h>

ULONG   DriveNumber;      /* Drive number                */
ULONG   FSInfoLevel;      /* File system data required   */
UCHAR   FSInfoBuf[40];    /* File system info buffer     */
ULONG   FSInfoBufSize;    /* File system info buffer size */
APIRET  rc;               /* Return code                 */

DriveNumber = 3;              /* Specify drive C               */

FSInfoLevel = FSIL_ALLOC;     /* Indicate that file system allocation */
                              /* information is requested      */

FSInfoBufSize = 40;           /* Size of return data buffer    */

rc = DosQueryFSInfo(DriveNumber, FSInfoLevel, FSInfoBuf, FSInfoBufSize);

if (rc != 0) {
    printf("DosQueryFSInfo error: return code = %ld", rc);
    return;
}
```

Figure 2-5. Obtaining Information about the File System

In this example, the data buffer *FSInfoBuf* is used to receive information about space allocation within the specified file system.

Obtaining Information about a File

An application can retrieve and set information about a specific file by using DosQueryFileInfo and DosSetFileInfo. File information consists of the dates and times that the file was created, last accessed, and last written to; the size (in bytes) of the file; the number of sectors (or clusters) the file occupies; and the file attributes.

The following code fragment obtains file information for a specified file. The example obtains the Level 1 information set for the file. The Level 1 information set for a file includes the dates and times of creation, last access, and last writing. It also includes information about the size of the file and the file's standard attributes. Assume that the handle of the desired file has been placed into *FileHandle* already.

```
#define INCL_DOSFILEMGR   /* File System values */
#include <os2.h>
#include <stdio.h>

HFILE        FileHandle;      /* File handle                  */
ULONG        FileInfoLevel;   /* Level of file info required */
FILESTATUS3  FileInfoBuf;     /* File info buffer             */
ULONG        FileInfoBufSize; /* File data buffer size        */
APIRET       rc;              /* Return code                  */

FileInfoLevel = 1;     /* Indicate that Level 1 information is desired */

FileInfoBufSize = sizeof(FILESTATUS3);
                    /* Size of the buffer that will             */
                    /* receive the Level 1 information          */

rc = DosQueryFileInfo(FileHandle, FileInfoLevel, &FileInfoBuf,
                    FileInfoBufSize);

if (rc != 0) {
    printf("DosQueryFileInfo error: return code = %ld", rc);
    return;
}
```

Figure 2-6. Obtaining Information about a File

In this example, Level 1 file information is placed into the *FileInfoBuf* buffer.

Communicating with a File System

An extended standard interface between an application and a file system driver is provided by DosFSCtl. This function is similar to DosDevIOCtl, which provides a standard interface between an application and a device driver. An application sends a request to the file system driver by specifying a particular function code. Data is exchanged through data areas and parameter lists.

DosFSCtl can be used to establish open connections to file system drivers that are not attached to a name in the operating system's name space. (A name space is a set of names that are known to the file system. For example, CON and PRN are always in the OS/2 file system's name space.)

The following code fragment demonstrates how a process can communicate with a file system driver (FSD). Assume that the calling process has placed an appropriate file handle into *FileHandle*. Assume that the specified file system recognizes a function code of hex 8100, and that the function code accepts an ASCII string as input, requires no specific command parameter list, and returns a string of ASCII characters to the caller.

```
#define INCL_DOSFILEMGR   /* File System values */
#include <os2.h>
#include <stdio.h>

UCHAR   DataArea[100];    /* Data area                            */
ULONG   DataLengthMax;    /* Max. length of Data area             */
ULONG   DataLengthInOut;  /* Data area length, in and out         */
PVOID   ParmList;         /* Parameter list                       */
ULONG   ParmLengthMax;    /* Max. length of Parameter list        */
ULONG   ParmLengthInOut;  /* Parameter list length, in and out    */
ULONG   FunctionCode;     /* Function code                        */
PSZ     RouteName;        /* Path or FSD name                     */
HFILE   FileHandle;       /* File handle                          */
ULONG   RouteMethod;      /* Method for routing                   */
APIRET  rc;               /* Return code                          */

FunctionCode = 0x8100;    /* Indicate the function to request     */
                          /* of the file system                   */

strcpy(DataArea,"PARM1: 98");
                          /* ASCII string to pass to file system */

DataLengthMax = 100;      /* Tell the file system the maximum     */
                          /* amount of data it can return         */

DataLengthInOut = strlen(DataArea);
                          /* On input, this is the number of      */
                          /* bytes sent to the file system        */

ParmList = 0;             /* In this example, assume that no      */
ParmLengthMax = 0;        /* specific command parameter list      */
ParmLengthInOut = 0;      /* is required by the file system       */
                          /* for this function code               */

RouteMethod = 1;          /* Indicate that the file handle        */
RouteName = 0;            /* directs routing (this implies        */
                          /* that the RouteName variable is       */
                          /* unused in this example)              */

rc = DosFSCtl(DataArea, DataLengthMax, &DataLengthInOut,
              ParmList, ParmLengthMax, &ParmLengthInOut,
              FunctionCode, RouteName, FileHandle,
              RouteMethod);

if (rc != 0) {
    printf("DosFSCtl error: return code = %ld", rc);
    return;
}
```

Figure   2-7. Communicating with a File System Driver

In this example, the the *DataArea* buffer is used to store the ASCII string sent by the file system in response to the function request, and the *DataLengthInOut* variable is used to store the number of bytes placed in the buffer by the file system.

Preparing File Systems for System Shutdown

At any time during normal system operation, data destined for a disk might be in a cache. If this information is not written to disk before the system powered-off, the disk can become corrupted. To prevent this, applications call DosShutdown to ensure that the operating system writes the data in the cache to the disk and prevents any further data from being cached. The user can then safely power-off the system.

Note: This call prepares all file systems and device drivers for system shutdown. Therefore, it must be called only when system shutdown is about to occur. The user and applications will no longer have access to their storage devices.

The following code fragment locks out changes to all file systems, and writes system buffers to the disk in preparation for turning off power to the system.

```
#define INCL_DOSFILEMGR   /* File System values */
#include <os2.h>
#include <stdio.h>

ULONG   Reserved;   /* Reserved, must be zero      */
APIRET  rc;         /* Return code                 */

Reserved = 0;       /* Reserved, must be set to zero */

rc = DosShutdown(Reserved);

if (rc != 0) {
    printf("DosShutdown error: return code = %ld", rc);
    return;
}
```

Figure 2-8. Preparing to Turn Off Power to the System

Writing Cache Buffers

DosResetBuffer is used to write to disk (flush) the file system's cache buffers for a specific file handle. When called with a value of hex FFFF for the file handle, DosResetBuffer writes all files belonging to the requesting process to disk (this usage should be administered with care, so the user is not burdened with insertion and removal of a large number of removable media volumes).

When DosResetBuffer is called for single file handle, the directory entry for the file is updated as if the file had been closed. However, the file remains open.

DosResetBuffer can also be called with the name of a named pipe. The process that calls DosResetBuffer is blocked at one end of the pipe until all data it has written has been successfully read by the process at the other end of the pipe. This enables communicating processes to synchronize their dialogs. For information about using named pipes, see "Named Pipes" on page 9-2.

The following code fragment opens a file, writes some data to the file's buffer, then writes the file's system buffer to the disk.

```
#define INCL_DOSFILEMGR   /* File System values */
#include <os2.h>
#include <stdio.h>

#define OPEN_FILE 0x01
#define CREATE_FILE 0x10
#define FILE_ARCHIVE 0x20
#define FILE_EXISTS OPEN_FILE
#define FILE_NOEXISTS CREATE_FILE
#define DASD_FLAG 0
#define INHERIT 0x80
#define WRITE_THRU 0
#define FAIL_FLAG 0
#define SHARE_FLAG 0x10
#define ACCESS_FLAG 0x02

#define FILE_NAME "test.dat"
#define FILE_SIZE 800L
#define FILE_ATTRIBUTE FILE_ARCHIVE
#define EABUF 0L

HFILE   FileHandle;
ULONG   Wrote;
ULONG   Action;
PSZ     FileData[100];
APIRET  rc;                /* Return code */
```

Figure 2-9 (Part 1 of 2). Writing the Buffers to the Device

```
Action = 2;
strcpy(FileData, "Data...");

rc = DosOpen(FILE_NAME,                          /* File path name            */
             &FileHandle,                        /* File handle               */
             &Action,                            /* Action taken              */
             FILE_SIZE,                          /* File primary allocation   */
             FILE_ATTRIBUTE,                     /* File attribute            */
             FILE_EXISTS | FILE_NOEXISTS,        /* Open function type        */
             DASD_FLAG | INHERIT |               /* Open mode of the file     */
             WRITE_THRU | FAIL_FLAG |
             SHARE_FLAG | ACCESS_FLAG,
             EABUF);                             /* No extended attributes    */

if (rc != 0) {
    printf("DosOpen error: return code = %ld", rc);
    return;
}

rc = DosWrite(FileHandle,           /* File handle    */
              (PVOID) FileData,     /* User buffer    */
              sizeof(FileData),     /* Buffer length  */
              &Wrote);              /* Bytes written  */

if (rc != 0) {
    printf("DosWrite error: return code = %ld", rc);
    return;
}

rc = DosResetBuffer(FileHandle);    /* File handle    */

if (rc != 0) {
    printf("DosResetBuffer error: return code = %ld", rc);
    return;
}
```

Figure 2-9 (Part 2 of 2). Writing the Buffers to the Device

Summary

Following are the OS/2 functions and data structures used in file system management.

Table 2-1. File System Functions

Function	Description
DosFSAttach	Attaches a file system to a device.
DosFSCtl	Communicates with a file system.
DosQueryFSAttach	Obtains information about an attached file system.
DosQueryFSInfo	Obtains volume information.
DosResetBuffer	Writes (flushes) cache buffers to disk.
DosSetFSInfo	Sets volume information.
DosShutdown	Prepares file system for system shutdown.

Table 2-2. File System Data Structures

Data Structure	Description
FSALLOCATE	Used by a DosQueryFSInfo level 1 call; returns the size of the volume and the number of free bytes.
FSINFO	Used by a DosQueryFSInfo level 2 call; returns the serial ID and label of the volume.
FSQBUFFER2	Used by DosQueryFSAttach; returns which file system is managing an attachable device.

Chapter 3. File Names

File names are the identifiers used by the file system to uniquely identify files on a disk. All file systems have specific rules for constructing names of file objects. Different file systems can have different rules for naming file objects.

The OS/2 FAT file system supports the DOS naming conventions. The OS/2 High Performance File System (HPFS) supports a superset of the DOS naming conventions, allowing for long file names and characters illegal under DOS. Although different file systems can have different rules for naming file objects, all OS/2 file systems require that full path names consist of directory and file names separated by backslashes (\).

The OS/2 operating system views path names as ASCII strings and does not restrict file systems to the DOS file name format. Compatibility with existing DOS applications requires that all installable file systems support a superset of the 8.3 file name format used in the FAT file system.

The following topics are related to the information in this chapter:

- File Systems
- File Management
- Extended Attributes
- Device I/O.

File-Naming Conventions

File name conventions are the rules used to form file names in a given file system. Although each installable file system (IFS) can have specific rules about how individual components in a directory or file name are formed, all file systems follow the same general conventions for combining components. For example, although the FAT file system requires that file and directory names have the 8.3 file name format, and HPFS supports names of up to 255 characters long, both file systems use the backslash (\) character to separate directory names and the file name when forming a path.

When creating names for directories and files, or when processing names supplied by the user, an application must follow these general rules:

- Process a path as a NULL-terminated string. An application can determine maximum length for a path by using DosQuerySysInfo.

- Use any character in the current code page for a name, but do not use a path separator, a character in the range 0 through 31, or any character explicitly prohibited by the file system.

  The following characters are reserved by the operating system. Do not use them in directory or file names.

        <   >   :   "   /   \ |

Although a name can contain characters in the extended character set (128 - 255), an application must be able to switch code pages if necessary to access the corresponding file.

- Compare names without regard to case. Names such as "ABC", "Abc", and "abc" are considered to be the same.

- Use the backslash (\) or the forward slash (/) to separate components in a path. No other character is accepted as a path separator.

- Use the dot (.) as a directory component in a path to represent the current directory.

- Use two dots (..) as a directory component in a path to represent the parent of the current directory.

- Use a period (.) to separate components in a directory name or file name. Unless explicitly defined by a file system, no restrictions are placed on the number of components in a name.

File Names in the FAT File System

Valid file names in the OS/2 FAT file system have the following form:

```
[drive:][directory\]filename[extension]
```

The *drive* parameter must name an existing drive and can be any letter from A through Z. The drive letter must be followed by a colon (:).

The *directory* parameter specifies the directory that contains the file's directory entry. The directory name must be followed by a backslash (\) to separate it from the file name. If the specified directory is not the current directory, *directory* must include the names of all the directories in the path, separated by backslashes. The root directory is specified by using a backslash at the beginning of the name.

For example, if the directory ABC is in the directory SAMPLE, and SAMPLE is in the root directory, the directory specification is:

```
\SAMPLE\ABC.
```

A directory name can also have an extension, which is any combination of up to three letters, digits, or special characters, preceded by a period (.).

The *filename* and *extension* parameters specify the file.

FAT File-Naming Rules

For file objects managed by the FAT file system, the following rules apply:

- File names are limited to 8 characters before and three characters after a single dot. This is referred to as the 8.3 file name format.

   The 8 characters before the dot are blank-filled. Embedded blanks are significant, trailing blanks and blanks immediately preceding the dot are not significant. Trailing blanks are truncated.

For example, "FILE.A" is really "FILE   .A ". "FILE.A" and "FILE   .A " are treated as the same file by the operating system and refer to the same file. Also, "FILE.TXT   " and "FILE.TXT" are treated as the same file.

Blanks elsewhere in the name are significant—"F I L E.TXT" is not the same as "FILE.TXT".

- Names are not case sensitive. This means that "FILE.TXT" and "file.txt" refer to the same file. Lowercase and uppercase characters are folded together for name comparison purposes.

- Names returned by file system functions are in uppercase. This means that if "file.txt" is created, DosFindFirst returns "FILE.TXT".

- Directory and file names can be any combination of up to eight letters, digits, or the following special characters:

  $ %   '   -   _   @   {   }   ˜   `   !   #   (   )

  File extensions can be any combination of up to three letters, digits, or special characters, preceded by a period.

- Invalid characters for directory names, file names, and volume labels are:

  - the range 0 - 1Fh

  - and the characters:

    <   > | +   =   :   ;   ,   .   "   /   \   [   ]

File Names in the High Performance File System

In HPFS, file names can be up to 255 characters long (one must be a terminating NULL, "\0"). Directory names can also be 255 characters long, but the length of the complete path, including drive, directories, and file name, cannot exceed 260 characters.

Certain characters that are illegal in the FAT file system are legal in HPFS file names:

  +   =   ;   ,   [   ]

Also, blank spaces can be used anywhere in an HPFS file name or directory name, but blank spaces and periods at the end of a file name are ignored. Additionally, the period (.) is a valid file name character and can be used as many times as desired. There is no requirement that HPFS file names have extensions; however, many applications still create and use them.

An HPFS file name can be all uppercase, all lowercase, or mixed case. The case is preserved for directory listings but is ignored in file searches and all other system operations. Therefore, in a given directory, there cannot be more than one file with the same name when the only difference is case.

File-Naming Rules for Installable File Systems

For file objects managed by OS/2 installable file systems, the following rules apply: ·

- Each element of a full path name residing on a disk managed by an installable file system can consist of up to 255 characters. File names can be up to 255 characters long (one of the characters must be a terminating NULL, "\0"). Directory names can also be 255 characters long, but the length of the complete path, including drive, directories, and file name, cannot exceed 260 characters. For example, in the path name "c:\XXX...XXX\YYY", "XXX...XXX" can include up to 255 characters. This is referred to as long file names.

- Names are not case sensitive.

- File name case as specified at create time is preserved. This means that if the file "file.TXT" is created, DosFindFirst returns "file.TXT". File name case may be modified using DosMove.

- Blanks immediately preceding a dot are significant. This means that "FILE.TXT" and "FILE   .TXT" refer to different files.

- Trailing blanks are truncated. This means that "FILE.TXT   " is the same as "FILE.TXT".

- Blanks elsewhere in the name are significant. This means that "F I L E.TXT" is not the same as "FILE.TXT".

- For compatibility reasons, trailing dots on component names are discarded. For Example, "\FILE.TXT...TEXT...\A..B...\C." becomes "\FILE.TXT...TEXT\A..B\C". This processing includes semaphore, queue, pipe, module, shared memory names, and device names.

- The set of legal characters is expanded to include

    + = ; , [ ]

  as well as all characters legal for the FAT file system.

- If an installable file system uses a component separator within a file name, it must be a dot (.). There are no restrictions on the number of components which can be allowed within a file name.

Long File Names

Programs that recognize long file names must indicate this by including the NEWFILES statement in their module definition file. This statement directs the linker to set a bit in the executable file header. It indicates that the module supports long file names. This bit is meaningless in a DOS Session and on versions of the OS/2 operating system prior to Version 1.2. Programs written for OS/2 Version 1.2 (and all later versions) installable file systems should set this bit. Bound programs that have this bit set can see files with long file names in OS/2 mode, but only files with 8.3 file name format in DOS Sessions.

This bit has meaning when attached to program modules, not when attached to DLLs. Whether the program recognizes long file names format is entirely dependent on the value of its NEWFILES bit and the effect of the bit extends into any calls to DLLs. In order to be compatible with all OS/2 file systems, dynamic link libraries must not create internal temporary files or directories that do not comply with 8.3 file naming conventions. In addition, dynamic link libraries cannot return long file names to an application. (The caller might be running on a file system that only supports 8.3 file names and use the returned name to create a file.)

OS/2 applications which do not recognize long file names can run with some restrictions. For these programs, long names (including device names) are filtered according to the following rules:

- Any name not representable in the 8.3 file name format is not returned from DosFindFirst or DosFindNext. This is because the application's buffers are unlikely to be large enough to handle longer names.

- Any long file name passed to the file system functions listed below are rejected in exactly the same way as under previous versions of the OS/2 operating system. It is not acceptable to create and manipulate a name that you cannot find.

      DosOpen
      DosDelete
      DosMove
      DosQueryPathInfo
      DosSetPathInfo
      DosCreateDir
      DosDeleteDir
      DosFindFirst
      DosFindNext
      DosQueryFSAttach
      DosFSAttach
      DosCopy
      DosSearchPath

- Long file names can be passed to DosSetCurrentDir and DosQueryCurrrentDir so that all programs can use all directories.

- Long names used with non-file system functions (for example, DosCreateSem) are not filtered.

For files located on file devices managed by the OS/2 FAT file system, long file names are handled differently in OS/2 mode than in DOS mode. In OS/2 mode, the long file name is considered an error. In DOS mode, the name is truncated and is not an error. The DOS mode treatment of file name formats provides compatibility with the PC-DOS environment for applications originally written for PC-DOS. However, if you are writing a family application to run under both the OS/2 operating system and the PC-DOS environment, your application must allow for this difference in operating environments.

Because long file names can be input to applications through program command lines, dialog boxes, or function calls, applications must provide their users with rules for how to enter file names. "File Names in User Input" on page 3-8 provides some general guidelines in this matter, that are applicable to both long file names and 8.3 file names.

Moving Files with Long Names

The OS/2 Workplace Shell supports copying files with long file names to media that is managed by a non-installable file system (IFS) and for returning these files to IFS media with the long name intact.

When a file with a long name is copied to media that does not support long file names, the OS/2 Workplace Shell stores the file's long name in the .LONGNAME extended attribute. When the file is copied back to a disk that does support long file names, the OS/2 Workplace Shell restores the long name from the extended attribute. See "The .LONGNAME Standard Extended Attribute" on page 5-13 for information on the .LONGNAME extended attribute.

If the new media does not support extended attributes, files that have long names cannot be moved to the media without having their names modified or truncated.

Note: The behavior described above only applies to the OS/2 Workplace Shell. The command processors, CMD.EXE and COMMAND.COM, do not automatically save the long file name; they require the user to enter a new file name that is legal on the new media. The DosCopy command also does not save the long file name automatically; the programmer must provide the target file name to DosCopy and the target file name must be a legal file name for the target media.

If you choose to store and restore the file's long name, you must do it yourself in the manner described above.

Metacharacters in File Names

Metacharacters are characters that can be used to represent placeholders in a file name. The asterisk (*) and the question mark (?) are the two metacharacters. The asterisk matches one or more characters, including blanks, but does not match the period. The question mark matches exactly one character, unless that character is a period. To match a period, the original name must contain a period. Metacharacters are illegal in all but the last component of a path. Metacharacters are also referred to as global file name characters, or as wildcard characters.

An application that allows more than one file name on its command line, can accept metacharacters to provide users with a shortcut for entering a long list of names. For instance, metacharacters can be used to reference a set of files with a common base name; to reference all files with an extension of EXE, the user would enter:

```
*.exe
```

Although a name that contains metacharacters is not a complete file name, an application can use functions, such as DosFindFirst and DosEditName, to expand the name (replace the metacharacters) and create one or more valid file names.

Metacharacters have two sets of semantics:

- As *search metacharacters*, which are used to select the files that are returned to the user when the user searches the disk for a file.

- As *edit metacharacters*, which are used to construct a new file name, given a source name and a target name specification.

Both asterisks and question marks, therefore, have two sets of rules, one for searching for file names and one for editing file names.

Search metacharacters are used in commands that search for files or groups of files, like DIR:

```
dir *.exe
```

An application can expand a name with metacharacters to a list of file names by using DosFindFirst and DosFindNext. These functions take a file name template (a name with metacharacters) and return the names of files on the disk that match the pattern in the template.

Edit metacharacters are used in commands that can change the names of files; for example, in a global copy command:

```
copy *.txt  *.old
```

An application can create a new file name from an existing name by using the DosEditName function. This function takes a template (a name with metacharacters) and expands it, using characters from an existing name. An asterisk in the template directs the function to copy all characters in the existing name until it locates a character that matches the character following the asterisk. A question mark directs the function to copy one character, unless that character is a period. The period in the template directs the function to look for and move to the next period in the existing name, skipping any characters between the current position and the period.

Searching for Files Using Metacharacters

An asterisk (*) matches 0 or more characters, any character, including blank. It does not cross NULL or \, which means it only matches a file name, not an entire path.

A question mark (?) matches 1 character, unless what it would match is a period (.) or the terminating NULL, in which case it matches 0 characters. It also does not cross the backslash character (\).

Any character, other than asterisks and question marks, matches itself, including a period.

Searching is case-insensitive. For example, "FILE.TXT" references the same file named "file.txt".

For compatibility reasons, any file name that does not have a dot in it gets an implicit one automatically appended to the end during searching operations. This means that searching for "FILE." would return "FILE".

Some file system functions accept file object name specifications using metacharacters. See the descriptions of the individual file system functions in the *Control Program Programming Reference* for details on the use of metacharacters.

Editing File Names Using Metacharacters

Metacharacters in a source name simply match files and behave just like any other search metacharacter.

Metacharacters in a target name are copy-edit commands and work as follows:

- A question mark (?) copies one character unless the character it would copy is a period (.), in which case it copies 0 characters. It also copies 0 characters if it is at the end of the source string.

- An asterisk (*) copies characters from the source name to the target name until it finds a source character that matches the character following it in the target.

- A period (.) in the target name causes the source pointer to match the corresponding "." in the target. They count from the left.

Editing is case-insensitive. If a case conflict between the source and editing string arises, the case in the editing string is used, thus:

```
copy file.txt *E.tmp
```

results in file.txt being copied as filE.tmp.

DosEditName provides applications with the ability to transform a file object name into another name, using an editing string that contains global characters.

Transforming File Names Using Metacharacters

File system functions that an application uses to copy, rename or move file objects do not support the use of global characters. For example, a user can perform a global copy of all files with the extension .EXE by entering the following on the command line:

```
copy *.exe
```

An application, however, cannot perform a similar global copy operation by making a single call to DosCopy or DosMove. These functions operate on a single, specific file object.

DosEditName, however, provides applications with the ability to transform an element of a full path name into another name, using an editing string that contains global characters. For example, for an application to copy all files with an extension of .SRC to files with an extension of .SAM, the application would:

1. Search for all files with the .SRC extension by using DosFindFirst and DosFindNext,

2. Transform the file names by using DosEditName with an editing string of "*.SAM",

3. Copy the files with the new extension with DosCopy.

File Names in User Input

Users often supply file names as part of an application's command line or in response to a prompt from the application. Traditionally, users have been able to supply more than one file name by separating the names with certain characters, such as a blank space. In some file systems, however, traditional separators are valid file name characters. This means additional conventions are required to ensure that an application processes all characters in a name.

When an application processes arguments (including file names) from its command line, the operating system treats the double quotation mark (") and the caret (^) as quotation characters. All characters between the opening and closing double quotation marks are processed as a single argument. The caret is used to quote characters that would otherwise have some special property. The character immediately following the caret is treated as a normal character; any special characteristics that the character has are to be ignored. For example, the greater-than symbol (>) normally causes a program's output to be redirected to a file or device. Typing "^>" causes the ">" to be included in the command line passed to the application. In both cases, the operating system discards the quotation characters and does not treat them as part of the final argument.

When a Presentation Manager (PM) application processes two or more file names from a dialog box or other prompt, it expects the user to enter each file name on a new line. Therefore, a PM application would use a multiple-line entry field to prompt for multiple file names. This often makes the use of quotation characters unnecessary.

When an application is started, the operating system constructs a command line for the application. If the command line includes file names, the operating system places a space character between names and marks the end of the list with two NULL characters. Applications that start other applications by using DosExecPgm can also pass arguments by using this convention or by using quotation characters. In practice, most applications receive a command line as a single, NULL-terminated string. Therefore, applications that use DosExecPgm should prepare command lines as a single string, and enclose any file names in quotation marks.

Device Names

Naming conventions for character devices are similar to those for naming files. The OS/2 operating system has reserved certain names for character devices supported by the base device drivers. These device names are listed below:

CLOCK$	Clock
COM1–COM4	First through fourth serial ports
CON	Console keyboard and screen
KBD$	Keyboard
LPT1	First parallel printer
LPT2	Second parallel printer
LPT3	Third parallel printer
MOUSE$	Mouse
NUL	Nonexistent (dummy) device
POINTER$	Pointer draw device (mouse screen support)
PRN	The default printer, usually LPT1
SCREEN$	Screen

These names can be used with DosOpen to open the corresponding devices. Reserved device names take precedence over file names; DosOpen checks for a device name before checking for a file name. Do not use a file name which is the same as a reserved device name; the file will never be opened, because the command will open the device instead.

COM1 through COM4 are reserved device names only when the ASYNC (RS-232C) device driver is loaded. The same is true for POINTER$ and MOUSE$, which are reserved only when a mouse device driver is loaded.

An application can call DosQueryFHState to verify that a file or device has been opened. See "Determining and Setting the State of a File or Device Handle" on page 4-16 for more information on getting the state of a file handle.

Chapter 4. File Management

The OS/2 operating system provides a standard set of file system functions. This means that applications can create, open, read, write, copy, and delete files and directories by using the same functions, regardless of which file system is used. When an application calls a file system function, the operating system passes the request to the dynamic link library that supports the file system. The dynamic link library carries out most file system processing, such as validating file names. If an error occurs, the file system returns the error to the operating system, which then passes it back to the calling application.

The OS/2 file system functions identify files and directories by their names. These functions store or search for the file or directory in the current directory on the current drive unless the name explicitly specifies a different directory and drive.

Occasionally, a file system has control functions in addition to the standard file system functions. The control functions are specific to the given file system. An application can call a control function by using DosFSCtl, which directs the operating system to pass the control-function information to the corresponding dynamic link library.

The following topics are related to the information in this chapter:

- Files Systems
- Files Names
- Extended Attributes
- Pipes
- Device I/O.

About Volumes and Drives

The OS/2 operating system allows more than one file system on a single storage device. If the device can have more than one partition (or volume), each partition can be initialized as an OS/2 partition and given a valid OS/2 file system. For each volume, the operating system determines the type of file system the first time the volume is accessed by a function or when the medium in the drive changes. After that, the operating system manages all input and output to that volume by using the corresponding dynamic link library.

The operating system uses the volume label and serial number to ensure that the medium in the drive does not change while there are outstanding requests for input and output. Each volume has a volume label and a 32-bit volume serial number, stored in a reserved location in logical sector 0 at the time of formatting. If the volume label and serial number do not match, the operating system signals the critical error handler to prompt the user to insert the volume that has the specified serial number and label. The operating system maintains the connection between the medium and the volume label and serial number until all open files on the volume are closed and all search references and cache buffer references are removed. The system redetermines the type of file system and the volume label and serial number only when the medium changes.

The OS/2 operating system enables applications to:

- Determine and set the default drive using DosQueryCurrentDisk and DosSetCurrentDisk, respectively.

- Determine and set drive information using DosQueryFSInfo and DosSetFSInfo.

- Determine and set the write verification switch using DosQueryVerify and DosSetVerify. If the write verification switch is on, each time data is written to the disk, the data is verified to ensure it has been recorded correctly. These functions are provided for recording critical data.

About Directories

When an application starts, it inherits the current directory and drive from the application that starts it. An application can determine which directory and drive are current by using DosQueryCurrentDir and DosQueryCurrentDisk. An application can change the current directory and drive of the file system by using DosSetCurrentDir and DosSetDefaultDisk.

When an application creates a new file, the system adds a file entry to the specified directory. Each directory can have any number of entries, up to the physical limit of the disk. An application can create new directories and delete existing directories by using DosCreateDir and DosDeleteDir. Before a directory can be deleted, it must be empty; if there are files or directories in that directory, they must be deleted or moved. An application can delete a file by using DosDelete or move a file to another directory by using DosMove.

Creating a Subdirectory

To create a new subdirectory, an application calls DosCreateDir and specifies a directory path name. If the call is successful, a new subdirectory is created at the end of the path on the specified disk. If no path name is specified, a new subdirectory is created at the end of the current directory for the process. If any subdirectories in the path do not exist, the subdirectory is not created.

Because a subdirectory is a file object, an application also can define an extended attribute for the directory when it is created during this call. See Chapter 5, "Extended Attributes" on page 5-1 for more information on extended attributes.

Determining and Changing the Current Directory

Calling DosQueryCurrentDir returns the full path name of the current directory for the specified drive. The string does not begin with a back slash (\) and it ends with a byte containing 00H, the NULL character.

To change the current directory, call DosSetCurrentDir with the path name of the directory you want to make the current directory.

Deleting a Directory

A subdirectory cannot be removed if it is the current subdirectory or if it contains hidden files or subdirectory entries other than the "." and ".." entries. When these requirements for removal are met, DosDeleteDir can be called with a path name to remove the subdirectory from the disk.

About Files

A file is one or more bytes of data, usually stored on a disk. While the application that creates the file determines the format of the file, the file system determines how the file is stored on the disk and what actions can be performed on it. The file system also stores information about the file in file attributes and extended attributes.

Files are accessed through the file system using file handles. File handles are returned by DosOpen when the file is opened and are used for all subsequent accesses to the file. Files can be be opened, read from, written to, closed, copied, moved, deleted, renamed, and locked. Files can be searched for based on a metacharacter template.

Each open file has a file pointer that indicates the current reading or writing location within the file. The file pointer moves automatically with each read or write operation on the file and can be moved manually by the application.

File Attributes

Each directory entry includes a set of file attributes. File attributes specify whether the directory entry is for a file, a directory, or a volume identifier. The attributes also specify if the file is read-only, hidden, archived, or a system file.

A *read-only* file cannot be opened for writing, nor can it be deleted. A *hidden* file (or directory) cannot be displayed by using an ordinary directory listing. A *system* file is excluded from normal directory searches. The *archived attribute* is for use by special purpose applications to mark a file that has been changed since the last time the file was examined.

An application can retrieve and set the file attributes by using DosQueryFileInfo and DosSetFileInfo.

File Handles

The operating system identifies each open file by assigning it a file handle when the application opens or creates the file. The file handle is a unique 32-bit integer. The application can use the handle in functions that read from and write to the file, depending on how the file was opened. The application can continue to use the handle until the file is closed.

The default maximum number of file handles for a process is 20. An application can change this maximum by using DosSetMaxFH. When this call is made, all currently open file handles are preserved.

When an application starts, it inherits all open file handles from the process that starts it. If the system's command processor starts an application, file handles 0, 1, and 2 represent the standard input, standard output, and standard error files. The standard input file is the keyboard; the standard output and standard error files are the screen. An application can read from the standard input file and write to the standard output and standard error files immediately; it does not have to open the files first.

An application can create a duplicate file handle for an open file by using DosDupHandle. A duplicate handle is identical to the original handle. Typically, duplicate handles are used to redirect the standard input and standard output files. For example, an application can open a disk file and duplicate the disk-file handle as handle 0. Thereafter, an application reading from the standard input file (handle 0) takes data from the disk file, not from the keyboard.

When devices and pipes are accessed through the file system functions (using DosOpen, DosRead, and so on), the devices and pipes are treated as files and are identified using file handles. The standard file handles can be redirected to a device or pipe.

File Pointer

Every open file has a file pointer that specifies the next byte to be read or the location to receive the next byte that is written. When a file is first opened, the system places the file pointer at the beginning of the file. As each byte is read or written, the operating system advances the pointer.

An application can also move the pointer by using DosSetFilePtr. When the pointer reaches the end of the file and the application attempts to read from the file, no bytes are read and no error occurs. Thus, reading 0 bytes without an error means the program has reached the end of the file.

When an application writes to a disk file, the data being written is usually collected in an internal buffer. The operating system writes to the disk only when the amount of data equals (or is a multiple of) the sector size of the disk. If there is data in the internal buffer when the file is closed, the system automatically writes the data to the disk before closing the file. An application can also flush the buffer (that is, write the contents of the buffer to the disk) by using DosResetBuffer.

Copying Files

DosCopy is used to copy files and subdirectories. Metacharacters (global file name characters) are not allowed, so only individual files or entire subdirectories can be copied with this function. The source and target can be on different drives.

When the source specified is a subdirectory and an I/O error occurs, the file being copied from the source directory to the target directory at the time of the error will be deleted from the target directory and DosCopy will be terminated.

When a file is being copied and an I/O error occurs,

- if the source file name is that of a file to be replaced, the file is deleted from the target path,

- if the source file name is that of a file to be appended, the target file is resized to its original size,

and the function is terminated.

DosCopy will copy the attributes of the source file, such as date of creation, and time of creation to the target file. Additionally, DosCopy will copy the extended attributes of the source file when creating a new subdirectory or a new file, or when replacing an existing file.

Moving Files

DosMove is used to move a file from one subdirectory to another on the same drive. In the process of moving the file, its name can be changed. Metacharacters (global file name characters) are not permitted.

Deleting Files

Calling DosDelete removes the directory entry associated with a file name. Metacharacters (global file name characters) are not permitted.

Files whose read-only attribute is set cannot be deleted.

Changing File Sizes

DosSetFileSize is used to extend or truncate the size of a file that is open for Read/Write or Write-Only access.

When a file is extended, for example to reserve disk space, the value of the additional bytes allocated by the system is undefined.

Locking and Unlocking File Regions

Because the OS/2 operating system permits more than one application to open a file and write to it, it is important that the applications not write over each other's work. An application can protect against this problem by temporarily locking a region in a file.

DosSetFileLocks provides a simple mechanism that temporarily prevents access by other processes to regions within a file. DosSetFileLocks specifies a range of bytes in the file that is locked by an application and that can be accessed only by the application locking the region. The application uses the same function to free the locked region.

Locking and unlocking regions in a file enables sharing processes to coordinate their efforts. A process can lock a region in a file so the process can read and update the file region. A sharing process that attempts to lock the region before the other process finishes its update and unlocks the region receives an error code. When a lock is unsuccessful because a lock is already in place, ERROR_LOCK_VIOLATION is returned.

A lock that extends beyond end-of-file is not considered an error. However, a locked region cannot overlap another locked region, nor can it encompass a locked region. Any such conflicting locks must be cleared before a region can be locked.

When a file handle is duplicated, the duplicate handle has access to any locked regions currently being accessed by the original handle. Although a child process created with DosExecPgm can inherit the file handles of its parent process, it does not inherit access to locked regions in effect for a file handle unless the file handle is duplicated and passed to it.

Notes:

1. File locks are intended to be in effect for only short periods of time.

2. When a file with locks is closed, the locks are released in no defined order.

Searching for Files

An application can use DosFindFirst, DosFindNext, and DosFindClose to search the current directory for all file names that match a given pattern.

The pattern must be an OS/2 file name and can include metacharacters (global file name characters). The wildcard characters are the question mark (?) and the asterisk (*). The question mark matches any single character; the asterisk matches any combination of characters. For example, the pattern "A*" matches the names "ABC", "A23", and "ABCD", but the pattern "A?C" matches only the name "ABC".

Determining the Maximum Path Length

An application that recognizes long file names might be run on systems with or without installable file systems. Additionally, the maximum length of a file name might vary from one installable file system to another. So that an application can properly handle this variable condition (and, for example, allocate large enough buffers to hold file names), the application should call DosQuerySysInfo to determine the maximum path length supported by the file system.

Make this call before calling file system functions that require full path names.

Devices

The OS/2 operating system enables you to access peripheral devices using file system commands, and treat those devices as file streams of data. These devices include:

Character devices	COM, clock, console (keyboard and screen), screen, keyboard, printer, null, pointer, and mouse devices.
Standard I/O devices	Character devices automatically installed by the operating system and recognized by the file system as the standard input, standard output, and standard error devices.
Pseudocharacter devices	An application can attach a device name to a file system and use the file system as a pseudocharacter device (also called a single-file device). Attaching a device name to a file system allows an application to open the device associated with the file system as if it were a character device (for example, a serial port) and read from and write to the device by using DosRead and DosWrite.

In addition, an application can use DosSetFilePtr and DosSetFileLocks with a pseudocharacter device. Also, pseudocharacter devices can be redirected.

A file system that can be attached to a pseudocharacter device is typically associated with a single disk file or with a |

special storage device, such as a tape drive. The file system establishes a connection with the device and transfers requests and data between the operating system and the device. The user perceives this file as a device name for a nonexistent device.

This file is seen as a character device because the current drive and directory have no effect on the name. A pseudocharacter device name is an ASCII string with the name of an OS/2 file in the form:

```
\dev\dev_name
```

The "\dev\" is a required part of the name, but there is no actual subdirectory named "\dev\". This just lets the operating system know that it is a pseudocharacter device name.

Logical file devices.   The hard disk or floppy disk drives, or the partitions on the hard disk or floppy disk drives.

Using File Commands

Files are accessed through the file system using file handles. File handles are returned by DosOpen when the file is opened and are used for all subsequent accesses to the file. Files can be be created, opened, read from, written to, closed, copied, moved, deleted, renamed, and locked. Files can be searched for based on a metacharacter pattern template.

Each open file has a file pointer that indicates the current reading or writing location within the file. The file pointer moves automatically with each read or write operation on the file and can be moved manually by the application.

The standard file handles—standard input, standard output, and standard error—provide redirectable input and output to applications. The standard file handles can be used to read input from the keyboard and write output to the display. Alternatively, they can be redirected to read input from and write output to a file. To an application reading and writing the standard file handles, there is no difference between the two.

Note: In the example code fragments that follow, error checking was left out to conserve space. Applications should always check the return code that the functions return. Control Program functions return an APIRET value. A return code of 0 indicates success. If a non-zero value is returned, an error occurred.

Creating Files

DosOpen is used to create files, which are then read from or written to. To create a file, specify FILE_CREATE as the sixth argument in the call to the function. DosOpen then creates the file, if it does not already exist. If the file already exists, the function returns the error value FILE_EXISTED.

In the following code fragment, DosOpen creates the file NEWFILE.TXT:

```
#define INCL_DOSFILEMGR    /* File System values */
#include <os2.h>

HFILE    hf;
ULONG    ulAction;
APIRET   rc;

rc = DosOpen("NEWFILE.TXT",          /* Name of file to create and open */
             &hf,                    /* Address of file handle          */
             &ulAction,              /* Action taken                    */
             0,                      /* Size of new file                */
             FILE_NORMAL,            /* File attributes                 */
             FILE_CREATE,            /* Creates the file                */
             OPEN_ACCESS_WRITEONLY | OPEN_SHARE_DENYNONE,
             (PEAOP2) NULL);         /* No extended attributes          */
```

Figure 4-1. Creating a New File

In this example, DosOpen creates the file and opens it for writing only. Note that the sharing method chosen permits other processes to open the file for any access. The new file is empty (contains no data).

When you use DosOpen to create (or replace) a file, you must specify the attributes the new file is to have. In the preceding example, this value is FILE_NORMAL, so the file is created as a normal file. Other possible file attributes include read-only and hidden, which correspond to FILE_READONLY and FILE_HIDDEN, respectively. The possible file attributes are:

File Attribute	Defined Constant
Normal file	FILE_NORMAL
Read-only file	FILE_READONLY
Hidden file	FILE_HIDDEN
System file	FILE_SYSTEM
Subdirectory	FILE_DIRECTORY
Archived file	FILE_ARCHIVED.

The file attribute affects how other processes access the file. For example, if the file is read-only, no process can open the file for writing. There is one exception—the process that creates the read-only file can write to it immediately after creating it. After closing the file, however, the process cannot reopen it for writing.

If you are creating a new file object (a new file or a replacement for an existing one), you must specify the size of the new file in bytes. For example, if you specify 256, the file size is 256 bytes. However, these 256 bytes are undefined. If the file being opened already exists, the file size parameter is ignored. It is up to the application to write valid data to the file. No matter what size you specify, the file pointer is set to point to the beginning of the file so a subsequent call to DosWrite starts writing data at the beginning of the file.

Extended attributes can be defined by an application when a file object is created. An application can define an extended attribute for a file when the file is created during a DosOpen call. (See Chapter 5, "Extended Attributes" on page 5-1 for more on extended attributes).

Applications can also control access to specific regions within a file by calling DosSetFileLocks.

Opening Files

Before performing input or output operations on a file, you must open the file and obtain a file handle. You obtain a file handle by using DosOpen. This function opens the specified file and returns a file handle for it. DosOpen can also be used to create new files.

DosOpen establishes a connection between a file object and an application. This connection is in the form of a 32-bit identifier called a *file handle*, which is used to refer to the file object and any information associated with it. DosOpen returns a handle that is used in other file system calls to gain access to the object. The file object can be a new file, an existing file, or a replacement for an existing file. It can also be a character device, a block device, or the client end of a named pipe. The type of object is determined by the file name you pass to DosOpen.

Note: If the object is a named pipe, it must be in a listening state for DosOpen to be successful. For more information about opening a named pipe, see "Opening Named Pipes" on page 9-14.

In the following code fragment, DosOpen opens the existing file SAMPLE.TXT for reading and puts the file handle into the *hf* variable:

```
#define INCL_DOSFILEMGR   /* File System values */
#include <os2.h>

HFILE   hf;
ULONG   ulAction;
APIRET  rc;

rc = DosOpen("SAMPLE.TXT",       /* Name of file to open       */
             &hf,                /* Address of file handle     */
             &ulAction,          /* Action taken               */
             0,                  /* Size of file               */
             FILE_NORMAL,        /* File attribute             */
             FILE_OPEN,          /* Open the file              */
             OPEN_ACCESS_READONLY | OPEN_SHARE_DENYNONE,
             (PEAOP2) NULL);     /* Extended attribute buffer */
```

Figure 4-2. Opening a File and Obtaining a File Handle

If DosOpen successfully opens the file, it copies the file handle to the *hf* variable and copies a value to the *ulAction* variable indicating what action was taken (for example, FILE_EXISTED for "existing file opened"). A file size is not needed to open an existing file, so the fourth argument is 0. The fifth argument, FILE_NORMAL, specifies the normal file attribute. The sixth argument, FILE_OPEN, directs DosOpen to open the file if it exists or return an error if it does not exist. The seventh argument directs DosOpen to open the file for reading only and enables other applications to open the file even while the current application has it open. The final argument is a pointer to a structure containing information on extended attributes. If the file has no extended attributes, this argument must be NULL.

DosOpen returns 0 if it successfully opens the file. Applications use the file handle in subsequent functions to read data from the file or to check the status and other file characteristics. If DosOpen fails to open the file, it returns an error value.

When you open a file you must specify whether you want to read from the file, write to it, or both read and write. Also, since more than one application might attempt to open the same file, you must also specify whether you want to allow other processes to have access to the file while you have it open. A file that is shared can be shared for reading only, writing only, or reading and writing. A file that is not shared cannot be opened by another application (or more than once by the first application) until it has been closed by the first application.

An application defines its file access rights (that is, I/O it needs to perform on a file) by setting the appropriate file access mode field in the file open-mode parameter. An application accesses a file as:

- Read-Only
- Write-Only
- Read/Write.

An application defines what I/O operations other processes can perform on a file by setting the appropriate sharing mode field in the *OpenMode* parameter. Other processes are granted:

- Deny Read/Write access
- Deny Write access
- Deny Read access
- Deny Neither Read or Write access (Deny None).

File sharing requires cooperation between the sharing processes. For example, if process A calls DosOpen to open a file with Deny Write sharing and process B calls DosOpen to open the same file with Read/Write access, the DosOpen call made by process B fails.

You indicate whether or not you want to permit another application to access your file by combining an OPEN_ACCESS_ value and an OPEN_SHARE_ value from the following list:

Table 4-1. File Access and Sharing Rights

Value	Meaning
OPEN_ACCESS_READONLY	Open a file for reading.
OPEN_ACCESS_WRITEONLY	Open a file for writing.
OPEN_ACCESS_READWRITE	Open a file for reading and writing.
OPEN_SHARE_DENYREADWRITE	Open a file for exclusive use, denying other processes read and write access.
OPEN_SHARE_DENYWRITE	Deny other processes write access to a file.
OPEN_SHARE_DENYREAD	Deny other processes read access to a file.
OPEN_SHARE_DENYNONE	Open a file with no sharing restrictions, granting read and write access to all processes.

In general, you can combine any access method (read, write, or read and write) with any sharing method (deny reading, deny writing, deny reading and writing, or grant any access). Some combinations have to be handled carefully, however, such as opening a file for writing without denying other processes access to it.

Note: For named pipes, the access and sharing modes must be consistent with those specified by DosCreateNPipe.

Other characteristics of the file handle that can be set:

Table 4-2. File Handle Characteristics

Flag	Purpose
Inheritance	Handle is inherited by a child process created with DosExecPgm, or is private to the calling process.
Write-Through	Actual I/O for synchronous writes is not guaranteed as complete or is guaranteed as complete before the write returns.
Fail-Errors	Media errors are reported by the system critical error handler, or by the application.
DASD	The file name parameter is the name of a file or device opened in the normal way, or a drive specification for a fixed disk or diskette drive. The DASD flag can be set for direct access to an entire disk or diskette volume, independent of the file system. When the DASD flag is set, the handle returned by DosOpen represents the logical volume as a single file. To block other processes from accessing the logical volume, a DosDevIOCtl Category 8, Function 0 call should be made using the handle returned by DosOpen. The DASD flag should be set only by systems programs, not by applications.
Cache	The file system caches or does not cache data for I/O operations on the file. This flag is advisory only.

See the DosOpen material in the *Control Program Programming Reference* for details of these characteristics.

After an object has been opened, its file handle state flags can be queried by calling DosQueryFHState and reset by calling DosSetFHState. See "Determining and Setting the State of a File or Device Handle" on page 4-16 for information on determining the state of a file handle.

When a child process inherits a file handle, it also inherits the sharing and access rights of the file.

You cannot use metacharacters (global file name characters; * and ?) in file names you supply to DosOpen.

Reading from Files

Once you open a file or have a file handle, you can read from and write to the file by using DosRead and DosWrite.

DosRead is called with a handle (obtained with DosOpen) for a file, pipe, or device. DosRead copies a specified number of bytes (up to the end of the file) from the file object to the buffer you specify. The operating system returns, in a parameter, the number of bytes actually read (which might not be the same as the number of bytes requested because the end of the file might have been reached).

To read from a file, you must open it for reading or for reading and writing.

The following code fragment shows how to open the file named SAMPLE.TXT and read the first 512 bytes from it:

```
#define INCL_DOSFILEMGR   /* File System values */
#include <os2.h>

#define BUF_SIZE 512

HFILE   hf;
ULONG   ulAction;
BYTE    abBuffer[BUF_SIZE];
ULONG   cbRead;
APIRET  rc;

rc = DosOpen("SAMPLE.TXT", &hf, &ulAction, 0, FILE_NORMAL, FILE_OPEN,
             OPEN_ACCESS_READONLY | OPEN_SHARE_DENYNONE,
             (PEAOP2) NULL);

if (!rc) {
    DosRead(hf, abBuffer, sizeof(abBuffer), &cbRead);
    DosClose(hf);
}
```

Figure 4-3. Opening and Reading a File

If the file does not have 512 bytes, DosRead reads to the end of the file and puts the number of bytes read in the *cbRead* variable. If the file pointer is already positioned at the end of the file when DosRead is called, the function puts a 0 in the *cbRead* variable.

Writing to Files

Once you open a file or have a file handle, you can read from and write to the file by using DosRead and DosWrite.

DosWrite copies bytes from a buffer you specify to a file, device, or pipe.

Calling DosWrite with a handle for a file, pipe, or device transfers the number of bytes specified from a buffer location to the object. The system returns, in a parameter, the number of bytes actually written (which in the case of a disk file might not be the same as the number requested because of insufficient disk space).

To write to a file, you must first open it for writing or for reading and writing.

The following code fragment shows how to open the file SAMPLE.TXT again and write 512 bytes to it:

```
#define INCL_DOSFILEMGR   /* File System values */
#include <os2.h>

#define BUF_SIZE 512

HFILE   hf;
ULONG   ulAction;
BYTE    abBuffer[BUF_SIZE];
ULONG   cbWritten;
APIRET  rc;

rc = DosOpen("SAMPLE.TXT", &hf, &ulAction, 0, FILE_NORMAL, FILE_CREATE,
             OPEN_ACCESS_WRITEONLY | OPEN_SHARE_DENYWRITE,
             (PEAOP2) NULL);

if (!rc) {
    DosWrite(hf, abBuffer, sizeof(abBuffer), &cbWritten);
    DosClose(hf);
}
```

Figure 4-4. Opening and Writing to a File

DosWrite writes the contents of the buffer to the file. If it fails to write 512 bytes (for example, if the disk is full), the function puts the number of bytes written in the *cbWritten* variable. The data is read and written exactly as given; the function does not format the data—that is, they do not convert binary data to decimal strings, or vice versa.

The Write-Through Flag

If an application requires data to be written in a specific order, setting the *Write-Through flag* to 1 guarantees that actual I/O for a synchronous write is completed before the DosWrite returns. If this flag has been set with DosOpen for buffered I/O, and multiple synchronous writes are performed, the system cannot guarantee the actual order in which the data is written. For details on changing the state of the *Write-Through flag*, see "Determining and Setting the State of a File or Device Handle" on page 4-16.

Moving the File Pointer

Every disk file has a corresponding file pointer that marks the current location in the file. The current location is the byte in the file that will be read from or written to on the next call to DosRead or DosWrite. Usually, the file pointer is at the beginning of the file when you first open or create the file, and it advances as you read or write to the file. You can, however, change the position of the file pointer at any time by using DosSetFilePtr.

DosSetFilePtr moves the file pointer a specified offset from a given position. You can move the pointer from the beginning of the file, from the end, or from the current position.

The following code fragment shows how to move the pointer 200 bytes from the end of the file:

```
#define INCL_DOSFILEMGR    /* File System values */
#include <os2.h>

#define HF_STDOUT 1         /* Standard output handle */
#define BUF_SIZE 255

BYTE abBuf[BUF_SIZE];
HFILE hf;
ULONG cbRead, cbWritten, ulAction, ulNewPtr;

DosOpen("SAMPLE.TXT", &hf, &ulAction, 0, FILE_NORMAL, FILE_OPEN,
        OPEN_ACCESS_READONLY | OPEN_SHARE_DENYNONE,
        (PEAOP2) NULL);

DosSetFilePtr(hf, -200, FILE_END, &ulNewPtr);

DosRead(hf, &abBuf, sizeof(abBuf), &cbRead);

DosWrite(HF_STDOUT, abBuf, cbRead, &cbWritten);
```

Figure 4-5. Moving the File Pointer

In this example, DosSetFilePtr moves the file pointer to the 200th byte from the end of the file. If the file is not that long, the function moves the pointer to the first byte in the file and returns the actual position (relative to the end of the file) in the *ulNewPtr* variable.

You can move the file pointer for disk files only. You cannot use DosSetFilePtr on devices, despite using other file functions (DosOpen, DosRead) to access a device.

If a file is read-only, write operations to the file will not be performed.

Moving the pointer from the end of the file can be used to determine the size of the file.

Closing Files

You can close a file by using DosClose. Since each application has a limited number of file handles that can be open at one time, it is a good practice to close a file after using it.

To do so, supply the file handle in DosClose, as shown in the following code fragment:

```
#define INCL_DOSFILEMGR    /* File System values */
#include <os2.h>

#define BUF_SIZE 80

HFILE    hf;
ULONG    ulAction;
BYTE     abBuffer[BUF_SIZE];
ULONG    cbRead;
APIRET   rc;

rc = DosOpen("SAMPLE.TXT", &hf, &ulAction, 0, FILE_NORMAL,
            FILE_OPEN, OPEN_ACCESS_READONLY | OPEN_SHARE_DENYNONE,
            (PEAOP2) NULL);

if (!rc) {
    DosRead(hf, abBuffer, sizeof(abBuffer), &cbRead);
    DosClose(hf);
}
```

Figure 4-6. Closing a File

If you open a file for writing, DosClose directs the system to flush the file buffer—that is, to write any existing data in the operating system's intermediate file buffer to the disk or device. The system keeps these intermediate file buffers to make file input and output more efficient. For example, it saves data from previous calls to DosWrite until a certain number of bytes are in the buffer then writes the contents of the buffer to the disk.

DosClose also closes the handle to the file (or pipe, or device). If one or more additional handles to a file have been created with DosDupHandle, the internal buffers for the file are not written to disk, and its directory entry is not updated, until DosClose has been called for all the handles.

For information on the effects of DosClose called with a named pipe handle, see "Named Pipes" on page 9-2.

Creating Duplicate File or Device Handles

DosDupHandle enables a process to create a duplicate handle for an open file, pipe, or device.

The value for the old-file-handle parameter is the handle of an open file, a pipe, or a device. The valid values for the new-file-handle parameter include FFFFH, 0000H (standard input), 0001H (standard output), and 0002H (standard error). Any value other than FFFFH is assumed to be the value of the new file handle.

A value of FFFFH causes the system to allocate a new file handle and send it to this location. If the value specified for the new-file-handle parameter is that of a currently open file, the file handle is closed before it is redefined.

An agreed upon value for a duplicate file handle can be established between a parent process and a child process. Avoid choosing arbitrary values for the new file handle.

The duplicate handle acquires the characteristics of the original. If you move the read/write pointer of the original file handle, for example by calling DosRead, DosWrite, or DosSetFilePtr, the pointer of the duplicate handle is also moved. If the original handle has access to regions in a file that have been locked by DosSetFileLocks, the duplicate also has access.

If inheritance was indicated when a file was opened with DosOpen, a parent process can create a duplicate handle for the file and pass it to a child process by means of shared memory. This permits the child to close the duplicate handle without affecting the file handle of the parent.

Because a parent process controls the meanings for standard I/O done by any child process it creates, the parent can use DosDupHandle to redefine unnamed pipe handles as standard I/O handles to communicate with a child. The steps involved are:

- The parent process creates two pipes and duplicates the read handle of one pipe as 0000 and the write handle of the other pipe as 0001.

- When the child process performs standard I/O, instead of reading from the keyboard and writing to the display, it reads from and writes to the pipes created by its parent.

- As the owner of the pipe, the parent process uses its read and write handles to write to the pipe defined to the child as standard input and read from the pipe defined to the child as standard output.

Determining and Setting the State of a File or Device Handle

After a file has been opened, the file handle state flags set with a DosOpen can be queried and reset by calling DosQueryFHState and DosSetFHState. The handle returned by DosSetFHState is used for subsequent input and output to the file.

The following code fragment calls DosSetFHState to set the File Write-Through flag for an opened file. Writes to the file may go through the file system buffer, but the sectors are to be written before any synchronous write call returns. DosQueryFHState is called first to obtain the file handle state bits. Assume that the appropriate file handle has been placed into *FileHandle* already.

```
#define INCL_DOSFILEMGR   /* File System values */
#include <os2.h>
#include <stdio.h>

HFILE   FileHandle;        /* File handle        */
ULONG   FileHandleState;   /* File handle state */
APIRET  rc;                /* Return code        */

rc = DosQueryFHState(FileHandle, &FileHandleState);

if (rc != 0) {
    printf("DosQueryFHState error: return code = %ld", rc);
    return;
}

FileHandleState |= OPEN_FLAGS_WRITE_THROUGH;

rc = DosSetFHState(FileHandle, FileHandleState);

if (rc != 0) {
    printf("DosSetFHState error: return code = %ld", rc);
    return;
}
```

Figure   4-7. Setting the State of a File Handle

Here are two scenarios involving the use of this function.

- An application requires that data be written in a specific order. To guarantee the order of the data written, it must perform separate synchronous write operations. The application can call DosSetFHState to set the Write-Through flag for the file. This action does not affect any previous asynchronous writes, whose data can remain in the buffers.

- An application cannot handle a certain critical error situation. DosSetFHState can be called to reset critical error handling as the operating system's responsibility. The I/O function that caused the critical error must be called again so the error can recur, causing control to be passed to the operating system. In the case where asynchronous I/O is being done, the precise time the results of this function will be available to the application is unpredictable.

Determining the Handle Type

DosQueryHType enables an application to determine whether a handle is to a file, a pipe, or a device. This function can be used when a file-oriented application needs to modify its behavior, depending on the source of its input. For example, CMD.EXE suppresses writing prompts when its input is from a disk file.

The following code fragment determines whether a given file handle refers to a file or a device. Assume that the desired file handle has been placed into *FileHandle* already.

```
#define INCL_DOSFILEMGR   /* File System values */
#include <os2.h>
#include <stdio.h>

HFILE   FileHandle;    /* File handle                          */
ULONG   HandType;      /* Handle type (returned)               */
ULONG   FlagWord;      /* Device driver attribute (returned)   */
APIRET  rc;            /* Return code                          */

rc = DosQueryHType(FileHandle, &HandType, &FlagWord);

if (rc != 0) {
    printf("DosQueryHType error: return code = %ld", rc);
    return;
}
```

Figure 4-8. Determining the Handle Type

In the preceding example, DosQueryHType returns a value that characterizes the type of file handle, and the associated device driver attribute word if handle type indicates that the file handle is associated with a local character device

Searching for Files

You can locate files with names that match a given pattern by using metacharacters in DosFindFirst and DosFindNext.

DosFindFirst searches the current directory and locates the first file name that matches the given pattern. DosFindNext locates the next matching file name and continues to find additional matches on each subsequent call until all matching names are found. The functions copy the file statistics on each file located to a data structure that you supply. The file information returned by a search includes file dates and times, length of data in the file, file size, file attributes, and file name.

To find all files that match the file specification, call DosFindNext repeatedly until the message ERROR_NO_MORE_FILES is returned. Then call DosFindClose to close the directory handle.

The following code fragment shows how to find all file names that have the extension ".C":

```
#define INCL_DOSFILEMGR    /* File System values */
#include <os2.h>

HDIR         hdir;
ULONG        cFilenames;
FILEFINDBUF  findbuf;
APIRET       rc;

cFilenames = 1;
hdir = HDIR_SYSTEM;

rc = DosFindFirst("*.C",
                   &hdir,              /* Directory handle                    */
                   FILE_NORMAL,        /* File attribute to look for          */
                   &findbuf,           /* Result buffer                       */
                   sizeof(findbuf),    /* Size of result buffer               */
                   &cFilenames,        /* Number of matching names to look for */
                   FIL_STANDARD);      /* Standard level of information       */

if (!rc) {
    do {
        .
        .         /* Use file name in findbuf.achName */
        .
        rc = DosFindNext(hdir, &findbuf, sizeof(findbuf), &cFilenames);

    } while (!rc);
}
DosFindClose(hdir);
```

*Figure   4-9. Finding All *.C Files*

In this example, DosFindNext continues to retrieve matching file names until it returns an error value (it returns ERROR_NO_MORE_FILES when it cannot find any more matching files).

To keep track of which files have already been found, both functions use the directory handle, *hdir.*

This directory handle must be set to HDIR_SYSTEM or HDIR_CREATE before the call to DosFindFirst. HDIR_SYSTEM (00000001H) tells the operating system to use the system handle for standard output, which is always available to the requesting process. HDIR_CREATE (FFFFFFFFH) tells the operating system to allocate a new, unused handle.

The directory handle returned by DosFindFirst must be used in subsequent calls to DosFindNext; it identifies for DosFindNext the name of the file being sought and the current position in the directory.

An attribute parameter for DosFindFirst allows hidden and system files, as well as normal files, to be included in searches.

After locating the files you need, use DosFindClose to close the directory handle. This ensures that when you search for the same files again, you will start at the beginning of the directory. After DosFindClose is called, a subsequent DosFindNext fails.

Searching Paths for Files

DosSearchPath searches directory paths for the name of a file object. The file specification can include metacharacters (global file name characters).

The path string used in the search consists of directory paths separated by semicolons. The caller can supply the path string, or it can supply the name of an environment variable whose value is the path string to be searched. The caller can request that the current working directory be searched before the path string is searched.

If the caller specifies an environment variable, DosSearchPath uses DosScanEnv to find the path string. DosScanEnv searches the environment segment for an environment variable name; for example, DPATH. The result pointer points to the string that is the value of the environment variable. The call to DosScanEnv can be made directly by the application, or it can be invoked by DosSearchPath.

If the file is found, its full path name is returned, with metacharacters left in place. The results might not be meaningful if a buffer overflow occurs.

As an example, assume that a string such as the following exists in the environment:

```
DPATH=C:\SYSDIR;C:\INIT
```

Two methods for searching directory paths to find a file are illustrated below.

```
#define INCL_DOSFILEMGR   /* File System values */
#include <os2.h>

#define ResultBufLen 255
  .
  .
  .
char  PathRef[255];
char  ResultBuffer[ResultBufLen];

DosScanEnv("DPATH", &PathRef);
DosSearchPath(0,                            /* Path Source Bit = 0 */
              PathRef, "MYPROG.INI",
              &ResultBuffer, ResultBufLen);
DosOpen(ResultBuffer, ... );
```

Figure 4-10. Method 1: Searching Directory Paths Using DosScanEnv and DosSearchPath

```
#define INCL_DOSFILEMGR    /* File System values */
#include <os2.h>

#define ResultBufLen 255
  .
  .
  .
char  ResultBuffer[ResultBufLen];

DosSearchPath(1,                           /* Path Source Bit = 1 */
            "DPATH", "MYPROG.INI",
            &ResultBuffer, ResultBufLen);
DosOpen(ResultBuffer, ... );
```

Figure 4-11. Method 2: Searching Directory Paths Using DosSearchPath

---

Standard File Handles

Every application, when it first starts, has three input and output file handles available to use. These file handles, called the standard input, standard output, and standard error files, enable the application to read input from the keyboard and display output on the screen without opening or preparing the keyboard or screen.

Standard Input, Output, and Error File Handles

As the operating system starts an application, it automatically opens the three standard files and makes the file handles—numbered 0, 1, and 2—available to the application. Applications can read from and write to the standard files as soon as they start.

Standard Input

File handle 0 is the standard input file. This handle can be used to read characters from the keyboard with DosRead. The function reads the specified number of characters unless the user types a *turnaround character*—that is, a character that marks the end of a line (the default turnaround character is a carriage-return/linefeed character pair).

As DosRead reads the characters, it copies them to the buffer you have supplied, as shown in the following code fragment:

```
#define INCL_DOSFILEMGR    /* File System values */
#include <os2.h>

#define HF_STDIN 0          /* Standard input handle */
#define BUF_SIZE 80

BYTE abBuffer[BUF_SIZE];
ULONG cbRead;

DosRead(HF_STDIN, abBuffer, sizeof(abBuffer), &cbRead);
```

Figure 4-12. Reading from Standard Input

In this example, DosRead copies to the *cbRead* variable the number of characters read from standard input. The function also copies the turnaround character, or characters, to the buffer. If the function reads fewer than 80 characters, the turnaround character is the last one in the buffer.

Standard Output

File handle 1 is the standard output file. This handle can be used to write characters on the screen with DosWrite. The function writes the characters in the given buffer to the current line. If you want to start a new line, you must place the current turnaround character in the buffer.

The following code fragment displays a prompt, reads a string, and displays the string:

```
#define INCL_DOSFILEMGR   /* File System values */
#include <os2.h>

#define HF_STDIN  0       /* Standard input handle  */
#define HF_STDOUT 1       /* Standard output handle */
#define BUF_SIZE 80

ULONG cbWritten, cbRead;
BYTE abBuffer[BUF_SIZE];
static UCHAR szEnterName[] = "Enter a name: ";

DosWrite(HF_STDOUT, szEnterName, sizeof(szEnterName), &cbWritten);

DosRead(HF_STDIN, abBuffer, sizeof(abBuffer), &cbRead);

DosWrite(HF_STDOUT, abBuffer, cbRead, &cbWritten);
```

Figure   4-13. Writing to Standard Output

Standard Error

File handle 2 is the standard error file. This handle, like the standard output handle, enables applications to write characters on the screen. Most applications use the standard error file to display error messages, enabling the application to redirect standard output to a file without also redirecting error messages to the file.

Redirecting Standard File Handles

The standard input, standard output, and standard error files are usually the keyboard and screen, but not always. For example, if you redirect standard output by using the greater-than (>) redirection symbol on the application's command line, all data written to the standard output file goes to the given file.

The following command line redirects standard output to the file SAMPLE.TXT and redirects error messages to the file SAMPLE.ERR:

```
type startup.cmd >sample.txt 2>sample.err
```

When a standard file is redirected, its handle is still available but corresponds to the given disk file instead of to the keyboard or screen. You can still use DosRead and DosWrite to read from and write to the files.

You can use DosDupHandle to redirect a standard file from inside your application. If you duplicate the standard input file handle, your application reads from the specified file rather than from the keyboard. Duplicating the standard output file handle causes output to be directed to a file or device instead of to the standard output device.

The following code fragment shows how to use the standard input handle to read from a file:

```
#define INCL_DOSFILEMGR    /* File System values */
#include <os2.h>

#define HF_STDIN  0        /* Standard input handle  */
#define HF_STDOUT 1        /* Standard output handle */
#define BUF_SIZE 80

BYTE    abBuffer[BUF_SIZE];
HFILE   hf, hfNew;
ULONG   cbRead, cbWritten, ulAction;
APIRET  rc;

rc = DosOpen("SAMPLE.C", &hf, &ulAction, 0, FILE_NORMAL, FILE_OPEN,
             OPEN_ACCESS_READONLY | OPEN_SHARE_DENYNONE, (PEAOP2) NULL);

if (!rc) {
    hfNew = 0;       /* Duplicates standard input */
    DosDupHandle(hf, &hfNew);
    DosRead(HF_STDIN, abBuffer, sizeof(abBuffer), &cbRead);
    DosWrite(HF_STDOUT, abBuffer, cbRead, &cbWritten);
}
```

Figure 4-14. Duplicating the Standard Input Handle

Summary

Following are the OS/2 functions and data structures used in file object management.

Table 4-3 (Page 1 of 2). File Management Functions	
File Functions	
DosClose	Closes a file handle.
DosCopy	Copies a file or subdirectory.
DosDelete	Deletes a file.
DosEditName	Transforms a file name.
DosMove	Moves a file or subdirectory.
DosOpen	Gets a handle to a file, pipe, or device.
DosRead	Reads from a file, pipe, or device.
DosSetFileInfo	Sets information for an open file.
DosSetFileLocks	Locks an unlocks a range in a file.
DosSetFilePtr	Moves the position of the file pointer.
DosSetFileSize	Changes the size of a file.
DosSetPathInfo	Sets information for a file or subdirectory.
DosSetVerify	Enables write verification.
DosWrite	Writes data to a file, pipe, or device.
File Handle Functions	
DosDupHandle	Duplicates a file handle.
DosQueryFHState	Gets the file handle state.
DosQueryHType	Gets the handle type.
DosSetFHState	Sets the file handle state.
DosSetMaxFH	Sets the maximum number of file handles.
File Query Functions	
DosEnumAttribute	Gets the name and size of a file object's extended attributes.
DosQueryFileInfo	Gets information for an open file.
DosQueryPathInfo	Gets information for a file or subdirectory.
DosQuerySysInfo	Gets values of system variables.
DosQueryVerify	Determines whether or not write verification is enabled.

Table 4-3 (Page 2 of 2). File Management Functions	
Directory Search (FileFind) Functions	
DosFindClose	Ends a search for matching file objects.
DosFindFirst	Begins a search for matching file objects.
DosFindNext	Continues a search for matching file objects.
Directory and Disk Functions	
DosCreateDir	Creates a subdirectory.
DosDeleteDir	Deletes an empty subdirectory.
DosQueryCurrentDir	Gets the current directory.
DosQueryCurrentDisk	Gets the current drive.
DosSetCurrentDir	Sets the current directory.
DosSetDefaultDisk	Sets the default drive.
Environment and Search Path Functions	
DosScanEnv	Scans environment variable.
DosQueryPathInfo	Gets information for a file or subdirectory.
DosSearchPath	Searches along a specified path.
DosSetPathInfo	Sets information for a file or subdirectory.

Table 4-4. File Management Data Structures	
Data Structure	**Description**
DENA1	Level 1 info. returned from DosEnumAttribute.
FDATE	A sub-structure used in the FILEFINDBUF and the FILESTATUS structures. Used to contain information about various dates associated with the file (creation, last change, and so on).
FILEFINDBUF	Used by DosFindFirst and DosFindNext to return information about files. There are also variations of the data structure called FILEFINDBUF2, FILEFINDBUF3, and FILEFINDBUF4.
FILELOCK	Used by DosSetFileLocks to indicate the range to lock within the file.
FILESTATUS	Used when querying and setting information about a file, such as the file's dates, times, and size.
FTIME	A sub-structure of FILEFINDBUF and FILESTATUS. Contains information about the time the file was created, last changed, and so on.
VOLUMELABEL	A sub-structure of the FSINFO data structure. It contains the volume's label.

Chapter 5. Extended Attributes

OS/2 file systems maintain a standard set of information on file objects. This standard set of information is referred to as *Level 1 file information*. Level 1 file information includes the name and size of the file object, and the date and time the file object was created, last accessed, and last written to.

Applications can attach additional information to a file object in the form of an *extended attribute* (EA). There can be many EAs associated with a file object and, because of their flexibility, almost any information about the file can be stored in one.

The following topics are related to the information in this chapter:

* Files Systems
* Files Names
* Files Management.

About Extended Attributes.

Level 1 file information is the basic information describing files that is stored by the file system. Level 1 file information includes the size of the file, and the date and time it was created, last written, and last accessed. A subset of this information is typically displayed by entering the DIR command on the OS/2 command line. Applications can obtain Level 1 file information by calling DosQueryPathInfo and DosQueryFileInfo. Applications can set Level 1 File Information by calling DosSetPathInfo and DosSetFileInfo.

Applications can attach additional information to a file object in the form of an *extended attribute* (EA). Extended attributes can be used to describe the file object to another application, to the operating system, and to the file system that is managing that object.

This information can be used to:

* Store notes on file objects (for example, the name of the file creator)
* Categorize file objects (for example, source, samples, icons, bit maps)
* Describe the format of data contained in the file object (for example, a data record)
* Append additional data to the file object.

An application uses extended attributes to provide a description of a file or directory but the application does not place the description in the file or directory itself. Extended attributes associated with a file object are not part of the file object or its data. They are stored separately from the file they are linked to and the file system manages the storage and maintenance of the EA.

Each extended attribute has two parts, a name and a value. The name is a NULL-terminated string; any convenient name can be chosen. EA names are restricted to the same character set as file names.

The value of the EA can be text, a bit map, binary data, anything at all. The operating system does not check data that is associated with an EA. The application that creates the extended attributes and the applications that read them must recognize the format and meaning of the data associated with a given EA name.

Applications can examine, add, and replace extended attributes at any time. Any application can read the extended attributes by using the DosQueryFileInfo or DosQueryPathInfo function. Applications can use DosFindFirst and DosFindNext to search for files that have specific extended attributes.

A file can have any number of extended attributes. This is illustrated in Figure 5-1. Each extended attribute can be up to 64KB in size. The sum of all extended attributes for a file must not exceed 64KB.

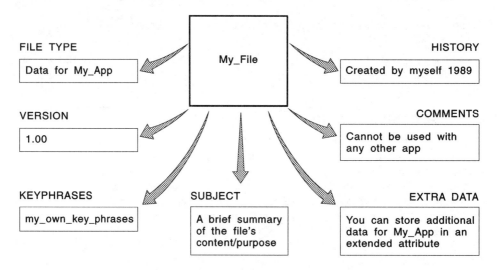

Figure 5-1. Extended Attributes of a File

In Figure 5-1, the file My_File has extended attributes with the following names and values:

Name	Value
FILE TYPE	Data for My_App
HISTORY	Created by myself 1989
VERSION	1.00
COMMENTS	Cannot be used with any other app
KEYPHRASES	my_own_key_phrases
SUBJECT	A brief summary of the file's contents or purpose
EXTRA DATA	I can store additional data for My_App in an extended attribute

So that extended attribute data can be understood by other applications, conventions have been established for naming EAs and indicating the type of data they contain.

In addition, a set of Standard Extended Attributes (SEAs) have been defined. SEAs define a common set of information that can be associated with most files (for example, file type and file purpose). Through SEAs, many applications can access the same, useful information associated with files.

Applications are not limited to using SEAs to associate information with files. They can define their own application-specific extended attributes.

Extended attributes associated with a file object are not part of the file object or its data.

Extended attributes are supported by the OS/2 High Performance File System and by the OS/2 FAT file system in versions of the OS/2 operating system including and following Version 1.2.

Applications define and associate extended attributes with a file object through file system functions. The file system functions that use and manipulate EAs are:

- DosOpen
- DosFindFirst
- DosQueryFileInfo
- DosQueryPathInfo
- DosSetFileInfo
- DosSetPathInfo.

Extended Attribute Data Type Conventions

Extended attributes (EAs) can contain any type of data. So that applications can understand the type of information stored in an EA, the first WORD of EA data must specify one of the following data types:

Table 5-1. Extended Attribute Data Types

Data Type	Value	Description
EAT_BINARY	FFFE	Binary (non-text) data; the first WORD following the data type specifies the length of the data.
EAT_ASCII	FFFD	ASCII text; the first WORD following the data type specifies the length of the data.
EAT_BITMAP	FFFB	Bit map data; the first WORD following the data type specifies the length of the data.
EAT_METAFILE	FFFA	Metafile data; the first WORD following the data type specifies the length of the data.
EAT_ICON	FFF9	Icon data; the first WORD following the data type specifies the length of the data.
EAT_EA	FFEE	ASCII name of another EA that is associated with the file. The contents of that EA are to be included into the current EA. The first WORD following the data type specifies the length of the data.
EAT_MVMT	FFDF	Multi-Valued, Multi-Typed data—two or more consecutive extended attribute values. Each value has an explicitly specified type.
EAT_MVST	FFDE	Multi-Valued, Single-Typed data—two or more consecutive extended attribute values. All values have the same type.
EAT_ASN1	FFDD	ASN.1 field data; an ISO standard for describing multivalue data streams.

Values of hex 8000 and up are reserved. Values between hex 0000 and hex 7FFF can be defined by the user.

Symbolic constants are defined in BSEDOS.H and BSEDOS.INC.

In all cases, the length specifies the number of bytes of data. Other values for data types, in the range hex 0000 through hex 7FFF, can be used for user-defined extended attributes.

All user-defined data types should be length-preceded, meaning that a WORD indicating the length of the data (in bytes) precedes the data.

For example, here is how to represent the string "Hello":

```
EAT_ASCII    0005    Hello
```

Figure 5-2. Extended Attribute ASCII Text String

Multi-Value Data Type Fields

In many cases, it is desirable for extended attributes (EAs) to store more than a single piece of information. For example, an extended attribute can store a list of names to which a document was sent. The multi-value formats specify how individual pieces of data are stored.

Data entries are length-preceded, making it easy to traverse a multi-valued list.

In order to allow EAs of different code pages, multi-valued EAs include a field in which the EA's code page is specified. For example, the code page field could be used to indicate that the comments for a Kanji file are written in Spanish. If this value is 0, the file default is assumed. (Code page data is for use by applications. The operating system does not examine or use EA code page information.)

When the concept of a default applies to a multi-valued EA, the first entry in the list is assumed to be the default. For example, suppose an EA entry contains the strings "Text" and "C Code". "Text" is considered the default type. If "C Code" were the first entry in the list ("C Code" then "Text"), then "C Code" would be considered the default type.

There are three multi-valued EA data types:

- Multi-Valued, Multi-Typed Data
- Multi-Valued, Single-Type Data
- ASN.1 Data.

Multi-Valued, Multi-Typed Data Type

This data type indicates that the value of a single extended attribute (EA) contains several pieces of information, each of a different data type. It is formatted as follows:

```
EAT_MVMT   Codepage   NumEntries   [DataType Data] ...
WORD       WORD       WORD          WORD
```

Figure 5-3. Format of Multi-Valued, Multi-Typed Extended Attributes

The first word indicates that the EA value is multi-valued, multi-typed. The second word indicates the code page associated with the language in which the EA value is written. The third word indicates the number of entries contained in this EA value. The next word indicates the data type for the first entry in this EA value, followed by the data for the first entry. The next word, if any, indicates the data type for the second entry in this EA value, followed by the data for the second entry. The pattern repeats— data type, followed by data—for any remaining entries.

For example, an extended attribute can have the following value:

```
EAT_MVMT   0000   0002   EAT_ASCII    000A Hello John
                         EAT_BINARY   0003 0x12 0x21 0x34
```

Figure 5-4. A Multi-Valued Multi-Typed Extended Attribute

This is a multi-valued extended attribute with two entries, using the default code page. The first entry is the string "Hello John", and the second is the binary data 0x12 0x21 0x34.

Whether or not the data is length-preceded is a function of the data type.

Multi-Valued, Single-Type Data Type

This data type indicates that the value of a single extended attribute (EA) contains several pieces of information, each of the same data type. For example:

```
EAT_MVST  Codepage  NumEntries  Data_Type  [data] ...
WORD      WORD      WORD        WORD
```

Figure 5-5. Format of Multi-Valued, Single-Typed Extended Attributes

The first word indicates that the EA value is multi-valued, single-typed. The second word indicates the code page associated with the language in which the EA value is written. The third word indicates the number of entries contained in this EA value. The next word indicates the data type of all the entries contained in this EA value, followed by the data for all entries.

For example, the following EA value contains three ASCII names:

```
EAT_MVST 0000 0003 EAT_ASCII 0004 Mark
                             0005 Ellen
                             0003 Liz
```

Figure 5-6. MVMT Extended Attribute Containing Three ASCII Names

Each name string is preceded by the length of the string. Whether or not the data is length-preceded is a function of the data type.

ASN.1 Data Type

This data type indicates that the extended attribute uses the ASN.1 ISO standard to describe a multi-valued data stream.

Including One Extended Attribute in Another

Extended attributes (EA) can contain pointers to data stored in other places.

This data type indicates that the data contained in another EA associated with the file object should be included into the current EA.

For example, the following EA value contains the string "Hello", followed by the data in the EA named AB.STUFF, followed by the string "Bye".

```
EA_MVMT 0000 0003 EAT_ASCII 0005  Hello
                  EAT_EA    0008  AB.STUFF
                  EAT_ASCII 0003  Bye
```

Figure 5-7. Extended Attribute Containing Data in Another Extended Attribute

Extended Attribute Naming Conventions

Because many applications use text, bit maps, and other binary data in extended attributes, standard names have been adopted to help identify these formats. An application is not limited to these Standard Extended Attributes but should use them when many applications will be accessing the same data.

Standard Extended Attributes (SEAs) have a dot (.) as a prefix. This identifies the extended attribute as a SEA. The leading dot is reserved, so applications should not define extended attributes that start with a dot. Also, extended attributes that start with the characters $, @, &, or + are reserved for system use.

To ensure that its extended attributes are unique, an application should use the name of the company and the name of the application (or suitable abbreviations of each) as a prefix for application-specific extended attributes.

For example, Company A has an OS/2 Application, B, that defines extended attributes STUFF, MORE_STUFF, and STILL_MORE_STUFF for its file objects. The names of these extended attributes could be represented by the following entry:

```
AB.STUFF   AB.MORE_STUFF   AB.STILL_MORE_STUFF
```

Figure 5-8. Extended Attribute Names

Standard Extended Attributes

There are nine OS/2 Standard Extended Attributes (SEAs).

The name of a SEA has a dot (.) as a prefix. This identifies the extended attribute as a SEA.

The values of Standard Extended Attributes can be multi- or single-valued, with formats following the data type conventions discussed previously.

Where entries for Standard EAs consist of ASCII characters, case is important.

The Standard EAs that have been defined are:

.ASSOCTABLE
.CODEPAGE
.COMMENTS
.HISTORY
.ICON
.KEYPHRASES
.LONGNAME
.SUBJECT
.TYPE
.VERSION

The .TYPE and .ASSOCTABLE extended attributes (EA) are two of the most useful SEAs.

The .TYPE extended attribute indicates what type of data is in a file. It also implies what programs can edit the file, and what icon is to be used for the file. The operating system can use the .TYPE EA to determine a default application to run and a default icon for a file of a particular type (if there is a .ICON EA, it will be used instead of the icon associated with a particular data type).

The .ASSOCTABLE extended attribute allows an application to indicate the type, extension, and icon for data files that it recognizes. It also contains an ownership flag. This data can be automatically installed by the operating system. When your program recognizes files created by other programs, you might want to install .ASSOCTABLE EA entries for those other programs.

The .ASSOCTABLE Standard Extended Attribute

The .ASSOCTABLE extended attribute (EA) contains information that associates data files with the applications that create them or that know how to use them. The .ASSOCTABLE extended attribute enables an application to indicate the type, extension, and icon for the data files it recognizes. The .ASSOCTABLE EA also contains an ownership flag. This tells the operating system which application to run when the user double-clicks the mouse on a given data file.

Because programs can understand and reference data files generated by other programs, this EA can be used to link a program with those files.

The name of this EA consists of the string ".ASSOCTABLE". The value of this EA contains application information and consists of multi-valued, multi-typed fields that link the application with:

- the file type (that is, the value of a .TYPE EA),
- the file extension,
- and icon data for data files that it generates or references. The .ASSOCTABLE EA associates icons by file-type. The data file's file-type is indicated in the .TYPE EA, or, if the data file does not have a .TYPE EA, by the extension.

This data can be installed automatically by the operating system.

The format of the EA is as follows.

```
EAT_MVMT 0000 0004 EAT_ASCII  .TYPE name
                   EAT_ASCII   file extension
                   EAT_BINARY  flags
                   EAT_ICON    icon data
```

Figure 5-9. Format of the Entries in the .ASSOCTABLE Extended Attribute

The source for the .ASSOCTABLE EA is contained in the resource file for an application. The .ASSOCTABLE EA is created using the Resource Compiler from a table with the following form:

```
ASSOCTABLE  assoctable -id
BEGIN
association_name,[extension],[flags], [icon_filename]
association_name,[extension],[flags], [icon_filename]
  .
  .
  .
END
```

Figure 5-10. .ASSOCTABLE Table Used by the Resource Compiler

The *association_name* is the name of a file type that the Resource Compiler understands. (This is the same name found in the .TYPE field of data files.)

The *extension* is the three letter file extension that is used to identify files of this type, if they have no .TYPE EA entry. (Three letter extensions should be used so that FAT file systems can make use of this EA). This field can be empty.

The *icon_filename* is the name of the file that contains the icon that is to be used to represent this file type. (This field can also be empty.)

The .ASSOCTABLE *flag* indicates that the program is the default application for data files with the specified type. This determines the program the operating system will start when the file is double-clicked with the mouse.

If more than one program has marked itself as the EAF_DEFAULTOWNER for a particular data file .TYPE, the operating system will not know which program to run when the file of this .TYPE is double-clicked on with the mouse. If no program is marked as the EAF_DEFAULTOWNER for a particular data file .TYPE, the operating system will be similarly confused. In both cases, the operating system provides the user with a list of applications that understand the file .TYPE, regardless of whether the application is the owner or not. The user selects the program to run from this list.

The *flag* entry indicates whether the application owns the file or merely recognizes the .TYPE. If this flag is set, the entry describing data files of this type cannot be edited. This flag is specified if a previously defined icon in the ASSOCTABLE is to be reused. Entries with this flag set have no icon data defined. The icon used for this entry will be the icon used for the previous entry.

EAF_ flags can be ORed together when specified in the ASSOCTABLE. The EAF_ flags are defined in PMWIN.H and PMWIN.INC.

.ASSOCTABLE Example

For example, My_Company's application, My_Application, generates or references data files that have the following .TYPE names:

```
My_Company My_Application documentation
My_Company My_Application macros
My_Company My_Application spreadsheet
My_Company My_Application chart
Your_Company Your_Application forecast
```

Figure   5-11. My_Application's .TYPE Extended Attribute

The source for the .ASSOCTABLE extended attribute in the resource file for My_Application could look like the following.

```
ASSOCTABLE
BEGIN
"My_Company My_Application documentation", "DOC", EAF_DEFAULTOWNER, My_App.ICO
"My_Company My_Application macros", "MAC", EAF_DEFAULTOWNER+EAF_REUSEICON
"My_Company My_Application spreadsheet", "SPR", EAF_DEFAULTOWNER+EAF_REUSEICON
"My_Company My_Application chart", "CHT", EAF_DEFAULTOWNER+EAF_REUSEICON
"Your_Company Your_Application forecast", "FOR", 0
END
```

Figure   5-12. Sample Resource Compiler Source File

My_Application can load and use some files generated by Your_Application. However, because My_Application is not the default owner of those files, the operating system does not run My_Application when the user double-clicks on the files with the mouse.

Figure 5-13 on page 5-11 illustrates how the value of the .ASSOCTABLE EA for My_Application might look. It is a multi-valued, multi-typed EA with five multi-valued, multi-typed entries (one for each file type referenced or generated by the application).

```
EAT_MVMT    0000 0005           ; There are 5 associated file types

EAT_MVMT    0000 0004           ; Description of 1st associated file type
EAT_ASCII   0027 My_Company My_Application documentation  ; File type
EAT_ASCII   0003 DOC            ; File extension
EAT_BINARY  flags              ; Flags
EAT_ASCII   icon data          ; Physical icon data

EAT_MVMT    0000 0004           ; Description of 2nd associated file type
EAT_ASCII   0020 My_Company My_Application macros
EAT_ASCII   0003 MAC
EAT_BINARY  flags
EAT_ICON    icon data

EAT_MVMT    0000 0004           ; Description of 3rd associated file type
EAT_ASCII   0025 My_Company My_Application spreadsheet
EAT_ASCII   0003 SPR
EAT_BINARY  flags
EAT_ICON    icon data

EAT_MVMT    0000 0004           ; Description of 4th associated file type
EAT_ASCII   001F My_Company My_Application chart
EAT_ASCII   0003 CHT
EAT_BINARY  flags
EAT_ICON    icon data

EAT_MVMT    0000 0004           ; Description of 5th associated file type
EAT_ASCII   001F Your_Company Your_Application forecast
EAT_ASCII   0003 FOR
EAT_BINARY  flags
EAT_ICON    icon data
```

Figure 5-13. .ASSOCTABLE EA Value for My_Application

The .CODEPAGE Standard Extended Attribute

The .CODEPAGE extended attribute (EA) contains the code page for the file. If this extended attribute is not provided, the code page of the file is the system default or is defined by the application.

The code page of the EA data associated with the file is assumed to be that of the file, unless the EA entry is specifically overridden in the code page field in the multi-valued extended attribute data type.

The .COMMENTS Standard Extended Attribute

The .COMMENTS extended attribute (EA) contains miscellaneous notes or reminders about the file (for example, peculiarities, restrictions, or requirements).

The name of this EA consists of the string ".COMMENT". The value of this EA consists of miscellaneous notes and can be multi-valued and of any type.

The .HISTORY Standard Extended Attribute

The .HISTORY extended attribute (EA) contains the modification history for a file object, indicating the author of the file and all subsequent changes. Each entry is separate field in a multi-value field and consists of be ASCII characters only.

The name of this EA consists of the string ".HISTORY". The value of this EA contains the modification history for a file object and can be multi-valued, with each action entry described in a separate field.

Each entry in the .HISTORY field has the following format:

```
PERSON  ACTION(created, changed or printed)  DATE
```

Figure   5-14. Format of the .HISTORY Extended Attribute

For example, the following .HISTORY extended attribute contains two entries:

```
EAT_MVMT 0000 0002
         EAT_ASCII 0017 Joe     Created  2/10/88
         EAT_ASCII 0017 Harry   Changed  2/11/88
```

Figure   5-15. .HISTORY Extended Attribute with Two Entries

This extended attribute can potentially become quite large. To avoid unwanted growth, an application can let the user decide when an entry should be added to this extended attribute. For example, there are some cases when it is important to note when a document is printed. However, it is probably unnecessary to note it every time the file is printed.

The .ICON Standard Extended Attribute

The .ICON extended attribute (EA) specifies the icon to be used for the file representation, for example when the application is minimized. This extended attribute contains the physical icon data used to represent the file object.

If there is no .ICON EA, the operating system can use the .TYPE entry to determine a default icon to use for the particular file. If there is an .ICON entry, however, it is used instead of the default icon.

The name of this EA consists of the string ".ICON". The value of this EA contains the physical icon data and has the following format:

```
EAT_ICON  data_length  data
WORD      DWORD
```

Figure   5-16. Format of the .ICON Extended Attribute

The data is of type BITMAPARRAYFILEHEADER and is used to specify an array of one device-dependent and one device-independent icon bit maps. The GpiLoadBitmap and WinLoadPointer functions support this icon file format.

It is best to provide as much icon information as possible. Ideally, an icon should be 64-by-64 bits in 8-color, device-independent format.

The Icon Editor is used to create the icon, which is saved in an icon file. The .ICON extended attribute for an application is created by the Resource Compiler as part of the compile process by specifying the DEFAULTICON keyword, as in:

```
DEFAULTICON <filename.ico>
```

This keyword uses the icon definition contained in the specified icon file (FILENAME.ICO) to create the .ICON EA for the application.

Applications store the binary icon data in this extended attribute. To install icons for data files, the applications can use the .ASSOCTABLE extended attribute, or DosSetPathInfo.

The .KEYPHRASES Standard Extended Attribute

The .KEYPHRASES extended attribute (EA) contains key text phrases for the file. Such phrases can be used in performing a database-type search or in helping the user understand the nature of the file.

The name of this EA consists of the string ".KEYPHRASES". The value of this EA consists of key phrases in ASCII.

Key phrases are represented as ASCII characters. Multiple key phrases can be stored in the value of this extended attribute, each stored in a separate entry in a multi-valued field.

For example, the following extended attribute contains three key phrases:

```
EAT_MVST 0000 0003 EAT_ASCII 0008 ABC Inc.
                   EAT_ASCII 000A Salesman A
                   EAT_ASCII 000F Product X sales
```

Figure 5-17. .KEYPHRASES Extended Attribute with Three Keyphrases

If there is more than one key phrase, each should be stored in a separate entry in a multi-value field.

The .LONGNAME Standard Extended Attribute

When an application attempts to write a file with a long name to a file system that does not support long names, it must generate a short name for the file. The application should notify the user of the new short name and save the original (long) name in the .LONGNAME extended attribute.

When a file is copied from a system that uses short names to a system that uses long names, the application should check the .LONGNAME extended attribute. If a value is

present, the application should rename the file to the long name, then remove the
.LONGNAME extended attribute.

See "Moving Files with Long Names" on page 3-5 for more information on moving files with
long file names.

The .SUBJECT Standard Extended Attribute

The .SUBJECT extended attribute (EA) contains a brief summary of the content or purpose
of the file object it is associated with.

The name of this EA consists of the string ".SUBJECT". The value of this EA consists of a
single-valued ASCII string that contains the purpose of the file object.

The length of this field must be less than 40 characters.

The .TYPE Standard Extended Attribute

The .TYPE extended attribute (EA) indicates the file-type of the file object it is associated
with. It is similar to a file name extension.

The name of this EA consists of the string ".TYPE". The value of this EA contains the file
object's file-type. The following file types are predefined:

Plain Text
OS/2 Command File
DOS Command File
Executable
Metafile
Bit map
Icon
Binary Data
Dynamic Link Library
C Code
Pascal Code
BASIC Code
COBOL Code
FORTRAN Code
Assembler Code
Library
Resource File
Object Code.

Data files only require identification of the file type. For data files without EAs, the file type is
derived from the file extension, if there is one.

File object types are represented as length-preceded ASCII strings, uniquely identifying the
file object's type. This identifier is referenced within the application's .ASSOCTABLE EA in
order to bind the data file type to the application. It is important that this name be a unique
identifier because all file type names are public data. For example, if application A and

application B both had a type name of SPREADSHEET, the filing system would not be able to identify A's SPREADSHEET from B's SPREADSHEET.

The recommended convention for defining file object types is:

- Company_name
- Application_name
- Application-specific_name

with spaces separating each.

For example, spreadsheet files generated by My_Application written by My_Company might have a file object type of the following.

```
My_Company My_Application Spreadsheet
```

Figure   5-18. My_Company My_Application Spreadsheet's File Type

Type names must be ASCII characters and case is significant.

Note: The performance of extended attributes is dependent on the file system. Because some file systems store extended attributes in first-in/first-out (FIFO) order, it is important to write the .TYPE entry first so the operating system can access that information quickly.

The .VERSION Extended Attribute

The .VERSION extended attribute (EA) contains the version number of the file format, as shown below.

```
My_Application 1.0
```

Figure   5-19. The .VERSION Extended Attribute

The name of this EA consists of the string ".VERSION". The value of this EA contains the file object version number. This attribute can be ASCII or binary. Only the application that created the file object should modify the value of this EA. It can also be used to indicate an application or dynamic link library version number.

Managing Extended Attributes

An application can create, query, and set extended attributes (EAs) for any file object.

The application can define extended attributes for a file when the file is created with DosOpen. Similarly, the application can define EAs for a directory when the directory is created using DosCreateDir.

An application can define EAs for existing file objects by referencing the file object by its handle and calling DosSetFileInfo, or by referencing the file object by its name and calling DosSetPathInfo.

An application can examine the EAs for a file object by referencing the file object by its handle and calling DosQueryFileInfo, or by referencing the file object by its name and calling DosQueryPathInfo. The application can also call DosEnumAttribute, using either the file object's handle or its name, to get information about the file object's EAs.

In addition, an application can search for file objects and specify that certain EAs be returned by calling DosFindFirst.

Controlling Access to Extended Attributes

Like the file objects they are associated with, extended attributes (EAs) can have more than one process accessing them at the same time. This means that one process could be querying EAs for a file object, while another is setting EAs for the same file object.

In addition, operations on EAs are not atomic. That is, a query or set operation might not complete before another query or set operation is performed on the same object. If an error occurs before an entire list of EAs has been set, all, some, or none of them may actually remain set on the file object. This means that EAs may not remain in a consistent state unless the order in which the operations are performed can be guaranteed.

Sharing protection is provided so that unpredictable results do not occur during multiple simultaneous operations on extended attributes. EA manipulation is associated with the access permission to the related file object (file or directory).

Handle-based access permission is controlled by the sharing/access mode of the associated file object:

- If the file object is open for read access, querying EAs (using DosQueryFileInfo) is permitted.

- If the file object is open for write access, setting EAs (using DosSetFileInfo) is permitted.

Path-based access permission is controlled by adding the file object to the sharing set for the duration of the call:

- For querying EAs (using DosQueryPathInfo), an application requires read access and file-sharing permission must be set to deny-write.

- For setting EAs (using DosSetPathInfo), an application requires write access and file-sharing permission must be deny-read-write.

Note: The functions that set and query EAs fail if another process holds conflicting sharing rights to the file object.

No explicit EA sharing is performed for DosEnumAttribute. Implicit sharing exists if the caller passes the handle of an open file, since sharing access to the associated file is required to modify its EA. No sharing is performed if the caller passes the path name. This means that if some other process is editing the EAs, and changes them between two calls to DosEnumAttribute, inconsistent results might be returned (for example, the same values might be returned twice, some values might be missed, and so on).

To prevent the modification of EAs for the handle case, the file should be opened in deny-write mode before calling DosEnumAttribute. To prevent the modification of EAs for the path name case, the file should be open in deny-write mode before calling DosEnumAttribute. For the directory name case, no sharing is possible.

Extended Attribute Data Structures

There are a series of data structures through which OS/2 functions manipulate extended attributes (EAs) for applications:

- Full EAs (FEA2s)
- A list of full EAs (FEA2List)
- Get EAs (GEA2)
- A list of get EAs (GEA2List)
- EAOP2s

Full Extended Attribute (FEA2) Data Structure

A *full EA* (FEA2) data structure contains the extended attribute name and value. The name length does not include the trailing NULL. The characters that form the name are legal file name characters.

An *FEA2List* is a list of FEA2 structures, preceded by the length of the list (including the length itself). FEA2Lists are used for querying, adding, deleting, or changing EAs. They are required input parameters for the functions that create or set extended attributes (DosSetFileInfo and DosSetPathInfo). They are required output parameters for the functions that query extended attributes (DosQueryFileInfo, DosQueryPathInfo, and DosEnumAttribute).

FEA2 data structures include the lengths of the extended attribute's names and values. EA name lengths of 0 are illegal and cause errors to be returned by EA functions. An EA value length of 0 has special meaning:

- Setting an EA with a value length of 0 in the FEA2 data structure causes that attribute to be deleted, if possible.

- Getting an EA with a value length of 0 in the FEA2 data structure indicates that the attribute is not present.

Get Extended Attribute (GEA2) Data Structure

A Get EA (GEA2) is an extended attribute name. The name length does not include the trailing NULL.

A GEA2List is a list of GEA2 structures, preceded by a length of the list (including the length itself). GEA2Lists are used for retrieving the values for a particular set of extended attributes. They are required input parameters for the functions that query extended attributes (DosQueryFileInfo, DosQueryPathInfo, and DosEnumAttribute).

Note: GEA2 data structures include the lengths of extended attribute's names and values. EA name lengths of 0 are illegal and cause errors to be returned by EA functions. An EA value length of 0 has special meaning. Setting an EA with a value length of 0 in the FEA2 data structure causes that attribute to be deleted, if possible. Getting an

EA with a value length of 0 in the FEA2 data structure indicates that the attribute is not present.

Extended Attribute Operation (EAOP2) Data Structure

An extended attribute operation (EAOP2) data structure consists of a GEA2List, an FEA2List, and an error field. All extended attribute manipulation is performed using this structure. Before calling an extended attribute function, an application must define an EAOP2 structure, with the GEA2List and FEA2List appropriately defined.

The use of GEA2List and FEA2List for each function is described further in the *Control Program Programming Reference*.

Preserving Extended Attributes

Extended attributes (EAs) are supported in the OS/2 operating system FAT file system and High Performance File System. Extended attributes are not supported by the FAT file system used in versions of Operating System/2 prior to Version 1.2, nor are they supported in the DOS operating system.

EAs associated with a file object are not part of a file object or of its data, but are maintained separately and managed by the file system that manages that object. EAs reside on the volume on which the file object resides and are connected to their file object by pointers from the file object.

Therefore, EAs belonging to a file object are lost when moving that file object from a storage device managed by an OS/2 FAT or installable file system to a storage device managed by the old FAT file system.

EAs can be lost under other circumstances, as well:

- When a program that does not recognize EAs (for example, an editor written for DOS) performs a non-truncating open on the files the EAs are associated with

- When the files they are associated with are sent over COM links.

So that files with EAs can be manipulated under these circumstances, without losing their EAs, the OS/2 operating system provides a utility called EAUTIL EAUTIL enables users to separate extended attributes from the specified file object, optionally disassociating them from the file object. The extended attributes are placed into a specified HoldFile. This utility also enables users to reattach the separated extended attributes with their file objects.

EAUTIL can be applied to subdirectories, as well as to files. It does not support global file name characters in parameters; it operates on a single file object at each invocation.

Users can use EAUTIL to:

- Strip EAs off files to be edited with a program that does not recognize EAs.

- Place the EAs into normal files so they can be dealt with by old tools (such as backup, restore, and so on) or easily transmitted.

- Reattach EAs to files after the files have been brought back from the systems where EAs are not supported.

For more information on EAUTIL, see the online *OS/2 Command Reference*.

Protecting Extended Attributes

Programs written for releases of the OS/2 operating system and DOS that do not support extended attributes (EAs) will tend to lose EAs simply because they do not know that they exist. The OS/2 operating system provides some controls that prevent old programs from destroying critical data without unduly restricting their activities. This is done by classifying programs and marking the extended attributes that are associated with files.

Programs are classified as:

- Those that recognize EAs. These include OS/2 Version 1.2 and later programs.

- Those that do not recognize EAs. These include programs written for releases of the OS/2 operating system and DOS that do not support EAs.

EAs associated with files are marked as critical or non-critical. Programs that do not recognize EAs are not permitted to manipulate files that have critical EAs associated with them. This protection does not apply to directories. EAs associated with directories cannot be marked as critical.

Critical Extended Attributes

Extended attributes (EAs) are non-critical by default. A non-critical EA is one that is not necessary to the functionality of the application. That is, if a non-critical EA is lost, the system continues to operate correctly. For example, losing the icons associated with data files does not generally cause any ill effect other than the inability to show the icon.

A *critical extended attribute* is one which is necessary to the correct operation of the operating system or of a particular application. EAs should be marked as critical if their loss would cause the system or program to perform incorrectly. For example, a mail program might store mail headers in EAs. The loss of the header from a message would normally render the mail program completely unable to further use that message. This would be unacceptable, so the mail program should mark this EA as critical.

A file has critical extended attributes (EAs) if at least one EA attached to the file is marked as critical.

Marking EAs as critical only prevents programs that do not recognize EAs from losing the EAs from the file. It does not prevent deletion of files by any application.

Applications must be careful how they mark their EAs. If they are too aggressive marking EAs as critical, users might be prevented from accessing files that their application uses.

EAs are marked as critical by setting the critical bit. The critical bit is bit 7 of the flags byte of the FEA2 data structure. If this bit is 0, the EA is a non-critical EA. If it is 1, it is a critical EA. The symbolic constant FEA_NEEDEA can be used to indicate a critical EA.

The creator of the EA determines whether it is critical or not.

Programs that do not recognize extended attributes (EAs) are prevented from performing certain operations on files that have critical EAs associated with them. For example, a program that does not recognize EAs is not permitted to perform a non-truncating open on a file with critical EAs associated with it, because programs cannot be permitted to read the data and ignore the EAs.

Programs that do not recognize EAs are, however, permitted to perform those operations that they can do completely. For example, they can delete files with critical EAs associated with them. Programs that do not recognize EAs are not prevented from accessing files whose EAs are not critical.

Programs that recognize EAs have no restrictions placed on their actions with respect to critical EAs.

Programs that recognize extended attributes must identify themselves to the operating system. This is done by including the NEWFILES declaration in the program's module definition file. The NEWFILES declaration is also how programs indicate that they understand and use long file names.

Searching for Extended Attributes

An application can search for file objects that have specific extended attribute names by calling DosFindFirst twice. The steps involved are:

1. Call DosFindFirst for FileInfoLevel = 2, to get the length of the buffer required to hold the EAOP2 data associated with a matching file object.

2. Call DosFindFirst for FileInfoLevel = 3, to get the EAOP2 data associated with the matching file object.

Supporting Extended Attributes

To support extended attributes, applications should do the following:

1. Fill in the .ASSOCTABLE extended attribute for all major file types that the application recognizes or uses.

2. Fill in the .ICON extended attribute for executable files.

3. Set the .TYPE extended attribute for data files the application creates.

4. Fill in and use the .LONGNAME extended attribute as appropriate.

5. Support .HISTORY and .VERSION.

6. Support the other Standard Extended Attributes as appropriate.

Summary

Following are the OS/2 data structures used in managing extended file attributes.

Table 5-2. Extended Attribute Data Structures	
Data Structure	**Description**
EAOP2	Extended Attribute OPeration data structure. Contains a FEA2List data structure, a GEA2List data structure, and an error field. All EA manipulation is performed using this structure.
FEA2	Full Extended Attribute data structure. Contains an EAs name and value. Used in a FEA2List for querying, adding, deleting, and changing EAs.
FEA2List	List of FEA2 data structures. Used in an EAOP2 for the functions that create, set, or query EAs.
GEA2	Get Extended Attribute data structure. Contains an EAs name. Used in a GEA2List for querying certain EAs.
GEA2List	List of GEA2 data structures. Used in an EAOP2 for the functions that query certain EAs.

Chapter 6. Memory Management

This chapter describes the memory management features and functions of the OS/2 operating system. The key features of OS/2 memory management are paged virtual memory and a 32-bit linear (flat) address space that is mapped through page tables to physical memory. An OS/2 application can allocate memory for its own use or to be shared with other applications.

The following topics are related to the information in this chapter:

- Exception Handling
- Program Execution and Control
- Semaphores
- Queues.

About Memory Management

The OS/2 operating system offers developers a 32-bit, linear (flat) memory address space. The OS/2 operating system uses a paged memory structure. The operating system allocates, protects, and manipulates memory in terms of pages.

Process Address Space

The OS/2 memory allocation functions return a 32-bit pointer to the allocated memory object. While a 32-bit pointer is sufficient to address the entire 4 gigabyte global address space, applications can access only the first 512MB of linear memory, called the *process address space*. Of this 512MB process address space, a minimum of 64MB is reserved for shared memory regions, leaving 448MB. Of this 448MB, some will be used by the application itself and a small amount will be taken by operating system overhead. The remainder is available for allocation. The amount of memory that can actually be committed and used is, of course, determined by the physical memory and hard disk space available on the machine.

Figure 6-1 shows how memory is apportioned by the OS/2 operating system. A minimum of 64MB is reserved for both the shared memory region and the private memory region.

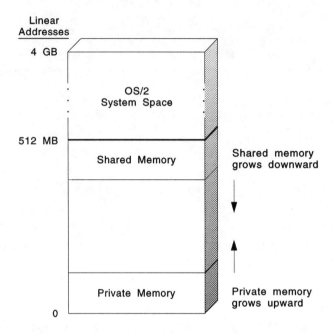

Figure 6-1. How Memory is Divided by the OS/2 Operating System

Figure 6-2 on page 6-3 shows a more detailed view of how the process address space (memory below 512MB) is used. The shared memory region is used for DLL code and data, and for memory shared between processes. Each process in the figure below—A, B, and C—has access to the complete linear address range between 0 and 512MB. The linear address range of each process is virtual memory and is completely independent of the linear address ranges of any other process. Conceptually, the processes run side-by-side, in the same linear address space. Note that shared memory is allocated across all process address spaces, whether a process has access to the shared memory or not.

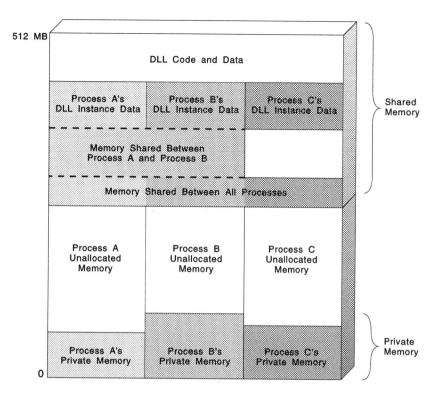

Figure 6-2. Process Address Spaces

Keep in mind that the amount of memory that can be committed for actual use is limited by the amount of physical memory and free hard disk space that is available on the computer on which the application is executing.

Memory Objects

Applications allocate and manipulate memory in terms of *memory objects*. A memory object consists of one or more pages of memory. An OS/2 application can allocate any number of memory objects, within the following limits:

- the physical memory in the system
- the free hard disk space on the hard disk containing the swap file
- the 512MB process address space limit (see "Process Address Space" on page 6-1).

When requesting memory, the size of the memory object is rounded up to the next higher multiple of 4KB. An application can suballocate a memory object into memory blocks whose size can range from 1 byte to the size of the memory object.

Memory objects have the following characteristics:

- They are not relocatable.
- They are allocated in units of 4KB. One 4KB unit is called a *page*.
- They can be larger than 64KB in size.

Memory Pages

The operating system allocates and commits memory objects in pages. A memory *page* is a 4KB (4096 bytes) piece of memory. Memory access protection is also done on a page-basis, rather than the segment-based protection used in previous versions of the operating system.

A *page range* is a linearly contiguous group of pages within a memory object. A page range can be:

- the entire memory object,
- part of the memory object, or
- a single page within a memory object.

If an application requests 512 bytes of memory, it will receive a 32-bit pointer to a 4KB page. All 4096 bytes are available to the application, even though the request specified only 512 bytes. If an application requests 62000 bytes, it will receive a pointer to a 65536-byte (64KB, 16-page) object. Again, all 65536 bytes are available for use.

Each page in the virtual address space of the process is either free (unallocated), private (available only to the process that allocated it), or shared (memory that is shared between processes).

Each page within a memory object can be in one of two states, either uncommitted (that is, the linear address range has been reserved, but is not yet backed by physical storage) or committed (physical storage has been allotted for the logical address range).

Access to a committed page is controlled by the page's access protection attribute. These protection attributes are read access, write access, execute access (on the 80386, this is the same as read access), and guard page access.

An uncommitted page is not accessible.

Memory Overcommitment and Swapping

Memory overcommitment occurs when applications allocate and commit more memory than is actually available in the computer. The operating system handles memory overcommitment by copying memory to the system swap file, SWAPPER.DAT, on the hard disk then reusing the memory for another allocation. The operating system copies as many pages of memory as are necessary to make room for the new allocation. The swapped memory can be retrieved the next time it is accessed; at that time, some other memory might be written to the swap file.

The operating system selects the memory to swap based on when it was last used. The page that is least-recently-used, that is, the page that has gone the longest since its last access, is the page chosen to swap to disk.

Swapping is transparent to an application, although excessive swapping can cause an application to run slowly.

Through swapping, the OS/2 operating system enables applications to allocate more memory than actually exists in the computer, bounded only by the amount of free space on the hard disk that contains the swap file.

User Configuration of Memory Swapping

Although an application cannot control swapping, the user can specify whether the system can swap memory by including the MEMMAN command in the CONFIG.SYS file.

If the MEMMAN command specifies SWAP, the operating system writes selected memory pages to the SWAPPER.DAT file whenever insufficient physical memory exists to satisfy an allocation request. This is the default choice. If the MEMMAN command specifies NOSWAP, the operating system does not swap memory.

Note: Be aware that disabling swapping will severely limit the number of applications that the user will be able to run concurrently; if there is not enough physical memory present, the operating system might not even boot.

The exact amount of memory available to an application depends on the amount of physical memory in the machine and the amount of free disk space on the partition that contains the SWAPPER.DAT file. The location of the SWAPPER.DAT file can be specified by including the SWAPPATH command in the CONFIG.SYS file. The SWAPPATH command specifies the location of SWAPPER.DAT and the amount of free space to reserve on the disk. The operating system adjusts the size of SWAPPER.DAT as necessary, leaving other files on the drive and the requested free space untouched.

Memory Allocation and Commitment

When an application asks the operating system to allocate memory, a linear address range is reserved. The range is not backed by physical memory until the memory is *committed*. Commitment assigns physical memory to the linear address range.

A memory object that is allocated, but not committed is called a *sparse memory object*. A sparse memory object must be committed before it can be used. An attempt to read from or write to uncommitted memory will cause an access violation.

An application can ask the operating system to commit the memory at the same time it is allocated, thus making it immediately usable, or the memory can be committed at a later time. If the application commits the memory at the same time the memory is allocated, the entire memory object is committed. If the application commits the memory at a later time, it can commit the entire sparse memory object or only commit a portion of it.

When multiple pages are committed at the same time (a page range), the pages will have sequential linear addresses.

Managing Memory Allocation and Commitment

The recommended way to manage memory is to make a large memory allocation early in program execution, then to commit or suballocate memory as the need occurs.

The initial allocation should be for as much space as you expect to use during program execution. Allocation without commitment does not actually use any physical memory, so there is no waste involved in allocating several megabytes.

After the memory object is allocated, the application uses one of two ways to manage the memory object:

- commit and decommit the memory as it is required
- set up the memory object as a heap and suballocate memory from the heap.

Committing and decommitting memory gives the application more control over the process, but the application will have to keep track of which pages are committed and which pages are not. When suballocating memory from a heap, the application can have the operating system track commitment and decommitment of physical memory pages, so the application does not have to. If you want DosSubAllocMem to manage the commitment of the pages spanned by the heap, all of the pages spanned by the memory object must be uncommitted initially.

Remember, no matter how much memory is originally allocated, the amount that an application will ultimately be able to commit and use is limited by the amount of physical memory and free disk space available on the machine.

Applications are not limited to a single large allocation of memory—other memory allocations can be made as necessary during execution—but large allocations and small commitments or suballocations are the most efficient way to manage memory.

Memory Resizing and Reallocation

In earlier versions of the operating system, an application could increase or decrease the size of an allocated memory segment by reallocating the segment.

Memory objects cannot be resized. Instead, an application should allocate a sparse memory object of whatever size might be necessary, then commit or decommit portions of the object.

If the amount of memory required cannot be determined at the time the memory is allocated, the application should allocate a sparse memory object large enough to meet the largest memory requirement. The application can then change the amount of committed memory as necessary.

For example, if you anticipate your application will use around 512KB of memory for most purposes, but might use 5MB under certain circumstances, you might take the following steps:

- During program initialization, use DosAllocMem to allocate 5MB.
- Commit the first 512KB (or some part of it) using DosSetMem.
- Proceed with normal processing.
- If extra memory is required occasionally, commit it and decommit it using DosSetMem.

- When the situation arises that the application requires the full 5MB, commit it at that time, using DosSetMem, then decommit it after you are finished with it, also using DosSetMem.

- When the application is finished with the memory, use DosFreeMem to release the memory back to the system.

Memory Protection

When an application allocates a memory object, it can specify the type of access to allow to the object. Memory access protection provides a program with control over the type of access that its threads have to a page of memory.

Access protection can only be defined for committed pages of memory and is initially set at the time the memory is committed. Different pages within the same memory object can have different access attributes and access attributes can be changed on a page-by-page basis at any time.

An application can request any combination of the following access protection attributes:

Table 6-1. Memory Access Protection Attributes

Access	Defined Constant	Description
Read Access	PAG_READ	The object can be read from, but not written to.
Write Access	PAG_WRITE	The object can be written to. On the 80386 microprocessor, write access implies both read and execute access.
Execute Access	PAG_EXECUTE	This is equivalent to read access on the 80386.
Guard Page Access	PAG_GUARD	Causes a guard-page-entered exception to be raised in a process that attempts to access the memory. This exception can be ignored or handled by the application's exception handler, if one is registered.

The guard page attribute is intended to provide automatic stack growth and stack limit checking. An application can also use it in other data structures, such as arrays. For example, if an application is using an array of 4096 bytes (one page), the application can allocate and commit two pages, one with read and write access and one designated as a guard page. If the application tries to write past the end of the array a page guard exception will be generated.

Any reference—read, write, or execute—to a guard page causes an access violation (page fault) to be generated. This fault causes a Guard Page Entered exception to occur for the thread that referred to the guard page. The exception can be handled by the exception handler of the process, if one is registered. If the process does not have an exception handler registered, the operating system's default exception handler will handle the exception. The default action by the system exception handler is to convert the page from a guard page to a committed page, then try to mark the next page in memory as a guard page. If the system is not successful in marking the next page as a guard page, an Unable-To-Grow-Stack exception occurs. The thread is allowed to continue execution, but must be aware that it has at most 4KB of stack remaining.

Obtaining Information about a Page Range

DosQueryMem is used to obtain information about a range of pages within the virtual address space of the current process.

Each page in the virtual address space of a process is either free, private, or shared.

Each page within a memory object can be in one of two states, either committed or uncommitted.

A committed page has its access controlled by an access protection attribute. These protection attributes are read protection (PAG_READ), write protection (PAG_WRITE), execute protection (PAG_EXECUTE), and guard page protection (PAG_GUARD).

Protection Violations

The operating system fully utilizes the memory protection capabilities of the 80386 microprocessor. The operating system grants an application access to a memory object only if the object has been explicitly allocated by the application or made available for use by the application.

If an application attempts to access memory that it is not assigned, the system interrupts the application and executes the exception handling routine for protection violations. Protection violations can be handled by the application (in its own exception handling routines) or by the operating system. If the protection violation is handled by the operating system, the system exception handling routine determines the cause of the exception, displays an error message, and then terminates the application.

It is usually not possible for an application to recover from a protection violation. Therefore, programmers should ensure that all pointers are valid. Because protection violations commonly occur during application debugging, each message displayed for a protection violation includes the contents of the registers when the violation occurred. If the violation occurred as a result of passing an invalid pointer to a memory function, an error code is returned by the memory function.

In earlier versions of the operating system, protection violations could be used to find bugs when an application accessed memory that was not allocated to the application. This approach will no longer work because memory objects can be larger than the size requested by the application because the memory objects are allocated on 4KB page boundaries. For example, a pointer to the 513th byte of a 512 byte memory object is valid and does not cause a protection violation. This means that programmers cannot always rely on protection violations to spot memory addressing errors.

Memory Suballocation and Using Heaps

There are times when a process requires only small amounts of memory rather than an entire memory object. It would be wasteful to allocate an entire page of memory when only a few bytes are necessary, so a mechanism is provided for applications to allocate a large block of memory and then suballocate portions of the memory as necessary to fulfill small requests from an application. This is done by creating a heap.

A *heap* is a region of storage within a memory object from which an application can allocate blocks of memory. A *memory block* is a piece of memory within a heap. The size of the memory block is rounded up to the next higher multiple of 8 bytes.

Because the operating system allocates a 4KB page for each memory allocation, using a heap to suballocate amounts of memory smaller than 4KB is more efficient than using DosAllocMem.

When an application creates a heap, it can have the operating system track the committing and decommitting of memory within the heap. When the application commits and decommits memory itself, it has to keep track of the access state of each page as they are accessed.

Applications use DosSubSetMem to initialize a memory object for suballocation, then use DosSubAllocMem and DosSubFreeMem to allocate and free the memory.

Memory is still committed in pages when an application uses suballocation. If the application suballocates 512 bytes, 4096 bytes will be committed. Accessing the 513th byte will not cause a protection violation, but you could be accessing memory that was suballocated by another thread in the process.

Shared Memory

Shared memory is memory that two or more applications can read from and write to. Shared memory is prepared in such a way that any application can receive a pointer to the memory and access the data. Applications must explicitly request access to shared memory; the shared memory is protected from applications that are not granted access.

There are two kinds of shared memory: named and unnamed. For named shared memory, any application that knows the name of the shared memory can access it. For unnamed shared memory, a pointer to the shared memory must be passed from the process that created the shared memory to the process being given access. Access can be granted to any application; it is not necessary that the process being granted access be related (parent-child) to the application that created the shared memory.

Since memory sharing is done by sharing linear addresses, the linear address range of the shared memory object is reserved in all process address spaces.

There are two basic methods of managing shared memory:

- In one method, two or more applications share the same memory at the same time. These applications read from and write to the memory object, usually controlling access to the memory by using a semaphore.

- In the other method of managing shared memory, one application prepares data in memory, then passes that memory to another application for further processing. The first application releases the memory after passing it along, so that only one application accesses the memory at a time.

Using Memory Management

This section describes how to use the OS/2 memory management functions and configuration commands to control the use of memory for OS/2 applications.

Note: In the example code fragments that follow, error checking was left out to conserve space. Applications should always check the return code that the functions return. Control Program functions return an APIRET value. A return code of 0 indicates success. If a non-zero value is returned, an error occurred.

Allocating Private Memory

An application can allocate regions of storage within the virtual address space of the process. Such an allocated region is called a memory object.

DosAllocMem is used to allocate a memory object. You specify a variable to receive the pointer that will address the new object, the amount of memory needed, and the allocation attributes and access protection attributes of the new memory object. When choosing the size of the memory object to allocate, remember that the maximum size of the memory object is defined when it is allocated, and memory objects cannot be resized.

When applications call DosAllocMem, the operating system reserves a range of private pages large enough to fulfill the specified allocation request from the private virtual address space of the subject process.

DosAllocMem will reserve this linear space and return zero if the allocation was successful. If it was unsuccessful, DosAllocMem will return an error code. An application should always test the return value before attempting to use the memory.

The following code fragment requests an allocation of 512 bytes. Remember that 4096 bytes will actually be allocated for this request:

```
#define  INCL_DOSMEMMGR   /* Memory Manager values */
#include <os2.h>

PBYTE   pb;
APIRET  rc;

rc = DosAllocMem((PVOID *) &pb, 512, fALLOC);
    /* pb receives the base address of the 4KB memory object    */

if (!rc) {         /* If the allocation was successful, rc == 0 */
    *pb = 3000;    /* Use the allocated memory                  */
}
```

Figure 6-3. Requesting 512 Bytes of Memory

In this example, DosAllocMem returns a 32-bit pointer to a 4096 byte committed memory object and allows the application to write to and read from the memory. This pointer is valid only for the 4096 bytes allocated by the system. An attempt to use the pointer outside the allocated memory will cause a protection violation.

Committing and Decommitting Page Ranges

If an application allocates a sparse memory object, no physical memory location is committed for the object. Memory in a sparse object must be committed before it can be used. DosSetMem is used to commit or decommit a range of previously allocated pages in a private or shared memory object. Applications can make specific address ranges within a memory object valid or invalid. Commitment and decommitment always take place in multiples of one or more pages.

Applications can also use DosSetMem to change the access protection attributes of a range of pages within a memory object.

The following code fragment requests allocation of 2MB of uncommitted memory and then commits 4096 bytes of the memory:

```
#define  INCL_DOSMEMMGR   /* Memory Manager values */
#include <os2.h>

APIRET  rc;
PBYTE   pb;

/* Allocate 16KB object */
rc = DosAllocMem((PVOID *) &pb, 2097152, PAG_READ | PAG_WRITE);

/* Commit 4KB          */
rc = DosSetMem(pb, 4096, PAG_COMMIT | PAG_DEFAULT);
```

Figure 6-4. Allocating Uncommitted Memory and Committing Part of It

An application can also allocate a large committed object and then decommit portions of it as they are no longer needed. Decommitment, like commitment, is done on page boundaries; an application can decommit no less than a 4096 byte page.

The following code fragment allocates 16384 bytes of committed memory and then decommits the first 4096 bytes of the memory:

```
#define  INCL_DOSMEMMGR   /* Memory Manager values */
#include <os2.h>

APIRET  rc;
PBYTE   pb;

rc = DosAllocMem((PVOID *) &pb, 16384, fALLOC);    /* Allocate 16 K object */

rc = DosSetMem(pb, 4096, PAG_DECOMMIT);            /* Decommit 4KB        */
```

Figure 6-5. Allocating Committed Memory and Decommitting Part of It

After memory is decommitted, an attempt to access the decommitted memory will cause a protection violation.

You cannot pass an argument that crosses multiple memory objects. The function will return an error.

Establishing Access Protection

When an OS/2 application commits a memory object, it specifies the types of access permitted for the memory object. This can be done at the same time the memory object is allocated, with DosAllocMem, or at a later time, using DosSetMem.

Any combination of read, write, execute, or guard-page access can be set, but at least read or write access must be specified when the memory object is committed; it is not possible to commit an object with no access protection attributes.

The application can also use DosSetMem to change the access permission of pages within a previously committed memory object. An application can permit read access to one page of the memory object and write access to the rest.

When using DosSetMem, all the pages in the range being changed must be either committed or decommitted.

The following code fragment commits a region of two pages within a previously allocated memory object, and sets read-only access rights for the region. Assume that the base address for DosSetMem was previously obtained by the process.

```
#define  INCL_DOSMEMMGR    /* Memory Manager values */
#include <os2.h>
#include <stdio.h>

PVOID   BaseAddress;       /* Pointer to the range of pages to be changed */
ULONG   RegionSize;        /* Size, in bytes, of the region to be changed */
ULONG   AttributeFlags;    /* Flag describing the page range              */
APIRET  rc;                /* Return code                                 */

RegionSize = 8192;         /* Specify a two-page region                   */

AttributeFlags = PAG_COMMIT | PAG_READ;

rc = DosSetMem(BaseAddress, RegionSize, AttributeFlags);

if (rc != 0) {
    printf("DosSetMem error: return code = %ld", rc);
    return;
}
```

Figure   6-6. Setting Read-Only Access for a Region

Querying Memory Object Information

DosQueryMem is used to determine the allocation state and access protection for a specified memory object. The application can query an entire memory object or a range of pages within an object.

The following code fragment uses DosQueryMem to ensure that memory is committed before the application attempts to use the memory:

```
#define  INCL_DOSMEMMGR    /* Memory Manager values  */
#include <os2.h>
#define HF_STDOUT 1        /* Standard output handle */

PBYTE   pb;        /* Base address of an allocated object */
ULONG   ulSize, flFlags, ulWritten;
APIRET  rc;        /* Return Code                         */

ulSize = 4096;

rc = DosQueryMem(pb, &ulSize, &flFlags);     /* Queries first 4096 bytes */

if (flFlags & PAG_COMMIT) {              /* If memory is committed, use it */
    rc = DosWrite(HF_STDOUT, "\r\n 4KB is committed.\r\n", 21, &ulWritten);
}
```

Figure   6-7. Determining the Allocation State of a Memory Object

Freeing Memory

When memory object is no longer needed, the application uses the DosFreeMem function to release the memory.

If applications do not release memory, the operating system either swaps the memory to the hard disk (if swapping is enabled) or uses memory that could be used by other applications. If the operating system swaps the memory to the hard disk, the SWAPPER.DAT swap file could become very large. Therefore, applications should release memory as soon as it is no longer needed. Any memory that is still allocated when the application ends is released by the operating system.

DosFreeMem frees a private or shared memory object from the virtual address space of the process. The released pages are returned to the system.

The following code fragment allocates 8192 bytes of committed memory and then releases the memory:

```
#define  INCL_DOSMEMMGR   /* Memory Manager values */
#include <os2.h>

PBYTE   pb;
APIRET  rc;

rc = DosAllocMem((PVOID *) &pb, 8192, fALLOC);    /* Allocate 8KB object */
   .
   .
   .
rc = DosFreeMem(pb);                              /* Free the object    */
```

Figure 6-8. Allocating and Freeing Memory

Using Suballocation and Heaps

This section describes how you can use DosAllocMem, DosSubSetMem, DosSubAllocMem, DosSubFreeMem, and DosSubUnsetMem to manage a memory heap.

Suballocating Memory

DosAllocMem can be used to create a memory heap.

Before an application can allocate small portions of the heap, it must use the DosSubSetMem function to set up the memory for suballocation. The size of the heap is rounded up to the next higher multiple of 8 bytes.

Then, the application uses DosSubAllocMem to allocate sections of the heap and the DosSubFreeMem function to release the memory.

DosSubAllocMem returns a 32-bit pointer to a block of memory. The pointer can be used to access the memory without further modification.

The following code fragment sets up 8192 bytes for suballocation and then allocates two small blocks of memory:

```
#define  INCL_DOSMEMMGR   /* Memory Manager values */
#include <os2.h>

APIRET  rc;
PBYTE   pbBase, pb1, pb2;

rc = DosAllocMem((PVOID *) &pbBase, 8192, fALLOC); /* Allocate 8 K object   */

rc = DosSubSetMem(pbBase, DOSSUB_INIT, 8192);      /* Set up object         */
                                                   /* for suballocation     */

rc = DosSubAllocMem(pbBase, (PVOID *) &pb1, 100);  /* Suballocate 100 bytes */

rc = DosSubAllocMem(pbBase, (PVOID *) &pb2, 500);  /* Suballocate 500 bytes */

rc = DosSubFreeMem(pbBase, pb1, 100);              /* Free 1st suballocation*/

rc = DosSubAllocMem(pbBase, (PVOID *) &pb1, 50);   /* Suballocate 50 bytes  */
```

Figure 6-9. Suballocating Memory

Increasing the Size of a Heap

DosSubSetMem can also be used to increase the size of a previously initialized heap. The heap size can be increased up to the size of the memory object that contains it.

The size of the heap is rounded up to the next higher multiple of 8 bytes.

The following code fragment increases the size of a heap. Assume that a memory object was previously allocated for the heap, and that the *Offset* variable was previously loaded with the virtual address of the memory object.

```
#define  INCL_DOSMEMMGR    /* Memory Manager values */
#include <os2.h>
#include <stdio.h>

PVOID   Offset;   /* Address of the heap to be used for suballocation */
ULONG   Flags;    /* Flags describing the memory object being resized */
ULONG   Size;     /* Size in bytes to increase the size of the heap   */
APIRET  rc;       /* Return code                                      */

Size = 20000;     /* Indicate a heap size increase of 20000 bytes    */

Flags = DOSSUB_GROW | DOSSUB_SPARSE_OBJ;

rc = DosSubSetMem(Offset, Flags, Size);

if (rc != 0) {
    printf("DosSubSetMem error: return code = %ld", rc);
    return;
}
```

Figure   6-10. Increasing the Size of Suballocated Memory

In this example, the heap is incremented, and that memory commitment is managed internally within subsequent DosSubAllocMem calls.

When using DosSubSetMem to increase the size of the heap, the *Flags* parameter must have the same setting as when the heap was initialized.

Note: Do not call DosSetMem to change the allocation attribute or access protection attributes of any pages spanned by a memory object that the suballocation functions are managing. Otherwise, unpredictable results could occur.

Call DosSubUnsetMem when finished with the heap that was set up with DosSubSetMem. This enables the suballocation function to free the resources that it uses to manage the heap. When you are through with the memory object that the heap was part of, use DosFreeMem to free the memory object.

Allocating a Block of Memory from a Heap

DosSubAllocMem allocates a block of memory from a heap that was previously initialized by DosSubSetMem. This is used when an application needs an area of memory that is smaller than an entire heap.

The size of the memory block is rounded up to the next higher multiple of 8 bytes.

The following code fragment allocates a block of memory from a heap that was previously initialized by DosSubSetMem. Assume that the *Offset* variable has been set to the address of the initialized heap already.

```
#define  INCL_DOSMEMMGR   /* Memory Manager values */
#include <os2.h>
#include <stdio.h>

PVOID    Offset;        /* The heap to suballocate from           */
PPVOID   BlockOffset;   /* Pointer to the variable where the offset of */
                        /* the suballocated memory block is returned  */
ULONG    Size;          /* Size in bytes of the memory block requested */
APIRET   rc;            /* Return code                            */

Size = 102;             /* Ask for 102 bytes.  This will be rounded  */
                        /* to 104 bytes (a multiple of 8 bytes).     */

rc = DosSubAllocMem(Offset, &BlockOffset, Size);

if (rc != 0) {
    printf("DosSubAllocMem error: return code = %ld", rc);
    return;
}
```

Figure 6-11. Allocating a Block of Memory from a Heap

In this example, the address of the allocated block (from the heap) is stored in the *BlockOffset* variable.

Remember to call DosSubFreeMem to free this block of memory when you are finished with it.

Freeing Memory Blocks

DosSubFreeMem frees a block of memory that was previously allocated by DosSubAllocMem.

Call DosSubFreeMem to free a block of memory in the heap when you are finished with that memory block.

The following code fragment frees a block of memory that was previously allocated from a heap. DosSubFreeMem returns the block to the heap. Assume that the *Offset* variable has been previously set to the address of the initialized heap, and that the *BlockOffset* variable has been previously set to the address of the block to be returned to the heap.

```
#define INCL_DOSMEMMGR   /* Memory Manager values */
#include <os2.h>
#include <stdio.h>

PVOID   Offset;        /* Offset of the heap to which the         */
                       /* block is to be freed                    */
PVOID   BlockOffset;   /* Offset of memory block to be freed      */
ULONG   Size;          /* Size in bytes of block to be freed      */
APIRET  rc;            /* Return code                             */

Size = 102;            /* Return 102 bytes. This will be rounded  */
                       /* to 104 bytes (a multiple of 8 bytes).   */

rc = DosSubFreeMem(Offset, BlockOffset, Size);

if (rc != 0) {
    printf("DosSubFreeMem error: return code = %ld", rc);
    return;
}
```

Figure 6-12. Freeing a Block of Memory from a Heap

Ending the Use of the Heap

DosSubUnsetMem terminates the use of a heap within a memory object. All calls to DosSubSetMem must eventually be followed by a call to DosSubUnsetMem. This enables the suballocation function to free the resources that it uses to manage the heap.

The application must call DosSubUnsetMem before it frees the memory object that contains this heap (with DosFreeMem).

The following code fragment shows the termination of a heap. Assume that the address of the heap was placed into *Offset* already.

```
#define INCL_DOSMEMMGR   /* Memory Manager values */
#include <os2.h>
#include <stdio.h>

PVOID   Offset;   /* Offset of the heap whose use is being terminated */
APIRET  rc;       /* Return code                                      */

rc = DosSubUnsetMem(Offset);

if (rc != 0) {
    printf("DosSubUnsetMem error: return code = %ld", rc);
    return;
}
```

Figure 6-13. Ending the Use of a Heap

Using Shared Memory

This section describes how you can use DosAllocSharedMem, DosGiveSharedMem, DosGetSharedMem, and DosGetNamedSharedMem to use shared memory.

Using Named Shared Memory

An application uses DosAllocSharedMem to allocate shared memory. When allocating the shared memory, an application can assign a unique name to the memory. Any application that has the name of the shared memory can use DosGetNamedSharedMem to retrieve a pointer to the memory. This makes it possible for two or more applications to share memory at the same time.

The name of a shared memory object has the following form:

    \sharemem\name

The "\sharemem\" is required. The "name" parameter can be any name that conforms to the rules for an OS/2 file name. No file is actually created for the memory object. There is no actual "\sharemem\" subdirectory.

The following code fragment allocates 65536 bytes of named shared memory with the name "\sharemem\mymem".

```
#define  INCL_DOSMEMMGR   /* Memory Manager values */
#include <os2.h>

APIRET  rc;
CHAR    szMem[] = { "\\sharemem\\mymem" };
PULONG  pb;

rc = DosAllocSharedMem((PVOID *) &pb, szMem, 65536, fALLOC);

*pb = 2762;
```

Figure   6-14. Allocating Named Shared Memory

Once the named memory is allocated, any other process can retrieve a pointer to the named memory by using DosGetNamedSharedMem.

The following code fragment retrieves a pointer to the named memory allocated above:

```
#define  INCL_DOSMEMMGR     /* Memory Manager values */
#include <os2.h>
#define HF_STDOUT 1          /* Standard output handle */

APIRET  rc;
CHAR    szMem[] = { "\\sharemem\\mymem" };
PULONG  pb2;
ULONG   ulWritten;

rc = DosGetNamedSharedMem((PVOID *) &pb2, szMem, PAG_READ | PAG_WRITE);

if (*pb2 == 2762)
    rc = DosWrite(HF_STDOUT, "\r\n Success!\r\n", 13, &ulWritten);
```

Figure 6-15. Getting a Pointer to Named Shared Memory

Using Unnamed Shared Memory

An application can allocate unnamed shared memory by using DosAllocSharedMem with the object name set to NULL and the memory options set to OBJ_GIVEABLE or OBJ_GETTABLE. Sharing unnamed memory is more difficult than sharing named memory because the application allocating the memory must somehow pass a pointer to another application. This is typically done by using some form of interprocess communication, such as a queue or a named pipe.

If an application allocates shared memory with the OBJ_GETTABLE option, it can pass a pointer to another application. The second application can then gain access to the shared memory by using DosGetSharedMem to validate the passed pointer. If an application allocates shared memory with the OBJ_GIVEABLE option, the process that allocates the memory can validate the pointer in another process with DosGiveSharedMem. The allocating process must still pass a pointer to the second process, but the second process need not use DosGetSharedMem.

The following code fragment allocates 24576 bytes (24KB) of unnamed shared memory:

```
#define  INCL_DOSMEMMGR     /* Memory Manager values */
#include <os2.h>

APIRET  rc;
PBYTE   pb;

rc = DosAllocSharedMem((PVOID *) &pb, (PSZ) NULL, 24576,
                       fALLOC | OBJ_GETTABLE);
```

Figure 6-16. Allocating 24576 Bytes of Unnamed Shared Memory

Once the memory is allocated, the process can pass the memory pointer to a second process via interprocess communication. Once the second process receives the pointer, it can validate the memory with DosGetSharedMem, as shown in the following code:

```
#define  INCL_DOSMEMMGR    /* Memory Manager values */
#include <os2.h>

APIRET  rc;
PBYTE  pb2;

rc = DosGetSharedMem(pb2, PAG_READ | PAG_WRITE);
```

Figure 6-17. Validating Shared Memory

Summary

Following are the OS/2 functions used in memory management.

Table 6-2. Memory Management Functions	
Memory Functions	
DosAllocMem	Allocates a private memory object within the virtual address space.
DosSetMem	Commits or decommits a range of pages within a memory object, or alters their protection.
DosFreeMem	Frees a private or shared memory object from the virtual address space of the process.
DosQueryMem	Obtains information about a range of pages within the virtual address space of the subject process.
Memory Suballocation Functions	
DosSubSetMem	Initializes a heap for suballocation, or increases the size of a previously initialized heap.
DosSubAllocMem	Suballocates a block of memory from a heap that was previously initialized by DosSubSetMem.
DosSubFreeMem	Frees a block of memory that was previously suballocated by DosSubAllocMem.
DosSubUnsetMem	Terminates the use of a heap.
Shared Memory Functions	
DosAllocSharedMem	Allocates a shared memory object within the virtual address space.
DosGetNamedSharedMem	Obtains access to an existing named shared memory object.
DosGetSharedMem	Obtains access to an existing shared memory object.
DosGiveSharedMem	Gives a target process access to an existing shared memory object.

Chapter 7. Program Execution Control

Multitasking is the ability of the operating system to manage the execution of more than one application at a time. A multitasking operating system, such as OS/2 2.0, enables users to run many applications simultaneously.

For the programmer, the OS/2 operating system supports two types of multitasking. An application can start other programs, in separate processes, that will execute concurrently with the application. These programs can be a new copy of the application, a related program that is designed to work with the application, or an unrelated program. Running multiple processes is the first type of multitasking provided for programmers.

Running multiple threads is the second type of multitasking supported by the OS/2 operating system. The OS/2 operating system enables applications to run multiple threads of execution within the same process; separate activities can be multitasked within the application. An example of multiple-thread multitasking would be for the application to dispatch a separate subroutine to load a file from the disk, and have the subroutine execute at the same time the main program continues to monitor and respond to user input.

This chapter describes processes, threads, and sessions, and the OS/2 functions used to create and manage them. Additionally, there is a section describing CPU scheduling.

The following topics are related to the information in this chapter:

- Memory
- Semaphores
- Queues
- Pipes
- Exception Handling
- Debugging.

About Program Execution Control—Thread, Processes, and Sessions

To successfully use multitasking—multiple processes and multiple threads—in your programs, you need to understand the difference between a thread, a process, and a session.

A *thread* is a dispatchable unit of execution that consists of a set of instructions, related CPU register values, and a stack. Each process has at least one thread, called the *main thread* or *thread 1*, and can have many threads running simultaneously. The application runs when the operating system gives control to a thread in the process. The thread is the basic unit of execution scheduling.

A *process* is the code, data, and other resources—such as file handles, semaphores, pipes, queues, and so on—of an application in memory. The OS/2 operating system considers every application it loads to be a process. System resources are allocated on a per-process basis.

A *session* is one (or more) processes with their own virtual console. (A virtual console is a virtual screen—either a character-based, full screen or a Presentation Manager window—and buffers for keyboard and mouse input.)

The OS/2 operating system supports up to 255 concurrent sessions and up to 4095 processes. The operating system supports a system-wide maximum of 4095 threads, but the number of threads available in a single process will be lower, and will vary, because of resource usage within the process.

Figure 7-1 on page 7-3 shows sessions, processes and threads, and their relationship with each other.

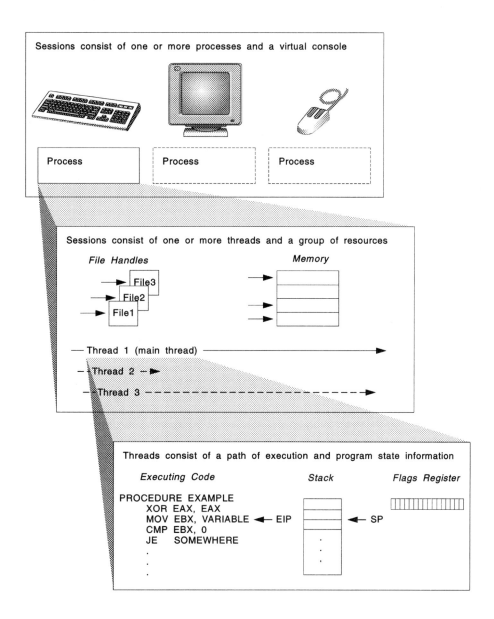

Figure 7-1. Sessions, Processes, and Threads

Threads

Applications always have at least one thread of execution—thread 1. Using multiple threads of execution, an application can do several things at the same time.

For example, a simple Presentation Manager application consists of a single process with two threads:

- A user interface thread that listens and responds to user requests, and that queues work for the second thread

- A processing thread that handles lengthy processing.

The operating system creates the first thread of execution for a process when it starts the executable file. To create another thread of execution, a thread calls DosCreateThread, specifying the address within the program module where the thread begins asynchronous execution. Although a thread can execute any part of the application, including a part being executed by another thread, threads typically are used to execute separate sections of the application. By using several threads, the system can distribute the available CPU time and enable an application to carry out several tasks simultaneously. For example, an application can load a file and prompt the user for input at the same time.

Each thread in a process has a unique stack and register context. Threads shares the resources of the process with the other threads in the process. For example, threads in the same process have access to the memory spaces of other threads within the process. However, threads of one process do not have access to the data spaces of other processes.

Each thread has a priority, that determines the amount of CPU time the thread is allocated. Threads inherit the priority of the thread that creates them. The priority of a thread can be changed by the application; see "Changing the Priority of a Thread" on page 7-30 for details.

An application can use DosSuspendThread and DosResumeThread to suspend and resume the execution of a given thread. When an application suspends a thread, the thread remains suspended until the application calls DosResumeThread.

When an application has more than one thread, it might be necessary to ensure that one thread is finished executing before another thread uses a shared resource, such as a disk file. DosWaitThread causes the application to wait until a specific thread has finished. DosWaitThread can also be used to determine the state of a thread; the function can return immediately with an error value if the identified thread is still running.

A thread ends when it calls DosExit.

Processes

An OS/2 application that has been loaded into memory and prepared for execution is called a process. As mentioned earlier, a process consists of the code, data, and other resources (for example, open file handles) that belong to the application. Each process has at least one thread, called the *main thread* or *thread 1*.

When the operating system executes an application, it confirms that the process code and data are in memory and that the main thread's registers and stack are set before starting the application. Each application has access to all resources of the computer, such as memory, disk drives, screen, keyboard, and the CPU itself. The system carefully manages these resources so that applications can access them without conflict.

A process can have more than one thread. The operating system creates the first thread of execution for a process when it starts the executable file. More threads can be created with

DosCreateThread. Each thread runs independently, with its own stack and register values. Unless the application changes a thread's priority, each thread gets a slice of the CPU in a round-robin strategy. All the threads in a process share the application's globally defined variables and other resources (open file handles, and so on).

A process or thread ends when it calls DosExit. The operating system automatically closes any files or other resources left open by the process when the process ends. When a thread ends, however, any open resources remain open until another thread closes them or the process ends. A process can direct the operating system to carry out other actions when the process ends, by using DosExitList to create a list of termination functions. The operating system calls the termination functions, in the order given, when the process is about to end. If the thread has registered any exception handlers, the exception handlers will also be called before the thread terminates.

Creating Processes

An application can load and execute other applications by using DosExecPgm. The new application, once loaded, is called a *child process*. The process that starts the new application is called the *parent process*.

A child process is like any other process. It has its own code, data, and threads. The child process inherits the resources—such as file handles, pipes, and queues—that belong to the parent process at the time the child process is created, although not necessarily with the same access rights. The parent process can place restrictions on the access of the child process to these resources:

- Files are inherited except for files that were opened with no inheritance indicated.

- Pipes are inherited.

Assuming that the parent process gives the child process appropriate access rights, the child process can use the inherited resources without preparing them. For example, if the parent process opens a file for reading and then starts a child process, the child process can read from the file immediately; it does not have to open the file. However, once the child process is created additional resources that the parent process creates are not available to the child process. Similarly, resources the child process creates are not available to the parent process.

The parent process also has control over the meanings of standard input, output, and error for the child process. For example, the parent can write a series of records to a file, open the file as standard input, open a listing file as standard output, and then execute a sort program that takes its input from standard input and writes to standard output.

Note that memory is not included in the list of things that a child process can inherit from its parent process. The child process is created with its own process address space that is separate and distinct from the memory of the parent process. A new linear address space is built for the new process. The only way for a parent process and a child process to access the same memory is to set up a shared memory area.

The executable file of the child process can be started either synchronously or asynchronously to the parent process. If the parent process starts the child process running *synchronously*, the parent process is suspended and waits until the child process ends before continuing. A child process running *asynchronously* executes independently of the parent process (that is, both run at the same time). The parent process specifies how the child process is to run by setting a parameter in the call to DosExecPgm.

Figure 7-2 shows the difference between synchronous and asynchronous program execution. In the first drawing, child process B is started and executes synchronously; parent process A is suspended while B executes. In the second drawing, child process B is started and executes asynchronously; parent process A continues to execute concurrently with B.

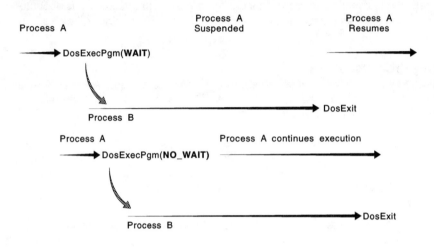

Figure 7-2. Starting a Child Process Synchronously and Asynchronously

The OS/2 command processor, CMD.EXE, starts most child processes synchronously. The parent process waits for each child process to end before it prompts the user for the next command. The command processor also enables the user to start asynchronous applications by using the DETACH command. When the user detaches an application, the command processor starts the application asynchronously, in the background, and continues to prompt for input.

Process Termination
A parent process can use DosWaitChild to determine the termination status of a child process that is running independently. The parent process can have one of its threads call DosWaitChild to wait for completion of the child process while other threads of the parent continue processing.

If the child has started another process, DosWaitChild waits for the completion of any grandchild processes before returning, but does not report their status. If the specified child process has multiple threads, DosWaitChild returns the result code of the last DosExit request.

If there are no child processes, either active or ended with a return code, DosWaitChild returns with an error code. If no child processes have terminated, DosWaitChild can optionally wait until one terminates before returning to the parent.

Process Exit Lists

Because any process can terminate any other process for which it has a process identifier, applications might lose information if a process terminates the application before it can save its work. To prevent this loss of data, you can create a list of functions to clean up data and files before the operating system terminates the process. This list is called an *exit list*. The operating system maintains an exit list for each process and calls these functions whenever the application is terminated, whether by another process or by itself.

You call DosExitList to add to the exit list a routine that is to be given control when a process is terminated (or finishes its execution). Multiple routines can be added to the list. When the process is terminating, the operating system transfers control to each address on the list.

Exit-list functions perform clean-up operations on resources. For example, an exit-list function can be used in a dynamic link library module to free resources or clear flags and semaphores when a client program has ended.

Multitasking with Threads and Multitasking with Processes

The creation and termination of a process is relatively slow compared to the creation and termination of a thread, and is more costly in terms of system resources.

For example, sharing data and resources between processes requires shared memory and the mechanisms of interprocess communication; threads, on the other hand, have full access to the memory and other resources that belong to the process the threads are part of and can be coordinated using semaphores. For these reasons, thread-to-thread task context switches are faster than process-to-process context switches.

Because the operating system can create and execute threads more quickly than processes, the preferred multitasking method for applications is to distribute tasks among threads in the same process instead of among processes.

Sessions

The OS/2 operating system uses sessions to help the user move from one application to the next without disrupting the screen display of an application.

A *session* consists of at least one process and a virtual console—buffers for keyboard and mouse input and either a character-based, full screen or a Presentation Manager window. When the system creates a session, the process in the session displays output in the screen or window. The user can view the output and supply input by moving to the session. The user moves to a session by pressing the Alt+Esc key combination, by selecting the title of the session from the Window List, or, for windowed sessions, by clicking the mouse in the session window.

A *child session* is under the control of the session that creates it. The session that starts the child session is called the *parent session*. Any process in the parent session can exercise control over a child session.

An *unrelated session* is not under the control of the session that started it. The process that creates the unrelated session cannot select it, make it nonselectable, bind it, or terminate it, nor can any other session. DosStartSession does not even return a session identifier when an unrelated session is started. Unrelated sessions are controlled entirely by the user. When the operating system starts new sessions, it starts them as unrelated sessions.

Creating Sessions

A process creates a new session by using DosStartSession. DosStartSession enables an application to start another session and to specify the name of the application to be started in that session.

DosStartSession also specifies which of the five session types is to be started:

- Full screen, protect mode,
- Text windowed, protect mode,
- Presentation Manager (PM),
- Full screen DOS Session, or
- Windowed DOS Session.

Protect mode applications run in full screen and text windowed sessions, PM and AVIO applications run in PM windows, and DOS applications run in full screen DOS Sessions and windowed DOS Sessions.

OS/2 applications running in any of the OS/2 session types—full screen, text windowed, and PM—can start sessions of any other type, including DOS Sessions. DOS Session applications cannot start other sessions.

An application can start another process in a separate session when the application will not manage any I/O done by the process. For example, an application that starts an unrelated application could start it in a separate session.

A session can be started as a related or an unrelated session. A related session is called a *child session*, and the session starting the child session is called the *parent session*. An application can control its child sessions by using the session identifier returned by DosStartSession with the DosSetSession, DosSelectSession, and DosStopSession. If an application starts an *unrelated session*, the new session cannot be controlled by the application. The Related field in the STARTDATA structure specifies whether the new session is related to the session calling DosStartSession.

After a process has started a child session, no other process in its session can start a child session until all dependent sessions started by this process have ended.

When a session is created, the title specified in the function call (or the application name if no title is specified) is added to the Window List.

DosStartSession can be used to start either a foreground or a background session, but a new session can be started in the foreground only when the caller's session, or one of the caller's descendant sessions, is currently executing in the foreground. The foreground session for windowed applications is the session of the application that owns the window focus.

Termination Queues

The parent session must create a *termination queue* prior to specifying the queue name in a call to DosStartSession. The operating system will continue to notify the parent session through the specified queue as long as the session calling DosStartSession remains a parent session. In other words, when all the child sessions for a particular parent session terminate, the termination queue is closed by the operating system. An existing queue name must be specified on the next DosStartSession call if the caller wants to continue receiving termination notification messages.

The operating system writes a data element to the specified queue when any child session terminates. The queue is posted regardless or who terminates the child session (the child, the parent, or the user) and whether the termination is normal or abnormal.

A parent session calls DosReadQueue to receive notification when a child session has terminated. The word that contains the request parameter, returned by DosReadQueue, will be 0. The data element has the following format:

Table 7-1. Termination Queue Element Format	
Size	**Description**
WORD	Session ID of the child session that terminated
WORD	Result code

The process that originally called the DosStartSession request should call DosReadQueue, with the NOWAIT parameter set to 0. This is the only process that has addressability to the notification data element. After reading and processing the data element, the caller must free the segment containing the data element by calling DosFreeMem.

When a child session terminates, the result code returned in the termination queue's data element is the result code of the program specified in the DosStartSession call, providing

- the program was executed directly, with no intermediate secondary command processor, or
- the program is executed indirectly through a secondary command processor, and the /C parameter is specified.

When a child session is running in the foreground at the time it terminates, the parent session becomes the new foreground session. When a parent session terminates, any child sessions are terminated. When an unrelated session terminates in the foreground, the operating system selects the next foreground session.

Child Session Control

A session can be either a child session or an unrelated session. A child session is under the control of the processes in the session that creates it (the parent session). A process can select, set, or stop a child session by using DosSelectSession, DosSetSession, or DosStopSession, respectively. DosStartSession returns a unique session identifier for the child session for use in these functions.

A session can run in either the foreground or background. A process can create a foreground session only if the creating process or one of its descendant sessions is executing in the current foreground session. A process can move a child session to the foreground by selecting the child session using the session identifier and calling DosSelectSession. A process can make a child session nonselectable by using DosSetSession to change the SelectInd field in the STATUSDATA structure. This prevents the user from selecting the session from the Window List but does not prevent a process from selecting the child session by using DosSelectSession.

A process can bind a child session to its own session by using DosSetSession. Binding a session causes that session to move to the foreground whenever the user selects the parent session from the Window List.

A parent session can use a session identifier with the DosSetSession function only if the parent session created the child session associated with that identifier. It cannot use identifiers for child sessions created by other parent processes. This is true for all session management functions.

Although a child session is related to the session that started it, the processes in the child and original sessions are not related. This means that even though DosStartSession supplies the process identifier of the process in the child session, the process identifier cannot be used with OS/2 functions such as DosSetPriority.

Child Session Termination

A parent session can stop a child session by using DosStopSession. Stopping the child session terminates the processes in that session. It also stops any sessions related to the child session. If a child session is in the foreground when it is stopped, the parent session becomes the foreground session. DosStopSession breaks any bond that exists between the parent session and the specified child session.

A process running in the session specified in the call to DosStopSession can ignore the request to terminate. If this happens, DosStopSession still returns 0 (indicating success). The only way to be certain that the child session has terminated is to wait for notification through the termination queue specified in the call to DosStartSession. The operating system writes a data element into the specified queue when the child session terminates. The process in the parent session must call DosReadQueue to retrieve this data element, which contains the session identifier for the child session and the return value for the process in the child session. Only the process that created the child session can read the data element.

About CPU Scheduling

The OS/2 operating system performs prioritized, preemptive, multitasking. *Prioritized* means that the operating system does not divide CPU time equally among all threads. All programs do not get equal access to the CPU. A prioritizing, time-slicing strategy is used to allocate access to the CPU among competing threads. Each thread has a priority and the operating system runs the highest priority thread that is ready to run. Programs with higher priorities (a real-time robotic application, for example), are given access to the CPU before programs with lower priorities. If a thread with a higher priority than the currently running thread becomes ready to run, the current thread is stopped immediately, or *preempted*, and the higher priority thread is given the CPU. The lower priority thread does not get to complete its time slice. Threads of equal priority are given CPU time in a round-robin manner.

Preemptive means that the multitasking activity needs no cooperation from the executing programs. The operating system maintains control over executing programs, and stops, or preempts, them when their time slice with the CPU is over or when a higher priority program is ready to run.

CPU scheduling is based on four priority classes—Time Critical, Fixed-High, Regular, and Idle-Time. Each class has 32 levels of execution ordering. Scheduling parameters are user-selectable at the time the system is started or can be varied dynamically based on system load.

Depending on a thread's priority class and level, the operating system periodically gives each thread in each process a small slice of CPU time. Threads with higher priorities always run before threads having lower priorities. A thread runs until its time is up or until a thread with a higher priority is ready to run. At that time, the operating system preempts the thread and starts another thread. Threads can also voluntarily relinquish the CPU (for example, by calling DosSleep).

The amount of time in each time slice is defined by the TIMESLICE command in the CONFIG.SYS file. The TIMESLICE command can be used by the user to customize the size of the time slices that a thread gets. The default is for the operating system to dynamically vary the size of the time slice based on the activity of the thread and the overall system load.

When a thread is created (using DosCreateThread), it inherits the priority of the thread that started it. DosSetPriority enables threads to change their priority classes and levels in response to changes in their execution environments. DosSetPriority enables a thread to change its own priority, or the priority of any thread within its process. DosSetPriority also enables changing priorities for the entire process and for descendant processes. Within each class, the priority level of a thread can vary because of a DosSetPriorty request or, if dynamic priority variation is being used, because of action taken by the operating system.

Priority Classes

The operating system uses four priority classes to determine when a thread receives a time slice:

Table 7-2. Priority Classes	
Priority	**Description**
Time-critical	Highest priority. For use when response time is critical.
Fixed-high	Used by threads that provide service to other threads. This priority class is to be used when it is desirable that the thread not be too sensitive to the foreground/background boost provided by dynamic priority variation. It is meant for programs that need to execute before regular programs, but without the immediate response time requirement called for by time-critical threads.
Regular	Default priority. Most threads belong in this class.
Idle-time	Lowest priority. This priority only gets CPU time when there is no other work to do.

A time-critical thread always receives a time slice before a fixed-high thread, a fixed-high thread always receives a time slice before a regular thread, and a regular thread always receives a time slice before an idle-time thread.

Time-Critical Threads

Time-critical threads have the highest priority class and execute before any fixed-high, regular, or idle-time threads.

The time-critical class is for threads that must react to events outside the system. For example, in a communications application, a thread responsible for reading data from the communications device needs enough time to read all incoming data. Because more than a regular time slice might be needed, a time-critical classification ensures that the thread gets all the time required.

Time-critical threads have a static priority that is not varied by the operating system. They are scheduled among themselves in priority level order, with round-robin scheduling of threads of equal priority.

Time-critical threads must be executed quickly, then free the CPU for other work until another time-critical event occurs. This is important to maintain good interactive responsiveness to the user and enable communications and other time critical applications to run concurrently. The time-critical activity should, when possible, be in a thread separate from the rest of the application, to isolate and minimize the time spent processing at the time-critical level. A good rule of thumb is that a time-critical thread should consist of no more than about 20,000 assembly language instructions.

Fixed-High Threads

A *fixed-high thread* has a priority class that is lower than time-critical but executes before any regular or idle-time threads. This class of threads should be used to provide service for other threads where it is desirable that the thread not be too sensitive to the foreground/background boost provided by dynamic priority variation. A messaging thread, would be a good example of this type of thread.

The operating system varies the priority of a fixed-high thread around a base value according to the activity of the thread and the system at any point in time. The base value can be set by the thread itself.

Regular Threads
A *regular thread* is the class that the majority of threads fall into. No explicit action is necessary by the application to run at this priority, it is the default.

The operating system varies the priority level of a regular thread around a base value according to the activity of the thread and the system at any point in time. The base value can be set by the thread itself.

Idle-Time Threads
An *idle-time* thread is one with very low priority that executes only when there are no regular, fixed-high, or time-critical threads to execute. Idle-time threads get CPU time only when there is no other work to do. The *idle-time* class is for threads that need very little CPU time.

Idle-time threads have a static priority that is not varied by the operating system.

Priority Levels

Within each class, the operating system maintains a priority level for a thread. For each of the four priority classes, there are 32 priority levels—0 to 31. A thread with priority level 31 always receives a time slice before a thread with priority level 30, and so on.

If two or more threads have the same priority level, the operating system distributes the CPU time equally by using a *round-robin scheme*; that is, the operating system gives a time slice to first one, then another, and so on, and then goes back to the first. A thread can use DosSetPriority to change its own priority or the priority of any other thread within its process.

Although an application can set the priority level of a thread at any time, only applications that use more than one thread or process should do so. The best use of priority is to speed up threads or processes on which other threads or processes depend. For example, an application might temporarily raise the priority of a thread loading a file if another thread is waiting for that file to be loaded. Because the priority of a thread is relative to all other threads in the system, raising the priority of the threads in an application merely to get the extra CPU time adversely affects the overall operation of the system.

There are other ways to affect the amount of CPU time a thread is given. A thread can define a critical section of code by using DosEnterCritSec and DosExitCritSec. While inside the critical section of code, a thread cannot be preempted by any other thread within its process (threads in other processes are still given their time slices). Using critical sections enables threads to get more CPU time, while not unduly affecting the rest of the system.

The priority class and priority level are set using DosSetPriority. The priority class is changed by passing the new priority class to the function. The priority level, however, is changed by passing a value, called the *priority-delta*, that is added to the existing priority level to produce the new priority level; changes to the priority level are relative to the current priority level. Specifying a positive priority-delta increases the priority level, enabling the thread to obtain more CPU time than it normally would. A negative priority-delta decreases the priority level, giving the thread less CPU time than it would normally receive. The value is restricted to the valid range, based upon the current priority class of the process.

If you change the priority level without changing the priority class, the priority-delta is relative to the current priority level. However, if you change the priority class at the same time that you change the priority level, the priority-delta value is relative to 0. Whenever DosSetPriority is called with a class specification, but no value is specified for priority-delta, the base priority level defaults to 0.

The process identifier parameter of DosSetPriority specifies which process is affected by the call. A process can change the priority of itself, of any process that is a descendant of itself, or of one of its threads.

A thread can change the priority of any thread within its current process. When a thread changes the priority of threads in a descendant process, however, only those threads running at the default priority will be changed. You cannot change the priority of a thread in a child process that has already changed its priority from the default.

The initial thread of execution for an application is given a regular class priority that varies by the system. When a thread is created, it is initially dispatched in the same class and priority as the thread that started it. A child process inherits the priority of the thread in the parent process that creates it.

Priority Guidelines

Within the two most common priority classes—time-critical and regular—there are certain broad guidelines recommended for choosing the priority level for a program.

- TIME-CRITICAL CLASS

  The guidelines for level within the time critical class are set to maximize the number of different applications that can successfully multitask in an OS/2 system. The guidelines are described in the following table.

Table 7-3. Recommended Priority Levels for Time-Critical Threads		
Activity	**Range of Recommended Priority Levels**	**Justification/Comments**
Robotics/Real time process control	20-31	OS/2 systems can be used on manufacturing lines to control equipment or in other real time process control applications. In this case a slow response from the PC could cause expensive damage to equipment or even human injury. Therefore the highest priority levels should be reserved for these applications.
Communications	10-19	In communications, the inability to get the processor could cause a loss of data or communications sessions. Therefore this class of applications is next highest.
Other	0-09	Other threads might need to preempt the foreground in special cases (for example, Control-Break). These should be set below the other 2 classes.

In general, application performance is not a good reason to make a thread time critical.

• REGULAR CLASS

In cases where explicit priority levels are set, they should follow the guidelines listed below.

Activity	Range of Recommended Priority Level	Justification
Communications	26-31	Communications should take priority over other background processing to increase overlap with transmission and processing on the partner PC or host. This gives the best system performance.
Other	0-25.	If an application has multiple threads it might be necessary to set them to several different priorities to optimize the order in which they run. A range of priority levels is provided to facilitate this. (The default priority is regular class, level = 0.)

Table 7-4. Recommended Priority Levels for Regular Priority Threads

Dynamic Priority Alteration

The operating system can be configured to dynamically alter the priority of a process. The PRIORITY statement in CONFIG.SYS can be set to either ABSOLUTE or DYNAMIC. If PRIORITY specifies the ABSOLUTE option, all processes receive CPU time based on the priority established by calls to DosSetPriority. If the PRIORITY command in the CONFIG.SYS file specifies the DYNAMIC option, the operating system adjusts process priorities based on system load and process activity, and on whether the process is in the foreground. DYNAMIC is the default setting; if the PRIORITY command is not specified, the system uses DYNAMIC priority. DYNAMIC is designed to gives the best overall system performance under most conditions.

When dynamic priority variation is enabled, the operating system grants higher priority to the foreground process than to background processes. System load and process activity are also taken into consideration. The priority of the process consists of a computed priority value that is based upon the display status of the process (foreground or background), and its recent I/O and CPU time usage history. When dynamic priority variation is enabled, I/O priority boosts are generated for keyboard input, window, foreground, processor starvation, device I/O, and DOS Session interrupts. This ensures that the foreground process—the process most likely to be in use—receives enough CPU time to provide quick response to user input.

Altering the Size of the Time Slice

The TIMESLICE command in CONFIG.SYS sets the minimum and maximum amount of processor time allocated to processes and programs for both OS/2 and DOS sessions.

The first parameter selects the minimum TIMESLICE value in milliseconds. This value is the minimum amount of time a thread is to be processed before yielding the processor to a thread of the same priority level. This value must be an integer greater than or equal to 32.

The second parameter selects the maximum TIMESLICE value in milliseconds. The value of this parameter is the maximum amount of time a thread can be processed before yielding processor time. This value must be an integer greater than or equal to the minimum value, and less than 65536.

The default is *dynamic time slicing*, which varies the size of the time slice depending on system load and paging activity. Dynamic time slicing is designed to give the best performance in most situations.

For examples and more details of the TIMESLICE command, see the online *OS/2 Command Reference*.

Using Processes

An OS/2 application that has been loaded into memory and prepared for execution is called a process. A *process* is the code, data, and other resources of the application, such as the open file handles, semaphores, pipes, queues and so on. The OS/2 operating system considers every application it loads to be a process.

Each process has at least one thread, called the *main thread* or *thread 1*. The application runs when the system scheduler gives control to a thread in the process. For more on thread management, see "Using Threads" on page 7-27.

Note: In the example code fragments that follow, error checking was left out to conserve space. Applications should always check the return code that the functions return. Control Program functions return an APIRET value. A return code of 0 indicates success. If a non-zero value is returned, an error occurred.

Starting a Child Process

You start a process by calling DosExecPgm. The process you start is a child of the calling, or parent, process and inherits many of the resources owned by the parent process, such as file handles.

DosExecPgm creates a process environment from an executable file. The target program is loaded into storage, and it begins execution.

The following code fragment starts an application named ABC:

```
#define INCL_DOSPROCESS        /* Process and thread values */
#include <os2.h>

CHAR szFailName[CCHMAXPATH];
RESULTCODES resc;

DosExecPgm(szFailName,         /* Object-name buffer  */
           sizeof(szFailName), /* Length of buffer    */
           EXEC_SYNC,          /* Sync flag           */
           (PSZ) NULL,         /* Argument string     */
           (PSZ) NULL,         /* Environment string  */
           &resc,              /* Address for result  */
           "ABC.EXE");         /* Name of application */
```

Figure 7-3. Starting a Child Process

In this example, ABC runs synchronously (as specified by EXEC_SYNC). This means the parent process temporarily stops while the child process runs. The parent process does not continue until the child process ends.

Starting an Asynchronous Child Process

To start a child process and enable it to run asynchronously (that is, without suspending the parent process until the child process ends), you use the EXEC_ASYNC constant in a call to DosExecPgm. If you start a process in this way, the function copies the process identifier of the child process to the *codeTerminate* field of the RESULTCODES structure that is returned by DosExecPgm. You can use this process identifier to check the progress of the child process or to terminate the process.

You can also run a child process asynchronously by using DosExecPgm with the EXEC_ASYNCRESULT constant. In addition to causing DosExecPgm to return to the parent process immediately, this constant also directs the operating system to save a copy of the termination status when the child process terminates. This status specifies the reason the child process stopped. The parent process can retrieve the termination status by using DosWaitChild.

The following code fragment starts the program SIMPLE.EXE, and then waits for it to finish. It then prints the termination code and the return code.

```
#define INCL_DOSPROCESS        /* Process and thread values */
#include <os2.h>
#include <stdio.h>

#define START_PROGRAM "SIMPLE.EXE"

CHAR        LoadError[100];
PSZ         Args;
PSZ         Envs;
RESULTCODES ReturnCodes;
APIRET      rc;

rc = DosExecPgm(LoadError,          /* Object name buffer        */
            sizeof(LoadError),  /* Length of object name buffer */
            EXEC_SYNC,          /* Asynchronous/Trace flags  */
            Args,               /* Argument string           */
            Envs,               /* Environment string        */
            &ReturnCodes,       /* Termination codes         */
            START_PROGRAM);     /* Program file name         */

printf("Termination Code %d  Return Code %d \n",
        ReturnCodes.codeTerminate,
        ReturnCodes.codeResult);

----------------SIMPLE.EXE------------------

#define INCL_DOSPROCESS        /* Process and thread values */
#include <os2.h>
#include <stdio.h>

#define RETURN_CODE 0

main()
{
    printf("Hello!\n");
    DosExit(EXIT_PROCESS,    /* End the thread or process */
            RETURN_CODE);    /* Result code               */
}
```

Figure   7-4. Retrieving the Termination Status of a Child Process

Starting a Background Process

You can start a child process in the background by specifying the EXEC_BACKGROUND constant in DosExecPgm. A background process runs independently of the parent process and is called a *detached process*. A detached process should not require any input from the keyboard or output to the video screen, but it can use interprocess communication, such as pipes, queues, and shared memory.

The following code fragment starts the program BATCH.EXE in the background.

```
#define INCL_DOSPROCESS        /* Process and thread values */
#include <os2.h>
#include <stdio.h>

#define START_PROGRAM "BATCH.EXE"

CHAR        LoadError[100];
PSZ         Args;
PSZ         Envs;
RESULTCODES ReturnCodes;
APIRET      rc;

rc = DosExecPgm(LoadError,           /* Object name buffer         */
                sizeof(LoadError),   /* Length of object name buffer */
                EXEC_BACKGROUND,     /* Asynchronous/Trace flags   */
                Args,                /* Argument string            */
                Envs,                /* Environment string         */
                &ReturnCodes,        /* Termination codes          */
                START_PROGRAM);      /* Program file name          */

if (rc != 0) {
    printf("DosExecPgm error: return code = %ld", rc);
    return;
}
```

Figure 7-5. Starting a Background Child Process

Setting the Command Line and Environment for a Child Process

When you start a process, it inherits many of the resources of the parent. This includes file handles, such as the standard input and standard output files. A child process also inherits the resources of the screen group, such as the mouse and video modes, and the environment variables of the parent process.

The call to DosExecPgm determines the command line and environment that the child process receives. The fourth and fifth parameters of the function are pointers to the command line and the environment, respectively. If these pointers are NULL, the child process receives nothing for a command line and only an exact duplicate of the environment of the parent process. The parent process can modify this information by creating a string (ending with two NULL characters) and passing the address of the string to the function. The command line string must include the name of the application, followed by a NULL character, and the command line arguments, followed by two NULL characters. Any number of arguments can be passed to the child process, as long as the argument string ends with two NULL characters.

The following code fragment passes to the child process the string "test -option1 -option2" as its command line:

```
#define INCL_DOSPROCESS    /* Process and thread values */
#include <os2.h>

RESULTCODES resc;
CHAR szFailName[CCHMAXPATH];

CHAR szCommandLine[] = "test\0-option1 -option2\0";

DosExecPgm(szFailName,          /* Object-name buffer  */
        sizeof(szFailName),     /* Length of buffer    */
        EXEC_SYNC,              /* Sync flag           */
        szCommandLine,         /* Argument string     */
        (PSZ) NULL,            /* Environment string  */
        &resc,                 /* Address of result   */
        "test.exe");           /* Name of application */
```

Figure   7-6. Setting the Command Line Environment for a Child Process

Changing the Priority of a Process

Changing the priority of a process is simply a matter of changing the priority of every thread executing in the process. For the details see the section on changing thread priorities, "Changing the Priority of a Thread" on page 7-30.

Obtaining Information about Child Processes

The operating system creates and maintains a Process Information Block for every process. An application can use DosGetInfoBlocks to access the Process Information Block. This function returns a pointer to a *pib_s* data structure, which contains the information from the Process Information Block.

The following code fragment returns the address of the Process Information Block of the current process. The calling thread can subsequently browse either the *pib_s* block.

```
#define INCL_DOSPROCESS    /* Process and thread values */
#include <os2.h>

PTIB    pptib;     /* Address of pointer to Thread Information Block  */
PPIB    pppib;     /* Address of pointer to Process Information Block */
APIRET  rc;        /* Return code                                    */

rc = DosGetInfoBlocks(&pptib, &pppib);
```

Figure   7-7. Obtaining Information about a Child Process

DosGetInfoBlocks also returns the address of the Thread Information Block of the current thread.

Waiting for a Child Process to Terminate

You can synchronize the execution of a process with the execution of one of its child processes by calling DosWaitChild. DosWaitChild does not return until the specified child process terminates. This can be useful, for example, if the parent process needs to ensure that the child process has completed its task before the parent process continues with its own task.

In the following code fragment, the parent process starts a child process and then waits for the child process to finish:

```
#define INCL_DOSPROCESS       /* Process and thread values */
#include <os2.h>

RESULTCODES resc;
PID pidEnded;
CHAR szFailName[CCHMAXPATH];

CHAR szCommandLine[] = "APP\0test\0";

DosExecPgm(szFailName,              /* Failed-name buffer     */
           sizeof(szFailName),      /* Length of buffer       */
           EXEC_ASYNC,              /* Sync flag              */
           szCommandLine,           /* Argument string        */
           (PSZ) NULL,              /* Environment string     */
           &resc,                   /* Address of result      */
           "APP.EXE");              /* Name of application     */

DosWaitChild(DCWA_PROCESS,          /* Only the process       */
             DCWW_WAIT,             /* Waits until it is done */
             &resc,                 /* Puts the result here   */
             &pidEnded,             /* PID of ended process   */
             resc.codeTerminate);   /* Child to wait for      */
```

Figure 7-8. Waiting for a Child Process to End

You can cause a process to wait for all its child processes to end by using the DCWA_PROCESSTREE constant in the call to DosWaitChild.

Ending the Current Process

You terminate the current process by calling DosExit. When you exit, the system stops the process and frees any existing resources the process owns.

In the following code fragment, DosExit is used to terminate the process if the given file does not exist:

```
#define INCL_DOSPROCESS      /* Process and thread values */
#include <os2.h>

#define HF_STDERR 2          /* Standard error handle    */

HFILE  hf;
ULONG  ulAction, cbWritten;
APIRET rc;

rc = DosOpen("SAMPLE.TXT", &hf, &ulAction, 0, FILE_NORMAL,
    FILE_OPEN, OPEN_ACCESS_WRITEONLY | OPEN_SHARE_DENYWRITE, (PEAOP2) NULL);

if (rc) {
    DosWrite(HF_STDERR, "Cannot open file\r\n", 18, &cbWritten);
    DosExit(EXIT_PROCESS, rc);
}
```

Figure   7-9. Ending the Current Process

EXIT_PROCESS directs DosExit to terminate all the threads in a process including the calling thread, thus terminating the process. DosExit includes an error value that is returned to the parent process through the RESULTCODES structure specified in the DosExecPgm call that started the process. If you started the application from the command line, the command processor, CMD.EXE, makes this value available through the ERRORLEVEL variable. If another process started the application, that process can call DosWaitChild to determine the error value.

If you want to exit only from a given thread, you can call DosExit with the EXIT_THREAD constant. This will terminate only the calling thread; other threads in the process are not affected. If the thread you terminate is the last thread in the process, the process also terminates. If the thread consists of a function, the thread terminates when the function returns.

Terminating a Process

A process can terminate the execution of a descendant process by calling DosKillProcess. This causes the operating system to send a XCPT_SIGNAL_KILLPROC exception to the target process. The child processes of the target process can also be terminated.

The following code fragment terminates the specified process and all child processes belonging to that process:

```
#define INCL_DOSPROCESS        /* Process and thread values */
#include <os2.h>

PID pidProcess;

DosKillProcess(DKP_PROCESSTREE, pidProcess);
```

Figure   7-10. Terminating a Process

In this example, the *pidProcess* parameter specifies which descendant process to terminate. The process identifier is returned by DosExecPgm in the *codeTerminate* field of the RESULTCODES structure when you start the child process.

The parameter DKP_PROCESSTREE in the example indicates that the specified process, *pidProcess*, and all of its descendant processes are to be terminated.

If you specify DKP_PROCESS in a call to DosKillProcess, only the specified process is terminated. Its child processes, if any, continue to run.

The process to be terminated must either be the current process, or it must have been directly created by the current process with DosExecPgm for asynchronous execution. That is, a process can terminate itself and its descendants.

The process to be terminated need not still be executing. If it has started its own child processes, but has stopped executing, its children can still be flagged for termination.

Obtaining the Termination Status of a Child Process

The operating system saves the termination status for a process if the process was started by using the EXEC_ASYNCRESULT constant in the call to DosExecPgm. You can retrieve the termination status of the most recently terminated process by using the DCWW_NOWAIT constant with DosWaitChild and setting the child process identification parameter to 0. The DCWW_NOWAIT constant directs the function to return immediately, without waiting for a process to end. Instead, the function retrieves the termination status from the process that most recently ended. If you specify a child process identification with DCWW_NOWAIT, DosWaitChild returns ERROR_CHILD_NOT_COMPLETE if the child process has not terminated. Once the specified process has ended, DosWaitChild returns its termination code.

The following code fragment starts a child session (the program SIMPLE.EXE), and then retrieves the termination status from the process that most recently ended.

```
#define INCL_DOSPROCESS         /* Process and thread values */
#include <os2.h>
#include <stdio.h>

#define START_PROGRAM "SIMPLE.EXE"

CHAR          LoadError[100];
PSZ           Args;
PSZ           Envs;
RESULTCODES   ReturnCodes;
ULONG         Pid;             /* Process ID (returned)            */
ULONG         Target;          /* Process ID of process to wait for */
APIRET        rc;              /* Return code                      */

strcpy(Args, "-a2 -1");       /* Pass arguments "-a2" and "-1"    */

Target = 0;       /* Process ID for the most recently terminated process  */

rc = DosExecPgm(LoadError,         /* Object name buffer            */
                sizeof(LoadError), /* Length of object name buffer  */
                EXEC_ASYNCRESULT,  /* Asynchronous/Trace flags      */
                Args,              /* Argument string               */
                Envs,              /* Environment string            */
                &ReturnCodes,      /* Termination codes             */
                START_PROGRAM);    /* Program file name             */

if (rc != 0) {
    printf("DosExecPgm error: return code = %ld", rc);
    return;
}

rc = DosWaitChild(DCWA_PROCESS,    /* Execution options             */
                  DCWW_NOWAIT,     /* Wait options                  */
                  &ReturnCodes,    /* Termination codes             */
                  &Pid,            /* Process ID (returned)         */
                  Target);         /* Process ID of process to wait for */
if (rc != 0) {
    printf("DosWaitChild error: return code = %ld", rc);
    return;
}
```

Figure 7-11. Obtaining the Termination Status of a Child Process

Creating an Exit List

You call DosExitList to add to the exit list a routine that is to be given control when a process is terminated (or finishes its execution). Multiple routines can be added to the list. When the process is terminating, the operating system transfers control to each address on the list.

If there are multiple addresses on the list, each function gets control in numerical order (with 0 being first and 0FFH being last), based on a value supplied by the application when it calls

DosExitList. In case of duplicate entries for this parameter, the routines will be executed in LIFO (last in, first out) order.

DosExitList requires a function code that specifies an action and a pointer to the function that is to receive control upon termination.

The following code fragment adds the locally defined function *SaveFiles* to the exit list:

```c
#define INCL_DOSPROCESS          /* Process and thread values */
#include <os2.h>

#define HF_STDOUT 1              /* Standard output handle    */

VOID main(VOID)
{
    .
    .
    .
    DosExitList(EXLST_ADD, (PFNEXITLIST) SaveFiles);
    .
    .
    .
    DosExit(EXIT_PROCESS, 0);
}

VOID APIENTRY SaveFiles(ULONG ulTermCode)
{
    ULONG cbWritten;

    switch (ulTermCode) {
        case TC_EXIT:
        case TC_KILLPROCESS:
            DosWrite(HF_STDOUT, "Goodbye\r\n", 10, &cbWritten);
            break;

        case TC_HARDERROR:
        case TC_TRAP:
            break;

    }
    DosExitList(EXLST_EXIT, 0);
}
```

Figure   7-12. Exit List Routines

Any function that you add to the list must take one parameter. The function can carry out any task, as shown in the preceding example, but as its last action it must call DosExitList, specifying the EXLST_EXIT constant. An exit-list function must not have a return value and must not call DosExit to terminate.

When an exit-list routine receives control, the parameter (located at ESP+4 on the stack) contains an indicator of why the process ended. The values returned are the same as those for termination codes returned by DosWaitChild or DosExecPgm requests. These values are:

TC_EXIT (0)   Normal exit
TC_HARDERROR (1)   Hard-error halt
TC_TRAP (2)   Trap operation for a 16-bit child process
TC_KILLPROCESS (3)   Unintercepted DosKillProcess
TC_EXCEPTION (4)   Exception operation for a 32-bit child process

To execute the exit-list functions, the operating system reassigns thread 1 after terminating all other threads in the process. If thread 1 has already exited (for example, if it called DosExit without terminating other threads in the process), the exit-list functions cannot be executed. In general, it is poor practice to terminate thread 1 without terminating all other threads.

Before transferring control to the termination routines, the operating system resets the stack to its initial value. Transfer is by way of an assembly language JMP instruction. The routine must be in the address space of the terminating process. The termination routine at that address takes the necessary steps and then calls DosExitList with FunctionOrder=EXLST_EXIT. Control is then transferred to the next address in the invocation order of the exit list. When all such addresses have been processed, the process completes exiting. If a routine on the list does not call DosExitList at the completion of its processing, the process waits, and the operating system prevents termination.

During DosExitList processing, the process is in a state of partial termination. All threads of the process are terminated, except for the one executing the exit-list routines. To ensure good response to a user request to end a program, there should be minimal delay in completing termination. Termination routines should be short and fail-safe.

You can use DosExitList with the EXLST_REMOVE constant to remove a function from the list.

The designer of an exit-list routine must carefully consider which functions will be used by the routine. In general, calls to most OS/2 functions are valid in a DosExitList routine, but certain functions, such as DosCreateThread and DosExecPgm, are not.

Using Threads

A *thread* is a dispatchable unit of execution that consists of a set of instructions, related CPU register values, and a stack. Every process has at least one thread and can have many threads running at the same time. The application runs when the operating system gives control to a thread in the process. The thread is the basic unit of execution scheduling.

Every process has at least one thread, called the *main thread* or *thread 1*. To execute different parts of an application simultaneously, you can start several threads.

A new thread inherits all the resources currently owned by the process. This means that if you opened a file before creating the thread, the file is available to the thread. Similarly, if the new thread creates or opens a resource, such as another file, that resource is available to the other threads in the process.

Creating a Thread

You use DosCreateThread to create a new thread for a process. DosCreateThread requires the address of the code to execute and a variable to receive the identifier of the thread. The address of the code is typically the address of a function that is defined within the application.

You can pass one ULONG parameter to the thread when you start it. To pass more information to the thread, pass the address of a data structure.

You specify how you want the thread to run when you call DosCreateThread. If bit 1 of the flag parameter in the function call is 0, the thread starts immediately. If bit 1 of the flag parameter is 1, the thread starts suspended and will not run until the application calls DosResumeThread.

Each thread maintains its own stack. You specify the size of the stack when you call DosCreateThread. The amount of space needed depends on a number of factors, including the number of function calls the thread makes and the number of parameters and local variables used by each function. If you plan to call OS/2 functions, a reasonable stack size is 8192 bytes (8KB); 4096 bytes (4KB) should be the absolute minimum. If bit 1 of the flag parameter is 0, the operating system uses the default method for initializing the thread's stack. If bit 1 of the flag parameter is 1, memory for the thread's entire stack is pre-committed.

The following code fragment creates a thread:

```
#define INCL_DOSPROCESS         /* Process and thread values */
#include <os2.h>

#define HF_STDOUT 1             /* Standard output handle   */

VOID main(VOID)
{
    ULONG ulBeepLen;
    TID   tidThread;

    ulBeepLen = 1000;
    .
    DosCreateThread(&tidThread,  /* Thread ID returned by DosCreateThread */
                    ThreadFunc,  /* Address of the thread function       */
                    ulBeepLen,   /* Parameter passed to thread           */
                    0,           /* Immediate execution, default stack   */
                                 /* initialization                       */
                    4096);       /* Stack size                           */
    .
    .
    .
    DosExit(EXIT_PROCESS, 0);
}

VOID ThreadFunc(ULONG ulBeepLen)
{
    DosBeep(750, ulBeepLen);

    DosWrite(HF_STDOUT, "Message from new thread\r\n", 25, 0);
}
```

Figure 7-13. Creating a Thread

A thread continues to run until it calls DosExit, returns control to the operating system, or is terminated by a DosKillThread call. In the preceding example, the thread exits when the function implicitly returns control at the end of the function.

Obtaining Information about a Thread

The operating system creates and maintains a Thread Information Block for each thread. An application can use DosGetInfoBlocks to access the Thread Information Block. This function returns a pointer to a *tib_s* data structure.

The following code fragment returns the address of the Thread Information Block of the current thread. The calling thread can subsequently browse the *tib_s* control block.

```
#define INCL_DOSPROCESS     /* Process and thread values */
#include <os2.h>

PTIB     pptib;      /* Address of pointer to Thread Information Block  */
PPIB     pppib;      /* Address of pointer to Process Information Block */
APIRET   rc;         /* Return code                                    */

rc = DosGetInfoBlocks(&pptib, &pppib);
```

Figure 7-14. Obtaining Information about a Thread

DosGetInfoBlocks also returns the address of the Process Information Block of the current process.

Changing the Priority of a Thread

You can use DosSetPriority to change the execution priority of threads in a process. The execution priority defines when or how often a thread receives an execution time slice. Threads with higher priorities receive time slices before those with lower priorities. When a thread that is higher in priority than the currently running thread becomes ready to run, it immediately preempts the lower priority thread (the lower priority thread does not get to complete its time slice). Threads with equal priority receive time slices in a round-robin order. If you raise the priority of a thread, the thread is executed more frequently.

You can use DosSetPriority to set the priority for one thread in a process, for all threads in a process (and thus the process itself), or for threads in a child process.

A process can change the priority of any thread within itself. When a process changes the priority of threads in a descendant process, however, only those with default priorities are changed. The priority of any thread in a descendant process that has already explicitly changed its priority from the default with DosSetPriority is not changed.

In the following code fragment, DosSetPriority lowers the priority of a process to be used as a background process:

```
#define INCL_DOSPROCESS         /* Process and thread values */
#include <os2.h>

PTIB ptib;    /* Thread Information Block  */
PPIB ppib;    /* Process Information Block */

DosGetInfoBlocks(&ptib, &ppib);

DosSetPriority(PRTYS_PROCESSTREE, PRTYC_IDLETIME, 0, ppib->pib_ulpid);
```

Figure 7-15. Changing the Priority of a Thread

DosGetInfoBlocks retrieves the Process Information Blocks and Thread Information Blocks. DosSetPriority then uses the process identifier to change the priority to idle time (idle-time processes receive the least attention by the operating system).

If you specify PRTYS_PROCESS when calling DosSetPriority, only the priority of the specified process changes. The priorities of all child processes remain unchanged.

If you specify PRTYS_THREAD in the call to DosSetPriority, you must specify a thread identifier as the last parameter. The priority of the specified thread changes, but the priorities of all other threads in the process remain unchanged.

Whenever DosSetPriority is called with a class specification, but no value is specified for priority-delta, the base priority level defaults to 0.

Suspending the Current Thread

You can temporarily suspend the execution of the current thread for a set amount of time by using DosSleep. This function suspends execution of the thread for the specified number of milliseconds. DosSleep is useful when you need to delay the execution of a task. For example, you can use DosSleep to delay a response when the user presses a DIRECTION key. The delay provides the user with enough time to observe the results and release the key.

The following code fragment uses DosSleep to suspend execution of a thread for 1000 milliseconds (1 second):

```
#define INCL_DOSPROCESS      /* Process and thread values */
#include <os2.h>

DosSleep(1000);
```

Figure   7-16. Suspending the Current Thread

Suspending and Resuming Execution of a Thread

DosSuspendThread and DosResumeThread are used to temporarily suspend the execution of a thread when it is not needed and resume execution when the thread is needed.

These functions are best used when it is necessary for a process to temporarily suspend execution of a thread that is in the middle of a task. For example, consider a thread that opens and reads files from a disk. If other threads in the process do not require input from these files, the process can suspend execution of the thread so that the operating system does not needlessly grant control to it.

The specified thread might not be suspended immediately if it has some system resources locked that must be freed first. However, the thread is not permitted to execute further application program instructions until a corresponding DosResumeThread is called.

A thread can only suspend another thread that is within its process.

DosResumeThread is used to enable the suspended thread to resume execution.

The following code fragment temporarily suspends the execution of another thread within the same process. A subsequent call to DosResumeThread restarts the suspended thread. Assume that the thread identifier of the target thread has been placed int *ThreadID* already.

```
#define INCL_DOSPROCESS      /* Process and thread values */
#include <os2.h>
#include <stdio.h>

TID     ThreadID;    /* Thread identifier */
APIRET  rc;          /* Return code       */

rc = DosSuspendThread(ThreadID);

if (rc != 0) {
    printf("DosSuspendThread error: return code = %ld", rc);
    return;
}

rc = DosResumeThread(ThreadID);

if (rc != 0) {
    printf("DosResumeThread error: return code = %ld", rc);
    return;
}
```

Figure 7-17. Suspending and Resuming Execution of a Thread

Entering Critical Sections

A thread can prevent execution of any of the other threads in its process by calling DosEnterCritSec. This function temporarily prevents a thread from being preempted by other threads within its process. The other threads in the process will not be executed until the current thread calls DosExitCritSec. This enables the calling thread to access a time-critical resource of the process.

The following code fragment enters a section that will not be preempted, performs a simple task, and then exits quickly.

```
#define INCL_DOSPROCESS      /* Process and thread values */
#include <os2.h>
#include <stdio.h>

BOOL    flag;           /* Program control flag */
APIRET  rc;             /* Return code          */

rc = DosEnterCritSec();

if (rc != 0) {
    printf("DosEnterCritSec error: return code = %ld", rc);
    return;
}

flag = TRUE;            /* Set the flag */

rc = DosExitCritSec();

if (rc != 0) {
    printf("DosExitCritSec error: return code = %ld", rc);
    return;
}
```

Figure 7-18. Entering and Exiting a Critical Section of Code

A count is maintained of the outstanding DosEnterCritSec requests. The count is incremented when a DosEnterCritSec request is made, and decremented when a DosExitCritSec request is made. A DosExitCritSec request will not cause normal thread dispatching to be restored while the count is greater than 0.

This count is maintained in a WORD-sized variable. If overflow occurs, the count is set to its maximum value, and an error is returned. The operation is not performed when this occurs.

Threads that call DosEnterCritSec must not must not make dynamic link calls within these critical sections. The dynamic link procedure could be using semaphores to serialize a resource. If a thread entering the critical section blocks another thread that already owns the resource which the dynamic link function is about to request, a deadlock occurs.

For example, threads of an application are serializing their access to a queue by means of a semaphore. A thread enters a critical section and makes a request to read the queue while another thread already has the semaphore that controls access to the queue. The thread that has the semaphore is now effectively blocked by DosEnterCritSec, and the thread that has requested the queue waits forever to access it.

Note: Thread 1 is the initial thread of execution. It handles all signals (Ctrl+C, Ctrl+Break, and KillProcess). If a signal occurs while DosEnterCritSec is active, thread 1 can begin execution to process the signal. Thread 1 must not access the critical resource that is being protected by the use of DosEnterCritSec.

Waiting for a Thread to Terminate

An application might need to ensure that one thread has finished executing before another thread continues with its own task. For example, one thread might have to finish reading a disk file into memory before another thread can use the information. You can use DosWaitThread to suspend a thread until another thread has terminated.

DosWaitThread places the current thread into a wait state until another thread in the current process has terminated. It then returns the thread identifier of the terminating thread.

The following code fragment creates three threads. The thread identifier for each thread is returned by DosCreateThread in the *atid* array. Using *&atid[0]* as a parameter in the call to DosWaitThread causes the operating system to wait until the thread with that identifier (the thread running Thread2Func) terminates.

```
#define INCL_DOSPROCESS        /* Process and thread values */
#include <os2.h>

#define HF_STDOUT 1            /* Standard output handle    */

TID atid[3];
ULONG cbWritten;

DosCreateThread(&atid[0], Thread2Func, 0, 0, 4096);
DosCreateThread(&atid[1], Thread3Func, 0, 0, 4096);
DosCreateThread(&atid[2], Thread4Func, 0, 0, 4096);
DosWaitThread(&atid[0], DCWW_WAIT);
DosWrite(HF_STDOUT, "The thread has terminated\r\n", 27, &cbWritten);
```

Figure   7-19. Waiting for a Certain Thread to End

If you set the *tid* parameter to 0 in the call to DosWaitThread, the operating system waits only until the next thread (any thread in the process) terminates. The identifier for the terminated thread is then returned in the *tid* parameter.

After the threads are created as in the preceding example, the following code fragment waits until one of the threads terminates, and then returns its thread identifier:

```
#define INCL_DOSPROCESS        /* Process and thread values */
#include <os2.h>

TID tid;

tid = 0;

DosWaitThread(&tid, DCWW_WAIT);
```

Figure   7-20. Waiting for Any Thread to End

The thread identifier of the next thread to terminate after the DosWaitThread call is returned in the *tid* parameter.

You can use DosWaitThread so that you can recover thread resources when the thread terminates, or to synchronize the execution of a thread with the execution of other threads.

Ending the Current Thread

To end the execution of the current thread, call DosExit, specifying the action code as 0. It is good practice to end each thread in the application individually.

If the thread that is ending is the last thread in the process, or if the request is to terminate all threads in the process, then the process also terminates. All threads except one are terminated, and that thread executes any routines in the list specified by DosExitList.

When this is complete, the resources of the process are released, and the result code that was specified in the DosExit call is passed to any thread that calls DosWaitChild for this process.

In the following code fragment, the main routine starts another program, SIMPLE.EXE, and then expects a return code of 3 to be returned. SIMPLE.EXE sets the return code with DosExit.

```
#define INCL_DOSPROCESS           /* Process and thread values */
#include <os2.h>
#include <stdio.h>

#define START_PROGRAM "SIMPLE.EXE"
#define RETURN_OK 3

CHAR        LoadError[100];
PSZ         Args;
PSZ         Envs;
RESULTCODES ReturnCodes;
APIRET      rc;

rc = DosExecPgm(LoadError,              /* Object name buffer         */
                sizeof(LoadError),      /* Length of object name buffer */
                EXEC_SYNC,              /* Asynchronous/Trace flags   */
                Args,                   /* Argument string            */
                Envs,                   /* Environment string         */
                &ReturnCodes,           /* Termination codes          */
                START_PROGRAM);         /* Program file name          */

if (ReturnCodes.codeResult == RETURN_OK)  /* Check result code       */
    printf("Things are ok...");
else
    printf("Something is wrong...");

----------------SIMPLE.EXE------------------

#define INCL_DOSPROCESS           /* Process and thread values */
#include <os2.h>
#include <stdio.h>

#define RETURN_CODE 3

main()
{
    printf("Hello!\n");
    DosExit(EXIT_THREAD,            /* End thread/process */
            RETURN_CODE);           /* Result code        */
}
```

Figure 7-21. Ending the Current Thread

When you specify DosExit for thread 1 (the initial thread of execution started by the operating system for this process), all of the threads in the process are terminated, and the process is ended.

Terminating a Thread

DosKillThread terminates a thread in the current process. DosKillThread enables a thread in a process to terminate any other thread in the process.

DosKillThread is used to force a thread within the current process to terminate without causing the entire process to be terminated.

```
#define INCL_DOSPROCESS        /* Process and thread values */
#include <os2.h>

TID tidThread;    /* ThreadID of the thread to be terminated */

DosCreateThread(&tidThread, ThreadFunction, 0, 0, 4096);
.
.
.
DosKillThread(tidThread);
```

Figure   7-22. Terminating a Thread within the Same Process

DosKillThread returns to the requestor without waiting for the target thread to complete its termination processing.

It is an invalid operation to use DosKillThread to kill the current thread.

Terminating thread 1 will cause the entire process to terminate similar to executing DosExit on thread 1.

If the target thread is executing 16-bit code or was created by a 16-bit requester, ERROR_BUSY is returned.

Using Sessions

A session consists of at least one process and a virtual console (either full screen, or Presentation Manager window, and buffers for keyboard and mouse input). An application can manage its own child sessions by using DosStartSession, DosStopSession, DosSelectSession, and DosSetSession.

Starting a Session

DosStartSession is used to start new sessions and to specify the name of the application to be started in the new session.

There are five types of sessions that you can start: full screen, text window, Presentation Manager (PM), full screen DOS Session, and windowed DOS Session. OS/2 applications running in any of the OS/2 session types—full screen, text window, and PM—can start a session for any other application type, including DOS Sessions. Applications running in DOS Sessions cannot start sessions.

DosStartSession can be used to start either a foreground or a background session, but a new session can be started in the foreground only when the session of the caller, or one of the descendant sessions of the caller, is currently executing in the foreground.

A session can be started as an unrelated session or as a child session.

In the following code fragment, an unrelated, foreground session is created, and the application, SIMON.EXE, is started in the new session:

```
#define INCL_DOSPROCESS          /* Process and thread values */
#define INCL_DOSSESMGR
#include <os2.h>

#define HF_STDOUT 1        /* Standard output handle */

STARTDATA  sd;
PID        pidProcess;
CHAR       szBuf[CCHMAXPATH];
ULONG      ulSessionID, cbWritten;
APIRET     rc;
CHAR       szPgmName[] = "SIMON.EXE";

sd.Length = sizeof(sd);                  /* Length of the structure */
sd.Related = SSF_RELATED_INDEPENDENT;    /* Unrelated session        */
sd.FgBg = SSF_FGBG_FORE;                 /* In the foreground        */
sd.TraceOpt = SSF_TRACEOPT_NONE;         /* No tracing               */
sd.PgmTitle = (PSZ) NULL;                /* Title is PgmName         */
sd.PgmName = szPgmName;                  /* Address of szPgmName      */
sd.PgmInputs = (PBYTE) NULL;             /* No command line args     */
sd.TermQ = (PBYTE) NULL;                 /* No terminal queue        */
sd.Environment = (PBYTE) NULL;           /* Inherits environment     */
sd.InheritOpt = SSF_INHERTOPT_PARENT;    /* Uses parent environment */
sd.SessionType = SSF_TYPE_PM;            /* PM session               */
sd.IconFile = (PSZ) NULL;                /* Uses default icon        */
sd.PgmHandle = 0;                        /* Used by Win calls        */
sd.PgmControl = SSF_CONTROL_MAXIMIZE;    /* Starts app maximized     */
sd.InitXPos = 0;                         /* Lower left corner        */
sd.InitYPos = 0;                         /* Lower left corner        */
sd.InitXSize = 0;                        /* Ignored for maximized    */
sd.InitYSize = 0;                        /* Ignored for maximized    */
sd.ObjectBuffer = szBuf;                 /* Fail-name buffer         */
sd.ObjectBuffLen = sizeof(szBuf);        /* Buffer length            */

rc = DosStartSession(&sd, &ulSessionID, &pidProcess);

if (rc) {
    DosBeep(750,250);
    DosWrite(HF_STDOUT, "error starting new session\r\n", 28, &cbWritten);
    DosExit(EXIT_PROCESS, rc);
}
```

Figure 7-23. Starting a Foreground Session

Before calling DosStartSession, you must create a STARTDATA data structure that defines the session to be started. Different lengths for the data structure are supported to provide compatibility and various levels of application control.

DosStartSession uses the STARTDATA structure to specify the details of the new session, such as the name of the application to start in the session, whether the new session should be started in the foreground or background, and whether the new session is unrelated or is a child session of the session calling DosStartSession.

When a session is created, the title specified in STARTDATA, (or the application title if no title is specified in STARTDATA) is added to the Window List.

The *Related* field in the STARTDATA structure specifies whether the new session is related to the session calling DosStartSession.

If the *InheritOpt* field in the STARTDATA data structure is set to 1, the new session inherits the environment and open file handles of the calling process. This applies for both unrelated and related sessions.

Controlling the Execution of Child Sessions

Once a process has started a child session, it can use DosSelectSession to control the child session.

A process calls DosSetSession to set the selectability and bonding of a child session.

Setting User Selectability of a Child Session

A process calls DosSetSession to set the *selectability* of a child session. When a child session is selectable, the user can select it from the Window List or by using Alt+Esc. When a child session is nonselectable, the user cannot select the session from the Window List or move to it by using the Alt+Esc keys.

In the following code fragment, DosSetSession makes a child session nonselectable:

```
#define INCL_DOSPROCESS        /* Process and thread values */
#define INCL_DOSSESMGR
#include <os2.h>

ULONG ulSessionID;
STATUSDATA stsdata;

stsdata.Length = sizeof(stsdata);
stsdata.SelectInd = SET_SESSION_NON_SELECTABLE;  /* Non-selectable     */
stsdata.BondInd = SET_SESSION_UNCHANGED;         /* Leaves session bonding */
                                                 /* index unchanged     */

DosSetSession(ulSessionID, &stsdata);
```

Figure 7-24. Making a Child Session Nonselectable

Once a child session is made nonselectable, the user cannot select the session from the Window List or move to it by using the Alt+Esc keys. However, the parent session can still bring the child session to the foreground by using DosSelectSession. If the session contains a Presentation Manager application or is a windowed session, the user will still be able to select it with a mouse.

The parent session can make a nonselectable child session selectable by setting the *SelectInd* field to SET_SESSION_SELECTABLE in the STATUSDATA structure.

DosSetSession can be called only by a parent session and only for a child session. That is, the calling process must be the process that started the child session using DosStartSession. Neither the parent session itself nor any grandchild, nor any other descendant session beyond a child session can be the target of this call.

Additionally, DosSetSession cannot be used to change the status of a session that was started as an unrelated session. The *Related* field in the STARTDATA structure must have been set to 1 when the session was started.

Binding Child Sessions to Parent Sessions

An application can use DosSetSession to establish a bond between a parent session and one of its child sessions. When the two sessions are bound, the operating system brings the child session to the foreground when the user selects the parent session.

In the following code fragment, a parent session is bound to the child session specified by the *ulSessionID* parameter:

```
#define INCL_DOSPROCESS          /* Process and thread values */
#define INCL_DOSSESMGR
#include <os2.h>

ULONG ulSessionID;
STATUSDATA stsdata;

stsdata.Length = sizeof(stsdata);
stsdata.SelectInd = SET_SESSION_UNCHANGED;   /* Leaves select setting alone */
stsdata.BondInd = SET_SESSION_BOND;          /* Binds parent and child     */

DosSetSession(ulSessionID, &stsdata);
```

Figure   7-25. Binding a Child Session to a Parent Session

When the application uses DosSetSession to establish a parent-child bond, any bond the parent has with another child session is broken. The application can remove the parent-child bond by calling DosSetSession with the BondInd field (in the STATUSDATA structure) set to SET_SESSION_NO_BOND.

A parent session can be executing in either the foreground or the background when it calls DosSetSession.

Switching a Session to the Foreground

An application can bring a session to the foreground, or *select* the session, by calling DosSelectSession.

DosSelectSession can only be used to select the current session or one of the current session's child sessions. It cannot be used to select a grandchild session, or any other descendant session beyond a child session, or any sessions that were started as unrelated sessions.

The session making the call, or one of its child sessions, must be executing in the foreground at the time the function is called. A process can call DosSelectSession with its own session identifier to switch itself to the foreground when one of its descendants is executing in the foreground.

The following code fragment uses DosSelectSession to switch the child session specified by the ulSessionID parameter to the foreground for five seconds. The application then switches the parent session back to the foreground:

```
#define INCL_DOSPROCESS        /* Process and thread values */
#include <os2.h>

ULONG ulSessionID;

DosSelectSession(ulSessionID);  /* Switches child to foreground */
DosSleep(5000);                 /* Sleeps for 5 seconds         */
DosSelectSession(0);            /* Switches parent back         */
```

Figure 7-26. Switching a Child Session to the Foreground

Terminating a Session

DosStopSession can be used by a parent session to stop one or all of its child sessions. If the child session specified in the call to DosStopSession has related sessions, the related sessions are also terminated. The parent session can be running in the foreground or the background when it calls DosStopSession. If the child session is running in the foreground when it is terminated, the parent session becomes the foreground session.

DosStopSession can only be called by a parent session for a child session. Neither the parent session itself, nor any grandchild, nor any other descendant session beyond a child session, nor any unrelated session, can be the target of this call.

In the following code fragment, the child session specified by the *ulSessionID* parameter is terminated:

```
#define INCL_DOSPROCESS        /* Process and thread values */
#define INCL_DOSSESMGR
#include <os2.h>

ULONG ulSessionID;

DosStopSession(STOP_SESSION_SPECIFIED, ulSessionID);
```

Figure   7-27. Terminating a Child Session

An application can terminate all its child sessions by setting the first parameter to STOP_SESSION_ALL in the call to DosStopSession. If this is specified, the second parameter is ignored.

A process running in a child session can ignore the request to terminate. If the process has set up its own exception handler, it might not terminate immediately after the call to DosStopSession. The only way the parent process can be certain that the child session has terminated is to wait for notification through the termination queue specified in the call to DosStartSession that started the session. When the child session terminates, the operating system writes a data element into the termination queue, specifying the child process identifier and the termination status.

If the process in the session specified by DosStopSession has not ended, then DosStopSession still returns a normal return code. You can ensure that a process in a session has ended by waiting for notification from the termination queue specified with DosStartSession.

Summary

Following are the OS/2 functions and data structures used for multitasking.

Table 7-5. Program Execution Control Functions	
Thread Control Functions	
DosCreateThread	Creates an asynchronous thread of execution under the current process.
DosEnterCritSec	Disables thread switching for the current process.
DosExit	Terminates thread execution in the current process.
DosExitCritSec	Enables thread switching for the current process.
DosGetInfoBlocks	Obtains the address of the Thread Information Block and the Process Information Block.
DosKillThread	Terminates a thread in the current process.
DosResumeThread	Restarts a thread that was previously suspended.
DosSetPriority	Changes the priority of a child process or thread in the current process.
DosSuspendThread	Suspends execution of another thread within the current process.
DosWaitThread	Waits for another thread in the current process to end.
Process Control Functions	
DosExecPgm	Executes another program as a child process.
DosExitList	Defines a list of routines to be executed when the current process ends.
DosGetInfoBlocks	Obtains the address of the Thread Information Block and the Process Information Block.
DosKillProcess	Flags a process or group of processes for termination.
DosWaitChild	Waits for a child process to end.
Session Control Functions	
DosSelectSession	Switches a child session to the foreground.
DosSetSession	Sets the status of a child session.
DosStartSession	Starts an unrelated or child session.
DosStopSession	Terminates one or all child sessions.

Table 7-6. Program Execution Control Data Structures

Data Structure	Description
RESULTCODES	Describes the reason a process terminated and contains the value returned by the process.
pib_s	Process Information Block.
STATUSDATA	Data structure for DosSetSession.
STARTDATA	Data structure for DosStartSession.
tib_s	Thread Information Block.

Chapter 8. Semaphores

Communication between processes is valuable in a multitasking operating system to enable concurrent processes to work together. Semaphores are one of three forms of interprocess communication (IPC), the other forms of IPC being pipes and queues.

This chapter describes how to create and use semaphores. Semaphores enable an application to signal the completion of tasks and control access to resources that are shared between more than one thread or process.

The following topics are related to the information in this chapter:

- Memory (Shared Memory)
- Program Execution and Control
- Pipes
- Queues.

About Semaphores

Semaphores signal the beginning or ending of an operation and provide mutually exclusive ownership of resources. Typically, semaphores are used to prevent more than one process or thread within a process from accessing a resource, such as shared memory, at the same time.

Semaphores are defined by the operating system and reside in an internal memory buffer. They are divided into three types, according to the functionality they provide:

- *Event semaphores* enable a thread to notify waiting threads that an event has occurred. The waiting threads then resume execution, performing operations that are dependent on the completion of the signaled event.

- *Mutual exclusion (mutex) semaphores* enable threads to serialize their access to shared resources. That is, ownership of a mutex semaphore is used by cooperating threads as a prerequisite for performing operations on a resource. (Threads cooperate by using the mutex semaphore functions to ensure that access to the resource is mutually exclusive.)

- *Multiple Wait (muxwait) semaphores* enable threads to wait either for multiple events to occur, or for multiple resources to become available. Alternatively, a flag can be set so that a thread waits for any one of multiple events to occur, or for any one of multiple resources to become available.

Event Semaphores

An event semaphore provides a signaling mechanism among threads or processes, ensuring that events occur in the desired sequence. Event semaphores are used by one thread to signal other threads that an event has occurred. An application can use this type of semaphore to block a thread or process until the event has occurred.

An event semaphore has two states, reset and posted. When an event semaphore is in the reset state, the operating system blocks any thread or process that is waiting on the

8-1

semaphore. When an event semaphore is in the posted state, all threads or processes waiting on the semaphore resume execution.

For example, assume thread 1 is allocating a shared memory object and threads 2 and 3 must wait for the memory to be allocated before they attempt to examine its contents. Before thread 1 allocates the memory, it creates an event semaphore, specifying the initial state of the semaphore as reset. (If the event semaphore has already been created, thread 1 simply resets the semaphore.) Threads 2 and 3 use DosWaitEventSem to wait for the semaphore to signal that the event, in this case the allocation and preparation of the shared memory object, has been completed. Because the semaphore was reset by thread 1, threads 2 and 3 are blocked when they call DosWaitEventSem. After thread 1 has finished allocating and placing data in the shared memory object, it signals the completion of its task by posting the event semaphore. The posting of the event semaphore unblocks threads 2 and 3, enabling them to resume execution. They can then proceed to examine the contents of the allocated memory.

In the example above, one thread controls the resetting and posting of the event semaphore, while other threads merely wait on the semaphore. Another approach could be for an application or thread to reset an event semaphore, then block itself on that semaphore. At a later time, another application or thread would post the event semaphore, unblocking the first thread. This method is shown in Figure 8-1. Process A resets the event semaphore, then blocks itself on the semaphore by calling DosWaitEventSem. At a later time, process B posts the event semaphore. This unblocks process A and enables it to continue execution. Note that in this example two different processes are accessing the event semaphore; this means that the event semaphore being used must be a *shared* semaphore. It might be a *named* semaphore, as well.

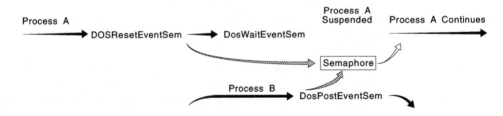

Figure 8-1. Resetting and Waiting for an Event Semaphore

Mutual Exclusion (Mutex) Semaphores

A mutual exclusion (mutex) semaphore protects resources (such as files, data in memory, and peripheral devices) from simultaneous access by several processes. Mutex semaphores enable threads to serialize their access to resources. It does so by preventing the processes from concurrently executing the sections of code through which access is made. These sections of code are called critical sections. For example, a mutex semaphore could be used to prevent two or more threads from simultaneously writing to the same file on a disk.

Before a thread can execute a mutex-protected critical section, it must request and receive ownership of the mutex semaphore. Only the thread that has gained ownership of the mutex semaphore is permitted to perform operations on the protected resource. Only one thread at a time can own the mutex semaphore, and the owner thread retains ownership until it finishes executing its critical section. When finished, the owner thread releases the mutex semaphore, enabling another thread to become the owner.

When a thread requests ownership of a mutex semaphore that is already owned, the operating system blocks the thread. When more than one thread requests ownership of the same semaphore, the operating system queues the requests and grants subsequent ownership based on the thread's priority and the order in which the requests were received.

If more than one thread is blocked on a DosRequestMutexSem request, then ownership is given to the thread that has the highest priority level. If more than one of the waiting threads have the same priority level, then FIFO ordering is used to determine which thread is unblocked and given ownership of the semaphore.

For example, both thread 1 and thread 2 must write information to the same disk file. Thread 1 claims ownership of an agreed-upon mutex semaphore and starts writing its information to the file. If thread 2 also requests ownership of the semaphore, it will be blocked. When thread 1 has finished writing to the file, it releases the semaphore. The operating system then unblocks thread 2 and designates it as the new owner of the semaphore so that it can write to the file.

During process termination, after delivery of process-termination exceptions and unwind exceptions, if any threads in the process aside from Thread 1 (the main thread) own a mutex semaphore, ownership of the semaphore (and therefore, the shared resource) passes to Thread 1. This gives Thread 1 a last chance to clean up the semaphore and the shared resource before the process ends. If Thread 1 ends without releasing the semaphore, all threads that are currently waiting on ownership of the semaphore will be unblocked with the SEM_OWNER_DIED return code. Any thread that attempts to open it or request ownership of the semaphore will receive a SEM_OWNER_DIED return code.

The recommended way to clean up semaphores, and other resources, is for each thread, especially Thread 1, to have an exception handler to handle clean up during process termination (the XCPT_PROCESS_TERMINATE or XCPT_ASYNC_PROCESS_TERMINATE exceptions). When it is not possible to register an exception handler for a thread, (a DLL, for example, must de-register its exception handlers when it returns control to the thread that called it), you should add a clean up routine to the exit list of the process.

Multiple Wait (Muxwait) Semaphores

A multiple wait (muxwait) semaphore enables a thread to wait on several event or mutex semaphores simultaneously. A muxwait semaphore is a compound semaphore that consists of a list of up to 64 event semaphores or mutex semaphores (the two types cannot be mixed).

A flag is set when the muxwait semaphore is created to enable threads to use the semaphore in either of two ways:

- Threads can wait for all of the mutex semaphores to be released, or for all of the event semaphores to be posted.

- Threads can wait for any one of the mutex semaphores in the list to be released, or for any one of the event semaphores in the list to be posted.

Depending on the value of the flag, a muxwait semaphore is said to have cleared when either any or all of the semaphores in the muxwait list have been posted or released.

For example, suppose a thread requires access to several regions of shared memory at the same time. The operating system blocks the thread until the thread acquires ownership of all the mutex semaphores protecting the shared regions. The thread can then access all the memory regions. Meanwhile, the operating system prevents access by other threads.

Named and Anonymous Semaphores

A semaphore can be either named or anonymous. A named semaphore is always shared; that is, it is always available to any process that knows the name. An anonymous semaphore can be either private to a process or shared among processes, depending on whether the application includes the DC_SEM_SHARED flag in the function that creates the semaphore. A semaphore intended for use solely among threads of the same process can be anonymous and private.

The operating system creates a named semaphore when an application specifies a name in the function that creates the semaphore. The name must have the following form:

    \SEM32\SemName

The "\SEM32\" is required, though it need not be uppercase. The semaphore name must conform to the rules for OS/2 file names, although no actual file is created for the semaphore. If the application does not specify a name in the function that creates the semaphore, the operating system creates an anonymous semaphore.

The OS/2 operating system permits a system-wide maximum of 65536 (64K) shared semaphores. In addition, each process can use up to 65536 (64K) private semaphores.

A shared muxwait semaphore must contain either all shared event semaphores or all shared mutex semaphores. However, a private muxwait semaphore can contain a combination of shared and private event or mutex semaphores. The operating system generates a unique handle when it creates a semaphore. Processes must obtain this handle before they can access the semaphore. A semaphore's handle is always available to the process that created the semaphore. A process can obtain the handle of a named semaphore created in another process by using the appropriate semaphore-opening function. A process that requires access to an anonymous shared semaphore that was created in another process must obtain the handle of the semaphore through some other form of interprocess communication, such as a pipe or a queue.

Semaphore Management

After one process creates a semaphore, threads in other processes must open the semaphore before they can access it. (Creating a semaphore automatically opens it for the creating process.) The open operation ensures that the process is a valid user of the semaphore. The operating system keeps track of the number of open operations that each process performs on a semaphore. A process can have up to 65535 (64K - 1) open operations performed on a semaphore at any one time.

If a process finishes using a semaphore and will not use it again, the process should close the semaphore so that the operating system can free the memory the semaphore is using. The operating system returns the ERROR_SEM_BUSY error value if a thread tries to close a semaphore that has another thread in the same process still waiting for it.

If a process terminates with open semaphores, the operating system automatically closes the semaphores for that process.

Semaphores reside in a memory buffer rather than a disk file. Therefore, when the last process that has a semaphore open exits or closes that semaphore, the operating system frees the associated handle or name.

When an application calls a function that causes a thread to wait on a semaphore, the application can specify the amount of time for the thread to wait. When the interval elapses without the semaphore being posted or released, the function returns the ERROR_TIMEOUT error value and the thread continues running. The application can provide a specific time-out value in milliseconds, or it can specify either the SEM_INDEFINITE_WAIT or the SEM_IMMEDIATE_RETURN flag. If a thread is interrupted while it is waiting on a semaphore, the ERROR_INTERRUPT error value is returned to the caller.

Using Event Semaphores

An application can use an event semaphore to trigger execution of other processes. This is useful if, for example, one process provides data to many other processes. Using an event semaphore frees the other process from the trouble of polling to determine when new data is available.

Note: In the example code fragments that follow, error checking was left out to conserve space. Applications should always check the return code that the functions return. Control Program functions return an APIRET value. A return code of 0 indicates success. If a non-zero value is returned, an error occurred.

Creating an Event Semaphore

Processes create an event semaphore by using DosCreateEventSem. The process that controls the event or resource is usually the one that creates the semaphore, but it does not have to be.

Threads in the process that creates the semaphore do not have to open the semaphore before using it. DosCreateEventSem obtains access to the semaphore for the calling process and its threads. Threads in other processes must call DosOpenEventSem to open the semaphore before they can use it.

Event semaphores can be defined as either private or shared:

- Private semaphores are always unnamed and are therefore always identified by their handles. They can be used only by threads within a single process.

- Shared semaphores can be either named or unnamed. If named, they can be opened using either the name or the handle. The handle returned by DosOpenEventSem is then used to identify the semaphore for all other functions. Semaphore names must include the prefix \SEM32\ and must conform to file system naming conventions. Shared semaphores can be used by threads in multiple processes.

In the following code fragment, the controlling process creates a named event semaphore and posts the semaphore after writing data to a shared file:

```
#define INCL_DOSSEMAPHORES    /* Semaphore values */
#include <os2.h>

HEV hevWriteEvent;

DosCreateEventSem("\\sem32\\wrtevent",          /* Named-shared semaphore */
                  &hevWriteEvent, 0, FALSE);    /* Initially reset        */
    .
    .
    /* Write data to shared file. */
    .
    .
DosPostEventSem(hevWriteEvent);                  /* Posts the event        */
    .
    .      /* Continue execution. */
    .
```

Figure 8-2. Creating and Posting a Named Event Semaphore

There is a system-wide limit of 65536 (64K) shared semaphores (including mutex, event, and muxwait semaphores); in addition, each process can have up to 65536 (64K) private semaphores.

When an event semaphore is created, a flag is used to specify the initial state of the event semaphore, either reset or posted. If the initial state is reset, a thread that calls DosWaitEventSem will be blocked until a process that has access to the semaphore uses DosPostEventSem to post the event semaphore. If the initial state is posted, then a thread that calls DosWaitEventSem will return immediately to continue its execution. If the thread calling DosWaitEventSem is not in the process that created the semaphore, the thread must open the semaphore with DosOpenEventSem before calling DosWaitEventSem.

The operating system maintains a usage count for each semaphore. DosCreateEventSem initializes the usage count to 1. Thereafter, each call to DosOpenEventSem increments the count, and each call to DosCloseEventSem decrements it.

Opening an Event Semaphore

When a process creates an event semaphore, all of the threads that belong to the process have immediate access to the semaphore.

Threads in other processes must open the semaphore by calling DosOpenEventSem before they can use the semaphore in any other event semaphore function.

The following code fragment shows how processes can open an event semaphore that was created in a different process and then wait for the event to be posted:

```
#define INCL_DOSSEMAPHORES     /* Semaphore values */
#include <os2.h>

HEV hevEventHandle = 0;                   /* Must be 0 because we are opening */
                                          /* the semaphore by name           */

DosOpenEventSem("\\sem32\\wrtevent", &hevEventHandle);

DosWaitEventSem(hevEventHandle,
                SEM_INDEFINITE_WAIT);   /* Waits until event is posted      */
    .
    .     /* Read from file when event is posted. */
    .
```

Figure 8-3. Opening an Event Semaphore and Waiting for It to be Posted

Applications can open an event semaphore by name or by handle. If the name is used to open the semaphore, as in the code fragment above, the handle parameter must be 0. If the handle is used to open the semaphore, the name parameter must be NULL.

Access to semaphores is on a per-process basis. Therefore, a semaphore that has been opened by one thread in a process is open to all other threads in that process as well.

DosOpenEventSem merely provides access to an event semaphore. In order to wait for an event semaphore to be posted, a thread must call DosWaitEventSem. In order to post or reset an open event semaphore, a thread uses DosPostEventSem or DosResetEventSem respectively.

When a process no longer requires access to an event semaphore, it closes the semaphore by calling DosCloseEventSem. If a process ends without closing an open semaphore, the semaphore is closed by the operating system.

Each call to DosOpenEventSem increments the usage count of the semaphore. This count is initialized to 1 when the semaphore is created and is decremented by each call to DosCloseEventSem. When the usage count reaches 0, the semaphore is deleted by the operating system.

Calls to DosOpenEventSem and DosCloseEventSem can be nested, but the usage count for a semaphore cannot exceed 65535. If an attempt is made to exceed this number, ERROR_TOO_MANY_OPENS is returned.

Closing an Event Semaphore

When a process no longer requires access to an event semaphore, it closes the semaphore by calling DosCloseEventSem.

The following code fragment closes an event semaphore. Assume that the handle of the semaphore has been placed into *hev* already.

```
#define INCL_DOSSEMAPHORES   /* Semaphore values */
#include <os2.h>
#include <stdio.h>

HEV     hev;      /* Event semaphore handle */
APIRET  rc;       /* Return code            */

rc = DosCloseEventSem(hev);

if (rc != 0) {
    printf("DosCloseEventSem error: return code = %ld", rc);
    return;
}
```

Figure   8-4. Closing an Event Semaphore

Calls to DosOpenEventSem and DosCloseEventSem can be nested, but the usage count for a semaphore cannot exceed 65535. If an attempt is made to exceed this number, ERROR_TOO_MANY_OPENS is returned.

If a process ends without closing an open semaphore, the semaphore is closed by the operating system.

Each call to DosCloseEventSem decrements the usage count of the semaphore. This count is initialized to 1 when the semaphore is created and is incremented by each call to DosOpenEventSem. When the usage count reaches 0, the semaphore is deleted from the operating system. The call to DosCloseEventSem that decrements the usage count to 0 and causes the semaphore to be deleted is referred to as the *final close*. If a thread attempts to perform the final close for a semaphore while another thread in the same process is still waiting for it, ERROR_SEM_BUSY is returned.

Resetting an Event Semaphore

DosResetEventSem resets an event semaphore if it is not already reset, and returns the number of times the semaphore was posted since it was last reset. All threads that subsequently call DosWaitEventSem for this semaphore will be blocked.

Any thread belonging to the process that created the event semaphore can change the state of the semaphore to reset by calling DosResetEventSem. Threads in other processes can also call DosResetEventSem, but they must first gain access to the semaphore by calling DosOpenEventSem.

When an event semaphore is in the reset state, any thread that calls DosWaitEventSem to wait for the semaphore will be blocked. When the event semaphore is posted, all of the threads that are waiting for the semaphore are released to continue execution.

The following code fragment resets an event semaphore. Assume that the handle of the semaphore has been placed into *hev* already.

```
#define INCL_DOSSEMAPHORES    /* Semaphore values */
#include <os2.h>
#include <stdio.h>

HEV     hev;        /* Event semaphore handle                    */
ULONG   ulPostCt;   /* Post count for the event semaphore (returned) */
APIRET  rc;         /* Return code                               */

rc = DosResetEventSem(hev, &ulPostCt);

if (rc != 0) {
    printf("DosResetEventSem error: return code = %ld", rc);
    return;
}
```

Figure 8-5. Resetting an Event Semaphore

DosResetEventSem returns the post count of the event semaphore and resets the post count to 0. The post count is the number of times the semaphore has been posted (using DosPostEventSem) since the last time the semaphore was in the reset state. (An event semaphore can be reset when it is created, as well as by calling DosResetEventSem.) The post count can also be obtained by calling DosQueryEventSem.

If the event semaphore is already reset when DosResetEventSem is called, ERROR_ALREADY_RESET is returned, along with a post count of 0. The semaphore is not reset a second time.

Posting an Event Semaphore

DosPostEventSem posts the semaphore, if it is not already posted, and increments the post count. All threads that have called DosWaitEventSem for this semaphore are unblocked and resume execution. Threads that call DosWaitEventSem after the event semaphore has been posted and before the next time it is reset, will return immediately from a call to DosWaitEventSem and continue execution. If the semaphore is subsequently reset, threads that call DosWaitEventSem will again be blocked.

Any thread in the process that created an event semaphore can post the semaphore by calling DosPostEventSem. Threads in other processes can also call DosPostEventSem, but they must first gain access to the semaphore by calling DosOpenEventSem.

The following code fragment posts a system event semaphore. Assume that the handle of the semaphore has been placed into *hev* already.

```
#define INCL_DOSSEMAPHORES   /* Semaphore values */
#include <os2.h>
#include <stdio.h>

HEV     hev;     /* Event semaphore handle */
APIRET  rc;      /* Return code            */

rc = DosPostEventSem(hev);

if (rc != 0) {
    printf("DosPostEventSem error: return code = %ld", rc);
    return;
}
```

Figure 8-6. Posting an Event Semaphore

The operating system maintains a post count for each event semaphore. The post count is the number of times the semaphore has been posted (with DosPostEventSem) since the last time the semaphore was in the reset state.

If the event semaphore is reset when DosPostEventSem is called, the semaphore is posted and the post count is set to 1. If the event semaphore is already posted when DosPostEventSem is called, the post count is incremented, and ERROR_ALREADY_POSTED is returned to the calling thread.

The post count is returned as output by DosResetEventSem; it can also be obtained by calling DosQueryEventSem.

The maximum number of times an event semaphore can be posted is 65535. The value of the post count cannot exceed 65535. If an attempt is made to exceed this number, DosPostEventSem returns ERROR_TOO_MANY_POSTS.

Waiting for an Event Semaphore

Any thread in the process that created an event semaphore can wait for the semaphore to be posted by calling DosWaitEventSem. Threads in other processes can also call DosWaitEventSem, but they must first gain access to the semaphore by calling DosOpenEventSem.

If the semaphore is already posted when DosWaitEventSem is called, the function returns immediately, and the thread continues to run. Otherwise, the thread is blocked until the semaphore is posted.

The following code fragment causes the calling thread to wait until the specified event semaphore is posted. Assume that the handle of the semaphore has been placed into *hev* already. *ulTimeout* is the number of milliseconds that the calling thread will wait for the event semaphore to be posted. If the specified event semaphore is not posted during this time interval, the request times out.

```
#define INCL_DOSSEMAPHORES   /* Semaphore values */
#include <os2.h>
#include <stdio.h>

HEV     hev;         /* Event semaphore handle       */
ULONG   ulTimeout;   /* Number of milliseconds to wait */
APIRET  rc;          /* Return code                  */

ulTimeout = 60000;   /* Wait for a maximum of 1 minute */

rc = DosWaitEventSem(hev, ulTimeout);

if (rc == ERROR_TIMEOUT) {
    printf("DosWaitEventSem call timed out");
    return;
}

if (rc == ERROR_INTERRUPT) {
    printf("DosWaitEventSem call was interrupted");
    return;
}

if (rc != 0) {
    printf("DosWaitEventSem error: return code = %ld", rc);
    return;
}
```

Figure   8-7. Waiting for an Event Semaphore

If the time limit specified in *ulTimeout* is reached before the semaphore is posted, ERROR_TIMEOUT is returned. If the waiting period is interrupted for some reason before the semaphore is posted, ERROR_INTERRUPT is returned. If SEM_IMMEDIATE_RETURN is specified for the time limit, DosWaitEventSem returns to the calling thread immediately. If SEM_INDEFINITE_WAIT is specified for the time limit, the thread waits indefinitely.

Unlike multiple event semaphores in a muxwait list, which are level-triggered, single event semaphores are *edge-triggered*. This means that if an event semaphore is posted and then reset before a waiting thread gets a chance to run, the semaphore is considered to be posted for the rest of that thread's waiting period; the thread does not have to wait for the semaphore to be posted again.

Querying an Event Semaphore

DosQueryEventSem returns the current post count of a semaphore. The post count is the number of times that the semaphore has been posted (with DosPostEventSem) since the last time the semaphore was reset. A count of 0 indicates that the semaphore is in the reset state; therefore, the operating system will block any threads that call DosWaitEventSem to wait on the semaphore.

Any thread in the process that created an event semaphore can obtain the post count for the semaphore by calling DosQueryEventSem. Threads in other processes can also call DosQueryEventSem, but they must first gain access to the semaphore by calling DosOpenEventSem.

The following code fragment retrieves the post count for an event semaphore. Assume that the handle of the semaphore has been placed into *hev* already.

```
#define INCL_DOSSEMAPHORES   /* Semaphore values */
#include <os2.h>
#include <stdio.h>

HEV    hev;       /* Event semaphore handle                     */
ULONG  ulPostCt;  /* Current post count for the semaphore (returned) */
APIRET rc;        /* Return code                                */

rc = DosQueryEventSem(hev, &ulPostCt);

if (rc != 0) {
    printf("DosQueryEventSem error: return code = %ld", rc);
    return;
}
```

Figure 8-8. Querying an Event Semaphore

If the specified event semaphore does not exist, ERROR_INVALID_HANDLE is returned.

Using Mutex Semaphores

An application can use a mutual exclusion (mutex) semaphore to protect a shared resource from simultaneous access by multiple threads or processes. For example, if several processes must write to the same disk file, the mutex semaphore ensures that only one process at a time writes to the file.

Creating a Mutex Semaphore

Mutex semaphores are created by calling DosCreateMutexSem. This function also opens the semaphore for the calling process and its threads.

When a mutex semaphore is created, a flag is set to specify the initial state of the semaphore, owned or unowned. If the semaphore is owned by a thread, other threads requesting the semaphore are blocked. If the semaphore is unowned—not owned by any thread— then any thread requesting ownership will be granted ownership immediately.

If the calling thread sets the initial state to owned, it owns the semaphore as soon as the operating system creates the semaphore and can proceed to access the resource that the semaphore was created to protect.

If the semaphore is unowned, any thread in the creating process can subsequently request ownership of the semaphore by calling DosRequestMutexSem. Threads in other processes can gain ownership of the semaphore, but they must call DosOpenMutexSem to acquire access to the semaphore before they can call DosRequestMutexSem.

Mutex semaphores can be defined as either private or shared.

- Private semaphores are always unnamed and are therefore identified by their handles. They can be used only by threads within a single process.

- Shared semaphores can be either named or unnamed. If named, they can be opened using either the name or the handle. The handle returned by DosOpenMutexSem is then used to identify the semaphore for all other functions. Semaphore names must include the prefix \SEM32\ and must conform to file system naming conventions. Shared semaphores can be used by threads in multiple processes.

The following code fragment creates a mutex semaphore:

```
#define INCL_DOSSEMAPHORES    /* Semaphore values */
#include <os2.h>

HMTX hmtxProtFile;

DosCreateMutexSem("\\sem32\\ProtFile",          /* Named-shared semaphore */
              &hmtxProtFile, 0, FALSE);     /* Initially unowned      */
    .
    .      /* Get data to write to shared file. */
    .
```

Figure   8-9. Creating a Mutex Semaphore

There is a system-wide limit of 65536 shared semaphores (including mutex, event, and muxwait semaphores); in addition, each process can have up to 65536 private semaphores.

The operating system maintains a usage count for each semaphore. DosCreateMutexSem initializes the usage count to 1. Thereafter, each call to DosOpenMutexSem increments the count, and each call to DosCloseMutexSem decrements it.

Opening a Mutex Semaphore

All of the threads belonging to the process that creates a mutex semaphore have immediate access to the semaphore. Threads in other processes must request access to the semaphore by calling DosOpenMutexSem before they can use the semaphore in other mutex semaphore functions.

Access to system resources is granted on a per-process basis. Therefore, a semaphore that has been opened by one thread in a process is open to all other threads in that process as well.

DosOpenMutexSem merely provides access to a mutex semaphore. To request ownership of a mutex semaphore, a thread must call DosRequestMutexSem.

When a process no longer requires access to a mutex semaphore, it should close the semaphore by calling DosCloseMutexSem. However, if a process ends without closing an open semaphore, the semaphore is closed by the operating system.

Each call to DosOpenMutexSem increments the usage count of the semaphore. This count is initialized to 1 when the semaphore is created and is decremented by each call to DosCloseMutexSem. When the usage count reaches 0, the semaphore is deleted by the system.

Calls to DosOpenMutexSem and DosCloseMutexSem can be nested, but the usage count for a semaphore cannot exceed 65535. If an attempt is made to exceed this number, ERROR_TOO_MANY_OPENS is returned.

If a process ends without releasing a mutex semaphore that it owns, any other thread that subsequently tries to open the semaphore will receive ERROR_SEM_OWNER_DIED. This return code indicates that the owning process ended abnormally, leaving the protected resource in an indeterminate state. However, the semaphore is still opened for the calling thread, enabling the thread to call DosQueryMutexSem to find out which process ended without releasing the semaphore. The thread can then take appropriate action concerning the semaphore and the protected resource.

Requesting a Mutex Semaphore

In order to access a shared resource, a process must own the mutex semaphore that is protecting the shared resource. Ownership is obtained by first opening the mutex semaphore with DosOpenMutexSem, then using DosRequestMutexSem to request ownership of the semaphore. If another process already owns the semaphore, the requesting process is blocked. If the semaphore is not owned, the operating system grants ownership to the requesting process and the process can access the shared resource. When the process is finished using the shared resource, it uses DosReleaseMutexSem to relinquish its ownership of the semaphore, thereby enabling another process to gain ownership.

A process can gain ownership of a mutex semaphore in three ways:

1. The thread that creates a mutex semaphore can designate itself as the owner by setting a flag when it calls DosCreateMutexSem.

2. Any thread in the process that created the semaphore can request ownership by calling DosRequestMutexSem.

3. A thread in another process must request access to the semaphore with DosOpenMutexSem before it can call DosRequestMutexSem.

Note that ownership of a mutex semaphore is given only to the requesting thread; it is not shared by other threads in the same process.

If a mutex semaphore is unowned, DosRequestMutexSem sets it as *owned* and returns immediately to the caller. If the semaphore is already owned, the calling thread is blocked until either the owning thread calls DosReleaseMutexSem to release the semaphore, or a specified time limit is reached.

The following code fragment shows how a process opens a mutex semaphore, requests it, and, after writing to the shared file, releases and closes the semaphore:

```
#define INCL_DOSSEMAPHORES    /* Semaphore values */
#include <os2.h>

HMTX hmtxProtFile;

DosOpenMutexSem("\\sem32\\ProtFile",
                &hmtxProtFile);             /* Opens for this process   */

DosRequestMutexSem(hmtxProtFile, 5000);    /* Returns in 5 seconds if   */
    .                                       /* Ownership not obtained    */
    .       /* Write data to shared file. */
    .
DosReleaseMutexSem(hmtxProtFile);          /* Releases ownership        */
    .
    .       /* Continue execution. */
    .
DosCloseMutexSem(hmtxProtFile);            /* Finished with shared file */
```

Figure 8-10. Opening, Requesting, Releasing, and Closing a Mutex Semaphore

If more than one thread is blocked on a DosRequestMutexSem request, the thread with the highest priority level is the first to be unblocked and given ownership of the semaphore. If more than 1 of the waiting threads have the same priority level, then FIFO ordering is used to determine which thread is unblocked and given ownership.

The *time-out* parameter (5000 milliseconds in the example above) places a limit on the amount of time a thread blocks on a DosRequestMutexSem request. If the time limit is reached before the thread gains ownership of the semaphore, ERROR_TIMEOUT is returned. If SEM_IMMEDIATE_RETURN is specified for the time limit, DosRequestMutexSem returns without blocking the thread. The thread can then perform other operations and call DosRequestMutexSem again later if it still requires access to the protected resource. If SEM_INDEFINITE_WAIT is specified for the time limit, the thread waits indefinitely. If the thread is unblocked by an external event while it is waiting for the mutex semaphore (as when a *No Wait* I/O request has just been completed), ERROR_INTERRUPT is returned to the caller.

In addition to the usage count that the operating system maintains for all semaphores, the operating system maintains a request count for each mutex semaphore. Each call to DosRequestMutexSem increments the count, and each call to DosReleaseMutexSem decrements it.

Calls to DosRequestMutexSem and DosReleaseMutexSem can be nested, but the request count for a semaphore cannot exceed 65535. If an attempt is made to exceed this number, ERROR_TOO_MANY_SEM_REQUESTS is returned. When calls to DosRequestMutexSem and DosReleaseMutexSem are nested, a call to DosReleaseMutexSem merely decrements the request count for the semaphore; the semaphore is not actually released to another thread until its request count is 0.

If a process ends while it owns a mutex semaphore, all of the currently blocked DosRequestMutexSem requests, as well as any future requests for the semaphore, return ERROR_SEM_OWNER_DIED. This return code indicates that the owning process ended abnormally, leaving the protected resource in an indeterminate state. An application that receives this error should close the mutex semaphore (so that it can be deleted from the operating system), because it is no longer valid. Appropriate action should also be taken concerning the protected resource.

Releasing a Mutex Semaphore

A thread can release ownership of a mutex semaphore by calling DosReleaseMutexSem.

Each call to DosReleaseMutexSem decrements the request count that is maintained for the semaphore by the operating system. Each call to DosRequestMutexSem increments the count.

The following code fragment relinquishes ownership of a mutex semaphore. Assume that the handle of the semaphore has been placed into *hmtx* already.

```
#define INCL_DOSSEMAPHORES   /* Semaphore values */
#include <os2.h>
#include <stdio.h>

HMTX    hmtx;      /* Mutex semaphore handle */
APIRET  rc;        /* Return code            */

rc = DosReleaseMutexSem(hmtx);

if (rc != 0) {
    printf("DosReleaseMutexSem error: return code = %ld", rc);
    return;
}
```

Figure 8-11. Releasing a Mutex Semaphore

Calls to DosRequestMutexSem and DosReleaseMutexSem can be nested, but the request count cannot exceed 65535. If an attempt is made to exceed this number, ERROR_TOO_MANY_SEM_REQUESTS is returned. When calls to DosRequestMutexSem and DosReleaseMutexSem are nested, a call to DosReleaseMutexSem merely decrements the request count for the semaphore; the semaphore is not actually released to another thread until its request count is 0.

Closing a Mutex Semaphore

When a process no longer requires access to a mutex semaphore, it can close the semaphore by calling DosCloseMutexSem. However, if a process ends without closing an open semaphore, the semaphore is closed by the operating system.

The following code fragment closes a mutex semaphore. Assume that the handle of the semaphore has been placed into *hmtx* already.

```
#define INCL_DOSSEMAPHORES    /* Semaphore values */
#include <os2.h>
#include <stdio.h>

HMTX    hmtx;    /* Mutex semaphore handle */
APIRET  rc;      /* Return code            */

rc = DosCloseMutexSem(hmtx);

if (rc != 0) {
    printf("DosCloseMutexSem error: return code = %ld", rc);
    return;
}
```

Figure 8-12. Closing a Mutex Semaphore

Each call to DosCloseMutexSem decrements the usage count of the semaphore. This count is initialized to 1 when the semaphore is created and is incremented by each call to DosOpenMutexSem. When the usage count reaches 0, the semaphore is deleted by the operating system.

The call to DosCloseMutexSem that decrements the usage count to 0 and causes the semaphore to be deleted is referred to as the *final close*. The final close will not succeed if either of the following conditions exists:

- The semaphore is owned by another thread in the same process.
- Another thread in the same process is still blocked on a DosRequestMutexSem request for the semaphore.

For both conditions, ERROR_SEM_BUSY is returned.

ERROR_SEM_BUSY is also returned if a thread tries to close a mutex semaphore that it still owns. The thread must first relinquish ownership of the semaphore by calling DosReleaseMutexSem.

Calls to DosOpenMutexSem and DosCloseMutexSem can be nested, but the usage count for a semaphore cannot exceed 65535. If an attempt is made to exceed this number, ERROR_TOO_MANY_OPENS is returned.

Querying a Mutex Semaphore

An application can use DosQueryMutexSem to determine the current owner of a mutex semaphore and to obtain a count of the number of requests on it. If the mutex semaphore is not owned, the request count is 0.

Any thread in the process that created a mutex semaphore can obtain information about the semaphore by calling DosQueryMutexSem. Threads in other processes can also call

DosQueryMutexSem, but they must first gain access to the semaphore by calling DosOpenMutexSem.

If the mutex semaphore exists and is owned, DosQueryMutexSem returns the process and thread identifications of the owner, as well as the request count for the semaphore. The request count is the number of DosRequestMutexSem calls minus the number of DosReleaseMutexSem calls that have been made for the semaphore by the owning thread.

If DosQueryMutexSem returns a request count of 0, the mutex semaphore is unowned.

If the owning process ended without calling DosCloseMutexSem, then ERROR_SEM_OWNER_DIED is returned, and the output parameters contain information about the ended owning process.

Using Muxwait Semaphores

A process that requires exclusive use of several shared resources at once can use a multiple wait (muxwait) semaphore to obtain ownership of all the mutex semaphores protecting the shared resources. A process can also use a muxwait semaphore to wait on a group of event semaphores so that the process continues running whenever events of interest occur.

A muxwait semaphore can refer to up to 64 event or mutex semaphores. An application cannot refer to event and mutex semaphores in a single muxwait semaphore, or include a muxwait semaphore in another muxwait semaphore.

Creating a Muxwait Semaphore

DosCreateMuxWaitSem is used to create muxwait semaphores. This function also opens (obtains access to) the semaphore for the calling process and its threads. Threads in other processes must call DosOpenMuxWaitSem to open the semaphore before they can use it in any other muxwait semaphore function.

All the semaphores in the muxwait list must be created and opened before the muxwait list can be created.

The following code fragment creates five event semaphores and a corresponding array of semaphore records. The array is used to specify the semaphores included in the muxwait semaphore in the subsequent call to DosCreateMuxWaitSem.

```
#define INCL_DOSSEMAPHORES    /* Semaphore values */
#include <os2.h>

ULONG ulLoop, ulSem;
HMUX hmuxHandAny;
SEMRECORD apsr[5];

/* Create event semaphores and fill semaphore-record array. */

for (ulLoop = 0; ulLoop < 5; ulLoop++) {    /* Create 5 private events    */
    DosCreateEventSem((PSZ) NULL,
                      (PHEV) &apsr[ulLoop].hsemCur,
                      0,
                      FALSE);
    apsr[ulLoop].ulUser = ulLoop;           /* User-assigned data         */
}
    .
    .
    .


DosCreateMuxWaitSem((PSZ) NULL,
                    &hmuxHandAny,            /* Creates the muxwait semaphore */
                    sizeof(apsr),
                    apsr,                    /* Specifies semrecord array     */
                    DCMW_WAIT_ANY);

DosWaitMuxWaitSem(hmuxHandAny,               /* Waits until one is posted     */
                  SEM_INDEFINITE_WAIT, &ulSem);
    .
    . /* Execution will continue when any event is posted. */
    .
```

Figure 8-13. Creating and Waiting for a Muxwait Semaphore

Muxwait semaphores can be defined as either private or shared:

- Private semaphores are always unnamed and are therefore always identified by their handles. They can be used only by threads within a single process.

- Shared semaphores can be either named or unnamed. If named, they can be opened using either the name or the handle. The handle returned by DosOpenMuxWaitSem is then used to identify the semaphore for all other functions. Semaphore names must include the prefix \SEM32\ and must conform to file system naming conventions. Shared semaphores can be used by threads in multiple processes.

There is a system-wide limit of 65536 (64K) shared semaphores (including mutex, event, and muxwait semaphores); in addition, each process can have up to 65536 (64K) private semaphores.

The following conditions apply to the kinds of semaphores that can be included in a muxwait-semaphore list:

- The list must contain either mutex semaphores or event semaphores. It cannot contain both at the same time and it cannot contain other muxwait semaphores.

- If the muxwait semaphore is shared, then all the semaphores in the list must also be shared.

- If the muxwait semaphore is private, then the semaphores in its list can be either private or shared.

If any of these conditions is violated, ERROR_WRONG_TYPE is returned.

The muxwait list can contain a maximum of 64 event semaphores or mutex semaphores. If an attempt is made to exceed this maximum, ERROR_TOO_MANY_SEMAPHORES is returned.

If the owners of any of the *mutex* semaphores in the muxwait semaphore list have ended without releasing them, ERROR_SEM_OWNER_DIED is returned. The thread should call DosQueryMutexSem for each mutex semaphore in the muxwait-semaphore list so that it can determine which semaphores are in the *Owner Died* state.

Each mutex semaphore that returns ERROR_SEM_OWNER_DIED from the query should be closed by calling DosCloseMutexSem. Also, because semaphore handles can be reused, the mutex semaphores that are closed must be deleted from the muxwait-semaphore list by calling DosDeleteMuxWaitSem.

The operating system maintains a usage count for each semaphore. DosCreateMuxWaitSem initializes the usage count to 1. Thereafter, each call to DosOpenMuxWaitSem increments the count, and each call to DosCloseMuxWaitSem decrements it.

One parameter of this function is a pointer to an array of SEMRECORD data structures. Each data structure contains one semaphore record for each of the semaphores to be included in the muxwait semaphore. A semaphore record contains the handle and a programmer-defined identifier for that semaphore.

Opening a Muxwait Semaphore

Processes other than the semaphore-creating process must use DosOpenMuxWaitSem to gain access to the muxwait semaphore before they can use the semaphore in any other muxwait semaphore function. All of the threads that belong to the process that creates the muxwait semaphore have immediate access to the semaphore.

The following code fragment opens a system muxwait semaphore.

```
#define INCL_DOSSEMAPHORES   /* Semaphore values */
#include <os2.h>
#include <stdio.h>

UCHAR   Name[40];   /* Semaphore name           */
HMUX    hmux;       /* Muxwait semaphore handle */
APIRET  rc;         /* Return code              */

strcpy(Name, "\\SEM32\\MUXWAIT1");  /* Name of the system muxwait semaphore */

rc = DosOpenMuxWaitSem(Name, &hmux);

if (rc != 0) {
    printf("DosOpenMuxWaitSem error: return code = %ld", rc);
    return;
}
```

Figure 8-14. Opening a Muxwait Semaphore

On successful return, *hmux* contains the handle of the system muxwait semaphore.

Opening a muxwait semaphore does not open the semaphores in its muxwait list. A process must open each of the semaphores included in a muxwait semaphore before it opens the muxwait semaphore. Otherwise, DosOpenMuxWaitSem returns the ERROR_INVALID_HANDLE error value to the calling function.

Access to semaphores is on a per-process basis. Therefore, a semaphore that has been opened by one thread in a process is open to all other threads in that process as well.

Note that DosOpenMuxWaitSem merely provides access to a muxwait semaphore. In order to wait for a muxwait semaphore to clear, a thread must call DosWaitMuxWaitSem.

When a process no longer requires access to a muxwait semaphore, it closes the semaphore by calling DosCloseMuxWaitSem. However, if a process ends without closing an open semaphore, the semaphore is closed by the operating system.

Each call to DosOpenMuxWaitSem increments the usage count of the semaphore. This count is initialized to 1 when the semaphore is created and is decremented by each call to DosCloseMuxWaitSem. When the usage count reaches 0, the semaphore is deleted by the operating system.

Calls to DosOpenMuxWaitSem and DosCloseMuxWaitSem can be nested, but the usage count for a semaphore cannot exceed 65535. If an attempt is made to exceed this number, ERROR_TOO_MANY_OPENS is returned.

Even if the owner of a mutex semaphore in a muxwait-semaphore list has ended without releasing the semaphore, the muxwait semaphore is still opened. Subsequent calls to the muxwait semaphore will return ERROR_SEM_OWNER_DIED. But because the process has opened the semaphore, it can then call DosQueryMuxWaitSem to identify all the mutex semaphores in the muxwait list. Next, the process can call DosQueryMutexSem for each mutex semaphore in the list to find out which ones are in the *Owner Died* state. Each mutex semaphore that returns ERROR_SEM_OWNER_DIED from the query should be closed by calling DosCloseMutexSem. Also, because semaphore handles can be reused, the mutex semaphores that are closed should be deleted from the muxwait-semaphore list by calling DosDeleteMuxWaitSem.

Closing a Muxwait Semaphore

When a process no longer requires access to a muxwait semaphore, it closes the semaphore by calling DosCloseMuxWaitSem. However, if a process ends without closing an open semaphore, the semaphore is closed by the operating system.

Each call to DosCloseMuxWaitSem decrements the usage count of the semaphore. This count is initialized to 1 when the semaphore is created and is incremented by each call to DosOpenMuxWaitSem. When the usage count reaches 0, the semaphore is deleted by the operating system.

The call to DosCloseMuxWaitSem that decrements the usage count to 0 and causes the semaphore to be deleted is referred to as the *final close*. If a thread attempts to perform the final close for a semaphore while another thread in the same process is still waiting for it, ERROR_SEM_BUSY is returned.

Calls to DosOpenMuxWaitSem and DosCloseMuxWaitSem can be nested, but the usage count for a semaphore cannot exceed 65535. If an attempt is made to exceed this number, ERROR_TOO_MANY_OPENS is returned.

Waiting for a Muxwait Semaphore

A thread can wait on a muxwait semaphore by using DosWaitMuxWaitSem.

Any thread in the process that created a muxwait semaphore can wait for the semaphore to clear by calling DosWaitMuxWaitSem. Threads in other processes can also call DosWaitMuxWaitSem, but they must first gain access to the semaphore by calling DosOpenMuxWaitSem.

The following code fragment waits for a muxwait semaphore to clear. Assume that the handle of the semaphore has been placed into *hmux* already. *ulTimeout* is the number of milliseconds that the calling thread will wait for the muxwait semaphore to clear. If the specified muxwait semaphore is not cleared during this time interval, the request times out.

```
#define INCL_DOSSEMAPHORES   /* Semaphore values */
#include <os2.h>
#include <stdio.h>

HMUX     hmux;       /* Muxwait semaphore handle              */
ULONG    ulTimeout;  /* Number of milliseconds to wait        */
ULONG    ulUser;     /* User field for the semaphore that was */
                     /* posted or released (returned)         */
APIRET   rc;         /* Return code                           */

ulTimeout = 60000;   /* Wait for a maximum of 1 minute        */

rc = DosWaitMuxWaitSem(hmux, ulTimeout, &ulUser);

if (rc == ERROR_TIMEOUT) {
    printf("DosWaitMuxWaitSem call timed out");
    return;
}

if (rc == ERROR_INTERRUPT) {
    printf("DosWaitMuxWaitSem call was interrupted");
    return;
}

if (rc != 0) {
    printf("DosWaitMuxWaitSem error: return code = %ld", rc);
    return;
}
```

Figure   8-15. Waiting for a Muxwait Semaphore

On successful return, the *ulUser* variable contains the user identifier of the semaphore that caused the wait to terminate. If the caller had to wait for all the semaphores within the muxwait semaphore to clear, then the value corresponds to the last semaphore within the muxwait semaphore to clear. If the caller had to wait for any semaphore with the muxwait semaphore to clear, then the value corresponds to that semaphore.

An application can use the DCMW_WAIT_ANY flag in DosCreateMuxWaitSem to block a thread until any one of the event or mutex semaphores included in the muxwait semaphore is posted or released. If the muxwait semaphore refers to mutex semaphores, the thread only gains ownership of the one mutex semaphore that was released.

An application can use the DCMW_WAIT_ALL flag in DosCreateMuxWaitSem to block a thread until all of the event or mutex semaphores included in the muxwait semaphore are posted or released. If the muxwait semaphore refers to mutex semaphores, the thread does not gain ownership of any of the mutex semaphores until they are all released. When all are released, the thread becomes owner of all the mutex semaphores included in the muxwait semaphore. If the muxwait semaphore refers to event semaphores, the thread will not run until all of the event semaphores are in the posted state at the same time. This is because event semaphores in a muxwait list are *level-triggered*, unlike individual event semaphores, which are edge-triggered.

For example, suppose that a thread is waiting for five event semaphores in a muxwait list to be posted. The first semaphore is posted and then reset. Next, the remaining semaphores are all posted, and they remain in the posted state. The thread that is waiting for the muxwait semaphore will not run until the first semaphore is posted again.

If an application specifies the DCMW_WAIT_ANY flag when the semaphore is created, DosWaitMuxWaitSem returns the programmer-defined identifier of the semaphore that is subsequently posted or released. If an application specifies the DCMW_WAIT_ALL flag, DosWaitMuxWaitSem returns the programmer-defined identifier of the last semaphore that was posted or released.

The *ulTimeout* parameter places a limit on the amount of time a thread blocks on a DosWaitMuxWaitSem request. If the time limit is reached before the semaphore has cleared, ERROR_TIMEOUT is returned. If SEM_IMMEDIATE_RETURN is specified as the time limit, DosWaitMuxWaitSem returns without blocking the thread. The thread can then go on to perform other operations and call DosWaitMuxWaitSem again later to wait for the event or mutex semaphores in the muxwait list to be posted or released. If a time limit of SEM_INDEFINITE_WAIT is specified, the thread waits (is blocked) indefinitely. If the thread is unblocked by an external event while it is waiting for the muxwait semaphore (as when a "no wait" I/O request has just been completed), DosWaitMuxWaitSem returns ERROR_INTERRUPT.

When a thread is waiting for any one of the semaphores in a muxwait list to be posted or released, the semaphores are checked in the order in which they are defined in the list.

Waiting for Multiple Event Semaphores

The following information pertains only to muxwait semaphores that consist of multiple *event* semaphores:

Unlike individual event semaphores, which are edge-triggered, event semaphores in a muxwait list are *level-triggered*. This means that if a thread is waiting for all of the event semaphores in the muxwait list, it will not run until all of the event semaphores are in the posted state at the same time.

For example, a thread is waiting for five event semaphores in a muxwait list to be posted. The first semaphore is posted and then reset. Next, the remaining semaphores are all posted, and they remain in the posted state. The thread that is waiting for the muxwait semaphore will not run until the first semaphore is posted again.

Waiting for Multiple Mutex Semaphores

The following information pertains only to muxwait semaphores that consist of multiple *mutex* semaphores:

- If a thread is waiting for all of the mutex semaphores in a muxwait list to be released, it does not receive ownership of any of the semaphores until all of the semaphores have been released.

- If a thread is waiting for any one of the mutex semaphores in a muxwait list, then the thread gains ownership only of the first mutex semaphore that is released. The ownership of all other mutex semaphores in the muxwait list remains unchanged.

- If two threads have the same priority, then a thread that is waiting for a mutex semaphore in a muxwait list takes precedence over a thread that has requested ownership of only the individual semaphore, provided all other mutex semaphores in the muxwait list have been released. For example, a mutex semaphore that is part of a muxwait semaphore is released. One thread has requested ownership of that single mutex semaphore, and another thread with the same priority is waiting for the muxwait semaphore that contains the same mutex semaphore. If all of the other mutex semaphores in the muxwait list are *unowned* and ready to be given to the muxwait semaphore, then the thread that is waiting for the muxwait semaphore will run first.

- If the owners of any of the mutex semaphores in the muxwait semaphore list have ended without releasing them, ERROR_SEM_OWNER_DIED is returned. The thread must then call DosQueryMuxWaitSem to obtain the records of all the semaphores in the muxwait list. Next, the thread must call DosQueryMutexSem for each mutex semaphore in the muxwait-semaphore list so that it can determine which semaphores are in the *Owner Died* state.

  Each mutex semaphore that returns ERROR_SEM_OWNER_DIED from the query should be closed by calling DosCloseMutexSem. Also, because semaphore handles can be reused, the mutex semaphores that are closed should be deleted from the muxwait-semaphore list by calling DosDeleteMuxWaitSem.

- If any of the mutex semaphores in the muxwait list are owned by the calling thread, ERROR_MUTEX_OWNED is returned.

Adding a Semaphore to a Muxwait List

An application uses DosAddMuxWaitSem to add semaphores to a muxwait semaphore that has already been created, even while threads are waiting on the muxwait semaphore.

Any thread in the process that created a muxwait semaphore can add a mutex semaphore or an event semaphore to the muxwait list by calling DosAddMuxWaitSem. Threads in other processes can also use this function, but they must first gain access to the semaphore by calling DosOpenMuxWaitSem.

A maximum of 64 semaphores can be included in a muxwait-semaphore list. If an attempt is made to exceed this maximum, ERROR_TOO_MANY_SEMAPHORES is returned.

All of the semaphores in a muxwait-semaphore list must be of the same type. That is, if a mutex semaphore is being added, then the other semaphores in the list must be mutex semaphores. If an event semaphore is being added, then the other semaphores in the list must be event semaphores. A shared muxwait semaphore can contain only shared semaphores in its list. A private muxwait semaphore can contain both private and shared semaphores. If any of these conditions is violated, ERROR_WRONG_TYPE is returned.

If the semaphore is successfully added to the muxwait list, DosAddMuxWaitSem checks to see whether each thread that is waiting for the muxwait semaphore has the newly added semaphore open in its process. The muxwait semaphore is invalid for any waiting threads that do not have the newly added semaphore open in their process; these threads are unblocked with a return code of ERROR_INVALID_HANDLE. Any processes that opened the muxwait semaphore before the add operation and that do not have the new semaphore open, will have to open the new semaphore before making any further use of the muxwait semaphore. Any future calls concerning the muxwait semaphore by processes that do not have the new semaphore open will have ERROR_INVALID_HANDLE returned until the new semaphore is opened.

A thread that receives a return code of ERROR_INVALID_HANDLE can take the following corrective action:

1. First, the thread can obtain the records of all the semaphores in the muxwait list by calling DosQueryMuxWaitSem.

2. Next, it can query each semaphore in the muxwait list, using DosQueryMutexSem or DosQueryEventSem, to find out which semaphore is not open to its process.

3. Finally, it can open the semaphores that are not open by calling DosOpenMutexSem or DosOpenEventSem.

As soon as this semaphore is opened, the muxwait semaphore becomes valid again for the process, as long as no other changes have been made to the muxwait list to make it invalid. However, in order to successfully wait for the muxwait semaphore, the process must call DosWaitMuxWaitSem again.

A semaphore must be open for a process before the process can add that semaphore to a muxwait semaphore. If it is not open and a thread is waiting on the muxwait semaphore, DosAddMuxWaitSem returns ERROR_INVALID_HANDLE to the process adding the new semaphore, and the waiting thread continues waiting.

Deleting a Semaphore from a Muxwait List

An application can delete semaphores from a muxwait semaphore by using DosDeleteMuxWaitSem.

Any thread in the process that created a muxwait semaphore can delete a mutex or event semaphore from the muxwait list by calling DosDeleteMuxWaitSem. Threads in other processes can also use this function, but they must first gain access to the semaphore by calling DosOpenMuxWaitSem.

Semaphores can be deleted from the muxwait list even while threads are currently waiting for the semaphore. If the deleted semaphore is the only one in the muxwait list that has not yet been posted or released, then threads that are waiting for the muxwait semaphore are unblocked. Also, if the deleted semaphore happens to be the last one that a particular thread was waiting for, that thread is unblocked. Also, if the deleted semaphore is the last one in the muxwait list (that is, if the list is now empty), then all the threads that are waiting for the muxwait semaphore are unblocked.

Querying a Muxwait Semaphore

Processes use DosQueryMuxWaitSem to obtain the semaphore records for each of the semaphores included in the muxwait semaphore.

Any thread in the process that created a muxwait semaphore can obtain information about the semaphores in the muxwait list by calling DosQueryMuxWaitSem. Threads in other processes can also use this function, but they must first gain access to the semaphore by calling DosOpenMuxWaitSem.

An application must provide this function with an array in which to store the semaphore records. If the array is not large enough to hold all of the semaphore records that are in the muxwait list, then ERROR_PARAM_TOO_SMALL is returned, and the record-counting parameter of DosQueryMuxWaitSem will contain the number of semaphore records that are in the muxwait list. The calling thread can then allocate the correct amount of space and call DosQueryMuxWaitSem again with the correct amount of space for the list of records.

If the owner of any mutex semaphore in the muxwait-semaphore list has ended without releasing the semaphore, the records of all the semaphores in the list are still returned, but DosQueryMuxWaitSem also returns ERROR_SEM_OWNER_DIED. The calling thread can call DosQueryMutexSem for each mutex semaphore in the muxwait-semaphore list so that it can determine which semaphores are in the *Owner Died* state. The process can then close the unowned mutex semaphores.

Each mutex semaphore that returns ERROR_SEM_OWNER_DIED from the query should be closed by calling DosCloseMutexSem. Also, because semaphore handles can be reused, the mutex semaphores that are closed should be deleted from the muxwait-semaphore list by calling DosDeleteMuxWaitSem.

If the specified muxwait semaphore does not exist, ERROR_INVALID_HANDLE is returned.

Summary

Following are the OS/2 functions and data structures used with semaphores.

Table 8-1. Semaphore Functions	
Event Semaphore Functions	
DosCloseEventSem	Closes an event semaphore.
DosCreateEventSem	Creates an event semaphore.
DosOpenEventSem	Opens an event semaphore for use.
DosPostEventSem	Posts an event semaphore.
DosQueryEventSem	Returns the post count of an event semaphore (the number of times the semaphore has been posted).
DosResetEventSem	Resets an event semaphore.
DosWaitEventSem	Waits for an event semaphore to be posted.
Mutex Semaphore Functions	
DosCloseMutexSem	Closes a mutex semaphore.
DosCreateMutexSem	Creates a mutex semaphore.
DosOpenMutexSem	Opens a mutex semaphore for use.
DosQueryMutexSem	Returns information about the owner of a mutex semaphore.
DosReleaseMutexSem	Releases a mutex semaphore.
DosRequestMutexSem	Requests ownership of a mutex semaphore.
Muxwait Semaphore Functions	
DosAddMuxWaitSem	Adds a mutex or event semaphore to a muxwait-semaphore list.
DosCloseMuxWaitSem	Closes a muxwait semaphore.
DosCreateMuxWaitSem	Creates a muxwait semaphore.
DosDeleteMuxWaitSem	Deletes a mutex or event semaphore to a muxwait-semaphore list.
DosOpenMuxWaitSem	Opens a muxwait semaphore.
DosQueryMuxWaitSem	Returns the semaphore records from a muxwait-semaphore list.
DosWaitMuxWaitSem	Waits for a muxwait semaphore to clear.

Table 8-2. Semaphore Data Structures	
Data Structure	**Description**
SEMRECORD	Used when adding a semaphore to a muxwait-semaphore list.

Chapter 9. Pipes

Communication between processes is valuable in a multitasking operating system to enable concurrent processes to work together. Pipes are one of three forms of interprocess communication (IPC), the other forms of IPC being semaphores and queues.

This chapter describes how to create, manage, and use pipes. Pipes enable two or more processes to communicate as if they were reading from and writing to a file.

The following topics are related to the information in this chapter:

- Memory (Shared Memory)
- Program Execution and Control
- Semaphores
- Queues.

About Pipes

A *pipe* is a named or unnamed buffer used to pass data between processes. A process writes to or reads from a pipe as if the pipe were standard input or standard output. A parent process can use pipes to control the input that a child process receives and to receive the output that the child process produces.

There are two types of pipes—named and unnamed.

Unnamed Pipes

An unnamed pipe is a circular buffer in memory. The buffer has *in* and *out* pointers that are maintained by the system.

An unnamed pipe can transfer information only between related processes. A child process started by a parent process with DosExecPgm inherits the handles to any unnamed pipes created by its parent. This inheritance enables the parent process and the child process to use the unnamed pipe to communicate with one another. This type of pipe is typically used to redirect the standard input and standard output of a child process.

To do this, a process opens a pipe and duplicates the read and write handles of the pipe as the standard input and standard output files for the child process. Once the handles are duplicated, the parent process can use DosExecPgm to start the child process. When the child process reads and writes to its standard input and standard output handles, it is reading and writing to the pipe. The parent process can also communicate with the child process through the pipe. Figure 9-1 on page 9-2 shows a parent process communicating with a child process through a pipe.

9-1

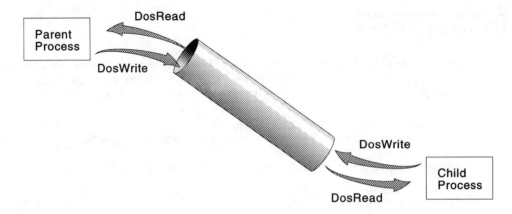

Figure   9-1. Redirecting Standard I/O through a Pipe

Using an unnamed pipe, a text editor could run another program, such as a compiler or assembler, and display the output of the compiler or assembler within the editor.

DosCreatePipe creates an unnamed pipe. This function returns two file handles for the pipe, one for writing to the pipe and another for reading from the pipe. A process can then write to the pipe by using DosWrite and read from the pipe by using DosRead.

A pipe exists until both handles are closed. The order in which the handles are closed is sometimes important. For example, DosWrite might wait for data to be read from the pipe before completing its operation. In this case, the read handle is closed before the write handle is closed, writing to the pipe generates an error.

No control or permission mechanisms or checks are performed on operations to unnamed pipes.

Named Pipes

Named pipes enable related or unrelated processes on either the same computer system or different systems to communicate with each other. Any process that knows the name of a pipe can open and use a named pipe. In addition, named pipe data can be transparently redirected across a network, such as a local area network (LAN). (Unnamed pipes, by contrast, can be used only by related processes that are on the same computer system.)

One process (the *server process*) creates the pipe and connects to one end of it. Other processes that access the named pipe are called *client processes*; they connect to the other end of the pipe. The server and client processes can then pass data back and forth by reading from and writing to the pipe. The server process controls access to the named pipe.

The client process can be either local or remote. A local client process is one that runs on the same computer system as the server process. A remote client process runs on a different system and communicates with the server process across a local area network (LAN).

When the server process creates a named pipe with DosCreateNPipe, it must specify the direction that data will flow through the pipe. The process specifies an inbound pipe if it intends to read data from the client process, an outbound pipe if it intends to write data to the client process, or a duplex pipe if it intends to read from and write to the client process.

The server process also specifies whether data passes through the pipe as bytes or messages. A message is a block of data, with a system-supplied header, that is read or written as a single unit. The server and client processes define the size and format of a message.

The server process also specifies whether child processes will inherit the named pipe and how information will be read from and written to the pipe. If the server specifies wait mode, DosRead will be blocked (it will not return to the process) until data is available in the pipe, and DosWrite will be blocked until there is enough room in the pipe to contain the entire data buffer. If the server specifies no-wait mode, reading from an empty pipe or writing to a full pipe immediately returns an error value.

A named pipe consists of two pipe buffers, one for each direction of communication. However, each end of the pipe has only one handle associated with it. The server receives the handle for its end when it creates the pipe with DosCreateNPipe. The client receives the handle for its end when it opens the pipe with DosOpen.

The server and the client use their respective handles both to read from the pipe and to write to it. (This is in contrast to unnamed pipes, for which both the server and the client read from one handle and write to another.) In other words, data that is written by the process at one end of the pipe is read by the process at the other end, as shown in the following diagram.

A named pipe can have multiple instances, up to the number specified when the pipe is first created. Pipe instances are actually separate pipes—that is, unique sets of pipe buffers with unique handles—that share the same name. The ability to create multiple pipe instances enables the server to communicate with multiple client processes at the same time.

See "Creating Multiple Instances of a Named Pipe" on page 9-13 for more information about named pipe instances.

Server-Client Communications Using Named Pipes

A server process initiates a connection to a client process by using DosConnectNPipe. Once the pipe has been connected by the server process, the client process must open the pipe by using DosOpen to complete the connection. If no client process has opened the pipe when the server process calls DosConnectNPipe, the function either waits until a client opens the pipe or returns ERROR_PIPE_NOT_CONNECTED, depending on whether the server process created the pipe to wait for data.

Each client process requires a separate instance of a pipe. For example, if a server process creates a named pipe and specifies that four instances of the pipe can be created, the process can then create three more instances of the named pipe (for a total of four pipes, including the original). Each instance has the same name, but each has a unique pipe handle. The process can then connect each pipe to the server. (Each instance must be connected by an explicit use of DosConnectNPipe.) In this example, the server must use each function four times to create and connect four separate instances of the named pipe. Each pipe is then available to a separate client process.

If a client process receives the ERROR_PIPE_BUSY return value from DosOpen, no instances of the given pipe are available. The process can use DosWaitNPipe to wait for an instance to become available. The function waits until an instance is free or until the specified time interval elapses. When an instance becomes free, the process can open the pipe. If several processes are waiting for an instance to become available, the system gives the named pipe to the process that has been waiting the longest.

The server process can disconnect a client process from a pipe by using DosDisConnectNPipe. Ideally, the client process closes the pipe by using DosClose before the server process disconnects the pipe. If the client process has not closed the pipe when the server process disconnects it, the server process forces the pipe closed and the client process subsequently receives errors if it attempts to access the pipe. Note that forcing the closure of the pipe might discard data in the pipe before the client process has had an opportunity to read it.

A process can read and write bytes to a named pipe by using DosRead and DosWrite. A process can read or write messages by using DosTransactNPipe. Depending on the access mode, DosTransactNPipe writes a message to the pipe, reads a message from the pipe, or both. If a named pipe contains unread data or is not a message pipe, DosTransactNPipe fails. If it is reading from the pipe, DosTransactNPipe does not return until a complete message is read, even if the server process specified no-wait mode when the pipe was created.

A process can also read data from a named pipe without removing the data from the pipe by using DosPeekNPipe. This function copies the specified number of bytes from the pipe and returns the number of bytes of data left in the pipe and the number of bytes left in the current message, if any.

DosPeekNPipe also returns the state of the pipe. A named pipe can be in one of the following states:

Table 9-1. Named Pipe States

State	Description
Connected	The pipe has been created and connected by the server process and has been opened by a client process. Only connected pipes can be written to or read from.
Closing	The pipe has been closed by the client process but has not yet been disconnected by the server process.
Disconnected	The pipe has been created by the server process but not connected, or has been explicitly disconnected and not yet reconnected. A disconnected pipe cannot accept a DosOpen request.
Listening	The pipe has been created and connected by the server process but has not yet been opened by a client process. A listening pipe is ready to accept a request to open. If the pipe is not in a listening state, DosOpen returns ERROR_PIPE_BUSY.

A process can open, read from, write to, and close a named message-format pipe by using DosCallNPipe. This function is equivalent to calling DosOpen, DosTransactNPipe, and DosClose. If no instances of the pipe are available, DosCallNPipe waits for an instance or returns without opening the pipe if the specified interval of time elapses.

A process can retrieve information about the handle state of a named pipe by using DosQueryNPHState. The handle state is a combination of the instance count, the access mode, and the pipe type (byte or message). DosQueryNPHState also specifies whether the process owning the handle is a server or client and whether the pipe waits if reading and writing cannot proceed.

A process can modify the handle state of a named pipe by using DosSetNPHState. For example, the process can change the reading mode for the pipe, enabling a process to read bytes from the pipe instead of messages.

Steps in Managing Server-Client Transactions

The following sequence summarizes the typical steps in the management of a named pipe:

1. The server process creates the pipe by calling DosCreateNPipe. DosCreateNPipe returns a handle for the server end of the pipe. (Note that the server uses the same handle to both read from and write to the pipe.) The pipe is now in the *disconnected state* and cannot be opened by a client process.

2. The server process calls DosConnectNPipe to put the pipe into a *listening state*. The pipe can now be opened by a client process.

3. A client process supplies the name of the pipe in a call to DosOpen and receives a pipe handle in return. (The client uses the same handle to both read from and write to the pipe.) The pipe is now in the *connected state* and can be read from or written to by the client.

4. The server and client processes communicate by calling DosRead and DosWrite. DosResetBuffer can be used to synchronize read and write dialogs. A server process that supports a large number of clients for a local named pipe can use DosSetNPipeSem and DosQueryNPipeSemState to coordinate access to the pipe.

   Server and client processes can also use DosTransactNPipe and DosCallNPipe to facilitate their communication.

5. After completing its transactions, the client process calls DosClose to close its end of the pipe. The pipe is now in the *closing state* and cannot be accessed by another client.

6. The server process calls DosDisConnectNPipe to acknowledge that the client has closed its end of the pipe. The pipe is now in the disconnected state again.

7. To enable another client process to open the pipe, the server must call DosConnectNPipe again. This puts the pipe back into the listening state. To end its access to the pipe, the server calls DosClose. When all of the handles for both ends of the pipe have been closed, the pipe is deallocated by the system.

Preparing a Named Pipe for a Client

A server process uses DosConnectNPipe to put a newly created named pipe into the listening state. The pipe must be in the listening state in order for a client process to gain access to the pipe by calling DosOpen.

After successfully opening the pipe and finishing its transactions, the client process calls DosClose to end its access to the pipe. The server process must acknowledge the close by calling DosDisConnectNPipe. It can then call DosConnectNPipe again to put the pipe into the listening state for the next client.

Together, DosConnectNPipe and DosDisConnectNPipe enable a server to create a named pipe and to reuse it for communication with different clients. Without these functions, the server would have to delete and re-create the pipe for each client.

Note: If multiple instances of a named pipe have been created, then each instance of the pipe must be put into the listening state before it can be opened by a client.

Facilitating Transaction Processing

DosTransactNPipe and DosCallNPipe facilitate the use of named pipes by combining other named pipe functions. Compared to calling the other functions separately, DosTransactNPipe and DosCallNPipe provide significant performance gains for applications that operate in a networked environment. They can also be used by local processes. However, both of these functions can be used only with duplex message pipes.

- DosTransactNPipe performs a transaction (a DosWrite followed by DosRead) on a duplex message pipe.

- DosCallNPipe has the combined effect of DosOpen, DosTransactNPipe, and DosClose, and is referred to as a *procedure call*. It provides an efficient means of implementing local and remote procedure call interfaces between processes.

Coordinating Access to a Local Named Pipe with Semaphores

When a process writes to a named pipe, the process at the other end (or handle) of the pipe might require notification that data is available to be read. Similarly, when a process reads from a named pipe, the process at the other end might require notification that write space has become available. As long as the communicating processes are on the same computer system, shared event semaphores and muxwait semaphores can be used to provide this notification. Using shared semaphores for this purpose is more efficient than dedicating a thread to periodically poll each pipe, particularly when a server process is communicating with a large number of client processes. The server or client (whichever is writing to the pipe) can post a semaphore whenever data is available in the pipe. This means that the reading process can use DosWaitEventSem or DosWaitMuxWaitSem to wait for data to arrive, rather than devote a thread to periodically polling the pipe.

A process associates a semaphore with a named pipe by using DosSetNPipeSem. First, create an event semaphore with DosCreateEventSem, specifying the initial state of the semaphore as *reset*. Then call DosSetNPipeSem to attach the event semaphore to a particular named-pipe handle. Up to two event semaphores can be attached to each named pipe, one for the server process and one for the client process. If there is already a semaphore associated with one end of the pipe, that semaphore is replaced. A process can check the state of the semaphores by using DosQueryNPipeSemState.

The server or client process must then call DosWaitEventSem. The particular thread that calls this function will block until data is either read from or written to the pipe. At that time, the system posts the event semaphore, enabling the blocked thread to resume its execution.

If a process requires notification whenever any one of multiple named pipes has been written to or read from, it can either attach the same event semaphore to multiple pipes, or it can create a muxwait semaphore:

- If the same event semaphore is attached to multiple pipes, then the *KeyHandle* parameter of DosSetNPipeSem is used to assign a unique value to each pipe. After the event semaphore has been posted, the process calls DosQueryNPipeSemState. This function returns information about each of the named pipes that are attached to the semaphore, including key-handle values. The calling process can use this information to determine which one of the named pipes has either data or write space available.

- To use a muxwait semaphore, a process first creates an event semaphore for each of the pipes that it wants to monitor. Each semaphore must then be attached to a pipe by calling DosSetNPipeSem. Again, a unique key-handle value must be assigned to each pipe.

  Next, the process calls DosCreateMuxWaitSem to create the muxwait semaphore, specifying DCMW_WAIT_ANY as one of the *flAttr* flags. The muxwait semaphore will consist of a linked list of the previously created event semaphores.

  The process calls DosWaitMuxWaitSem so that it will be notified the next time data is read from or written to any of the pipes. However, it must call DosQueryNPipeSemState to determine which one of the pipes is ready to be read from or written to.

Using Unnamed Pipes

Unnamed pipes are useful in applications that transfer data between related processes. They are commonly used to control the input and output of child processes by redirecting the standard input and output of the child process to a pipe controlled by the parent process.

Note: In the example code fragments that follow, error checking was left out to conserve space. Applications should always check the return code that the functions return. Control Program functions return an APIRET value. A return code of 0 indicates success. If a non-zero value is returned, an error occurred.

Creating Unnamed Pipes

DosCreatePipe creates an unnamed pipe. Two handles are returned: one for read access to the pipe and one for write access. The pipe size specified is advisory; its actual size is dependent on the amount of available memory. If the size parameter is 0, the pipe is created with the default size, which is 512 bytes.

This example creates an unnamed pipe. The current process can use the unnamed pipe for communication between itself and a child process.

```
#define INCL_DOSQUEUES    /* Queue values */
#include <os2.h>
#include <stdio.h>

HFILE    ReadHandle;    /* Pointer to the read handle    */
HFILE    WriteHandle;   /* Pointer to the write handle   */
ULONG    PipeSize;      /* Pipe size                     */
APIRET   rc;            /* Return code                   */

PipeSize = 4096;        /* Ask for 4KB of internal storage */
                        /* for the pipe                    */

rc = DosCreatePipe(&ReadHandle, &WriteHandle, PipeSize);

if (rc != 0) {
    printf("DosCreatePipe error: return code = %ld", rc);
    return;
}
```

Figure 9-2. Creating an Unnamed Pipe

On successful return, the *ReadHandle* variable contains the read handle for the pipe, and the *WriteHandle* variable contains the write handle for the pipe.

After a process creates a pipe, any child process started with DosExecPgm inherits the pipe handles. Using shared memory, the parent process can pass one of the pipe handles to the child process; thus, one process can store data in the pipe and the other can retrieve it.

Reading from and Writing to Unnamed Pipes

Applications use the OS/2 file system functions to read from and write to unnamed pipes. The handles returned by DosCreatePipe are used as file handles to DosRead and DosWrite.

To write (or add data) to an unnamed pipe, call DosWrite, specifying the write handle of the pipe in DosWrite's file handle parameter. DosWrite requests to a pipe are processed in the order in which they are made. Multiple calls to DosWrite can be made before data is read (or removed) from the pipe. When the pipe becomes full, write requests are blocked until space is freed by read requests.

To read from a pipe, call DosRead, specifying the read handle of the pipe in DosRead's file handle parameter. Subsequent calls to DosRead can empty the pipe if no further calls to DosWrite are made in the meantime.

If the process reading the pipe ends, the next DosWrite request for that pipe returns ERROR_BROKEN_PIPE.

Calling DosClose terminates access to an unnamed pipe. However, the pipe is not deleted from memory until all handles to the pipe have been closed, including any handles that were defined with DosDupHandle.

Redirecting Standard I/O for Child Processes

An application can use unnamed pipes to redirect the standard input and the standard output for a child process.

A typical use of an unnamed pipe is to read the output of a child process. An application creates a pipe and then duplicates the standard output handle. When the child process is started, its standard output will be written into the pipe, where the application can read and display it. The following code fragment shows how to do this:

```
#define INCL_DOSQUEUES    /* Queue values */
#include <os2.h>

#define PIPESIZE 256
#define HF_STDOUT 1        /* Standard output handle */

HPIPE hpR, hpW;
RESULTCODES resc;
ULONG cbRead, cbWritten;
CHAR achBuf[PIPESIZE], szFailName[CCHMAXPATH];

HFILE hfSave = -1,
      hfNew = HF_STDOUT;

DosDupHandle(HF_STDOUT, &hfSave);     /* Saves standard output handle    */

DosCreatePipe(&hpR, &hpW, PIPESIZE); /* Creates pipe                    */

DosDupHandle(hpW, &hfNew);           /* Duplicates standard output handle */

DosExecPgm(szFailName, sizeof(szFailName),  /* Starts child process     */
           EXEC_ASYNC, (PSZ) NULL, (PSZ) NULL, &resc,
           "DUMMY.EXE");

DosClose(hpW);                       /* Closes write handle to ensure   */
                                     /* Notification at child termination */

DosDupHandle(hfSave, &hfNew);        /* Brings stdout back              */

/*
 * Read from the pipe and write to the screen
 * as long as there are bytes to read.
 */

do {
    DosRead(hpR, achBuf, sizeof(achBuf), &cbRead);
    DosWrite(HF_STDOUT, achBuf, cbRead, &cbWritten);
} while(cbRead);
```

Figure 9-3. Redirecting the Standard I/O of a Child Process into an Unnamed Pipe

A parent process can also use unnamed pipes to communicate with a child process by redirecting both the standard input and the standard output for the child process. To do this, the parent process:

1. Creates two pipes with DosCreatePipe.
2. Uses DosDupHandle to redefine the read handle of one pipe as standard input (0000), and the write handle of the other pipe as standard output (0001).
3. Starts the child process with DosExecPgm.
4. Uses the remaining pipe handles to read and write to the pipes.

The parent process controls the meanings for standard I/O for the child process. Thus, when the child process uses standard I/O handles with DosRead and DosWrite, it reads from and writes to the pipes of its parent instead of reading from the keyboard and writing to the display.

Using Named Pipes

Named pipes are useful in applications that transfer data between processes. The processes using named pipes can be related, unrelated, or even on different computers.

Creating Named Pipes

The server process creates a named pipe by using DosCreateNPipe. You must specify the name of the pipe, the access modes, the type of pipe (byte or message), and the sizes of the input and output buffers. DosCreateNPipe returns a pipe handle that can be used in subsequent pipe operations.

Each named pipe must have a unique name of the following form:

```
\PIPE\PipeName
```

The "\PIPE\" in the name above is required, but need not be uppercase. It is not the name of a subdirectory.

To open a pipe on a remote computer, the client process must specify the name of the server process that opened the pipe as part of the pipe name, as follows:

```
\\Server\PIPE\PipeName
```

"\\Server" in the name above is the name of the remote computer; again, "\PIPE\" is required.

The name parameter must conform to the rules for OS/2 file names, but no actual file is created for the pipe.

In the following code fragment, DosCreateNPipe creates a pipe named \pipe\pipe1 and supplies a unique handle identifying the pipe. *OpenMode* is set to NP_ACCESS_DUPLEX. This activates full duplex access to the named pipe. There will be no inheritance to child process, and no write-through (write-through only affects remote pipes). *PipeMode* is set to "NP_WMESG | NP_RMESG | 0x01". This specifies that the pipe should be read as a message stream for both reading and writing and an instance count of 1 (only one instance of the named pipe can be created at a time). The pipe will block on Read/Write if no data is available.

```
#define INCL_DOSNMPIPES    /* Named-pipe values */
#include <os2.h>
#include <stdio.h>

UCHAR   FileName[40];  /* Pipe name               */
HPIPE   PipeHandle;    /* Pipe handle (returned) */
ULONG   OpenMode;      /* Open-mode parameters    */
ULONG   PipeMode;      /* Pipe-mode parameters    */
ULONG   OutBufSize;    /* Size of the out-buffer */
ULONG   InBufSize;     /* Size of the in-buffer  */
ULONG   TimeOut;       /* Default value for DosWaitNPipe time-out parameter */
APIRET  rc;            /* Return code             */

strcpy(FileName,"\\PIPE\\PIPE1");

OpenMode = NP_ACCESS_DUPLEX;              /* Full duplex, no inheritance,   */
                                         /* no write-through               */

PipeMode = NP_WMESG | NP_RMESG | 0x01;  /* Block on read and write, message */
                                         /* stream, instance count of 1     */

OutBufSize = 4096;   /* The outgoing buffer must be 4KB in size           */

InBufSize = 2048;    /* The incoming buffer must be 2KB in size           */

TimeOut = 10000;     /* Time-out is 10 seconds (units are in milliseconds) */

rc = DosCreateNPipe(FileName, &PipeHandle, OpenMode,
                    PipeMode, OutBufSize, InBufSize,
                    TimeOut);

if (rc != 0) {
    printf("DosCreateNPipe error: return code = %ld", rc);
    return;
}
```

Figure 9-4. Creating a Named Pipe

Once the named pipe is created, the application can call DosConnectNPipe to connect a client process to the pipe.

Once a client process connects to the pipe, the process can read from and write to the pipe. The preceding example creates a byte pipe, so the process can use DosRead and DosWrite to read from and write to the pipe.

After the client process finishes using the pipe, the server process can disconnect the pipe by using DosDisConnectNPipe. The server process can either connect again or close the named pipe by using DosClose.

When a server process creates a named pipe, it defines the pipe to the system by specifying the file write-through mode, the inheritance mode, the access and blocking modes, the pipe type, the read mode, the size of the in and out buffers, and the instance count. The following list describes these modes, types, and buffers.

- The *file write-through mode* has significance only for communication with remote client processes. When the file write-through bit is set, data is sent across the network as soon as it is written; otherwise, the operating system will in some cases hold data briefly in a local buffer before sending it across the network.

- The *inheritance mode* specifies whether or not the pipe handle will be inherited by a child process.

- The *access mode* specifies the direction in which data will flow through the pipe. The server creates an inbound pipe (a pipe with inbound access mode) if it intends to read data from the client process, an outbound pipe if it intends to write data to the client process, or a duplex pipe if it intends to both read from and write to the client process.

- The *blocking mode* specifies whether or not DosRead and DosWrite will block when no data is available.

- The *pipe type* is the form in which a stream of data is written to the pipe. If the pipe is a byte pipe, the server and client processes write data as an undifferentiated stream of bytes. If the pipe is a message pipe, the processes write data as a stream of messages; messages are blocks of data, each with a system-supplied header, that are written as single units. The server and client processes define the size and format of a message.

- The *read mode* is the form in which data is read from the pipe. The data in a pipe that was created as a byte pipe can only be read as bytes; therefore, a byte pipe will always be in byte-read mode. The data in a message pipe, however, can be read either as messages or as bytes. (If it is to be read as bytes, DosRead skips over the message headers). Therefore, message pipes can be in either message-read mode or byte-read mode.

  Note: The terms "byte pipe" and "message pipe" always refer to the pipe type—the form in which data is written to the pipe. When the read mode of a pipe is being referred to, it is always explicitly identified as either message-read mode or byte-read mode.

- The *in* and *out buffers* can be up to 64KB in size. If the pipe will be read in message-read mode, and if the message size is known, the server can control how many messages the buffer will hold at one time by specifying the appropriate buffer size.

- The *instance count* is the maximum number of instances of the named pipe that can be created. A pipe instance is actually a separate pipe—that is, a unique set of pipe buffers with unique handles. However, the term "pipe instance" is used to distinguish pipes that share the same name from pipes with different names. Because a client process uses only the name of the pipe when opening it, the existence of multiple pipe instances is transparent to a client process.

Creating Multiple Instances of a Named Pipe
Although each named pipe must have a unique name, a server process can create multiple *instances* of a pipe, all of which have the same name. A pipe instance is actually a separate pipe—that is, a unique set of pipe buffers with unique handles.

The ability to create multiple pipe instances enables the server to communicate with multiple client processes at the same time. Because a client process uses only the name of the pipe when opening it, the existence of multiple pipe instances is transparent to a client process.

The *ICount* parameter of DosCreateNPipe specifies the maximum number of named pipe instances that can be created. (An unlimited number can also be specified.) This parameter is specified only when the first instance of a named pipe is created; any subsequent attempt to redefine the instance count will be ignored.

If the instance count is greater than 1, the server process can create additional pipe instances by specifying the same pipe name in subsequent calls to DosCreateNPipe. Generally, the attributes of the subsequent pipe instances are defined to be the same as those of the original pipe instance, because a client process that requests the pipe has no way of controlling which pipe instance will be assigned to it.

After an additional pipe instance has been created, it is used in the same manner as the original pipe instance. That is, the same sequence of named pipe functions is used in the control or management of all named pipe instances. (See "Steps in Managing Server-Client Transactions" on page 9-5 for more information.)

Note: If all of the instances of a named pipe are in use when a client calls DosOpen, ERROR_PIPE_BUSY is returned. However, the client can wait for an instance of that pipe to become available by calling DosWaitNPipe.

Multiple instances of a named pipe can be created by different processes. That is, multiple server processes can create and use instances of the same named pipe to communicate with their clients.

Opening Named Pipes

A client process can open the client end of a named pipe by using DosOpen. DosOpen opens the client end of a pipe by name and returns a handle. The application must use the appropriate pipe name and access modes to open the pipe for reading, writing, or both. (To open a pipe on a remote computer, the client process must also specify the name of the computer system as part of the pipe name, as follows:

```
\\ComputerName\PIPE\PipeName.)
```

If a pipe name includes a remote LAN server name, DosOpen attempts to open the pipe on a remote computer. The server process can then read input from the client process through the pipe.

The following code fragment opens a remote pipe, reads from the standard input (usually the keyboard), and sends the information to the server process through the pipe:

```
#define INCL_DOSQUEUES   /* Queue values          */
#include <os2.h>

#define PIPESIZE 256
#define SERVER_PIPE_NAME "\\\\myserver\\pipe\\mypipe"
#define HF_STDIN 0        /* Standard input handle */

HPIPE    hp;
BYTE     abBuf[PIPESIZE];
ULONG    ulAction, cbRead, cbWritten;
APIRET   rc;

rc = DosOpen(SERVER_PIPE_NAME, &hp, &ulAction, 0,
            FILE_NORMAL, FILE_OPEN,
            OPEN_ACCESS_READWRITE | OPEN_SHARE_DENYNONE,
            (PEAOP) NULL);

if (rc)
    DosExit(EXIT_PROCESS, 0);                   /* Open pipe failed    */

do {                                            /* Open pipe succeeded */
    DosRead(HF_STDIN, abBuf, sizeof(abBuf), &cbRead);
    DosWrite(hp, abBuf, cbRead, &cbWritten);    /* Writes to the pipe  */
} while (cbRead > 2);                           /* Stop on a blank line */

DosClose(hp);
```

Figure 9-5. Opening and Writing to a Remote Pipe

The client process checks the return value from DosOpen to verify that the pipe was actually opened. If the server process has not yet created the pipe, DosOpen returns an error. When the client process finishes using the pipe, it closes the pipe by using DosClose.

When a named pipe is opened, its initial state is set by the system to block read and write operations (blocking mode), and to read data as a byte stream (byte-read mode). However, the client can change these modes by calling DosSetNPHState.

A call to DosOpen fails if all instances of the named pipe are already open. The open also fails if the pipe has been closed by a client, but the server has not called DosDisConnectNPipe (to acknowledge the client's close), followed by DosConnectNPipe (to prepare the pipe for the next client). In both of these situations, ERROR_PIPE_BUSY is returned.

If all instances of a named pipe are busy, a client process can call DosWaitNPipe to wait for an instance to become available before it calls DosOpen again.

After a pipe instance has been opened by a client, that same instance cannot be opened by another client at the same time. However, the opening process can duplicate the handle as many times as desired by calling DosDupHandle. This enables child processes to share access to a pipe instance with a parent process.

The access-mode and sharing-mode fields that are specified for DosOpen must be the same as those that were specified by the server when it created the pipe with DosCreateNPipe.

Reading from Named Pipes

Both the server and the client processes read data from a pipe by calling DosRead. The server reads from the handle that was returned when it created the pipe with DosCreateNPipe, and the client reads from the handle that was returned to it by DosOpen.

When a pipe is created, the *PipeMode* parameter is used to specify both the *pipe type* and the *read mode* for the server end of the pipe:

- A byte pipe can be read-only in byte-read mode. (DosCreateNPipe and DosSetNPHState return ERROR_INVALID_PARAMETER if message-read mode is specified for a byte pipe.) In byte-read mode, all currently available data is returned, up to the buffer size specified by DosRead.

- A message pipe can be read in either byte-read mode or message-read mode, as follows:

  - When a message pipe is read in byte-read mode, the message headers are skipped, and the pipe is read as if it were a byte pipe.

  - When a message pipe is read in message-read mode, each message is read either in its entirety, or not at all, depending on the size of the message and the buffer length:

    - If the buffer length that was specified for DosRead is larger than the next available message, then only that message is read, and the Bytes-Read parameter indicates the size of the message.

    - If the buffer length for DosRead is smaller than the next available message, DosRead returns the number of bytes requested and ERROR_MORE_DATA. Subsequent calls to DosRead are blocked until the rest of the message can be transferred. (DosPeekNPipe can be used to find out how many bytes are left in the message.)

The *PipeMode* parameter of DosCreateNPipe also specifies the *blocking mode* for the server end of the pipe:

- If nonblocking mode was specified, DosRead returns immediately with 0 in the Bytes-Read parameter if no data is available.

- If blocking mode was specified, DosRead blocks until data is available; the only time it will return with 0 in the Bytes-Read parameter is if it reaches end-of-file.

DosRead works the same for both ends of the pipe. However, the read mode and blocking mode are not necessarily the same for the client end of the pipe as they are for the server end, because DosOpen always opens the CLIENT end in byte-read mode and blocking mode.

The read mode and blocking mode for either end of the pipe can be changed by calling DosSetNPHState. The pipe type, however, is always the same for both the server and client ends of the pipe, and it cannot be changed.

Writing to Named Pipes

Both the server and the client processes write to a pipe by calling DosWrite. The server writes to the handle that was returned to it by DosCreateNPipe, and the client writes to the handle that was returned to it by DosOpen. This relationship is shown in Figure 9-6.

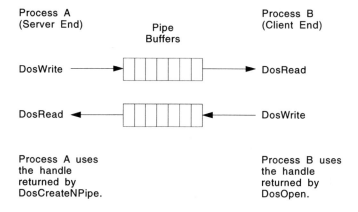

Figure   9-6. Client-Server Communications with a Named Pipe

Either bytes or messages can be written, depending on whether the pipe was created as a byte pipe or as a message pipe.

When a process writes to a message pipe, the buffer-length parameter for DosWrite holds the size of the message that the process is writing. Because DosWrite automatically encodes message lengths in the pipe, applications do not have to encode this information in the data buffers.

The action taken by DosWrite depends on the blocking mode of the pipe, which is not necessarily the same for the server and client ends of the pipe. For the server process, the blocking mode of the pipe is specified when the pipe is created. For a client process, the blocking mode is automatically set to blocking when the pipe is opened. The blocking mode can also be reset by calling DosSetNPHState.

If the end of the message pipe that is being written to is in blocking mode, DosWrite does not return until all of the requested bytes have been written. (It might have to wait for the first part of the message to be read before it can write the rest of the message.)

If the message pipe is in nonblocking mode, DosWrite takes the following action:

- If the message is larger than the pipe buffer, DosWrite blocks until the entire message has been written. (Again, it might have to wait for the first part of the message to be read before it can write the rest of the message.)

- If the message is smaller than the pipe buffer, but there is currently not enough room in the buffer, DosWrite returns with a value of 0 in the Bytes-Written parameter.

If a byte pipe is in nonblocking mode, and if there is more data to be written than will fit in the pipe buffer, then DosWrite writes as many bytes as will fit in the buffer and returns the number of bytes that were actually written.

If a process tries to write to a pipe whose other end is closed, ERROR_BROKEN_PIPE is returned.

Synchronizing Named Pipe Dialogs

Communicating processes can synchronize their named pipe dialogs by calling DosResetBuffer after each call to DosWrite.

When used with external files, DosResetBuffer flushes the buffer cache of the requesting process to disk. When used with named pipes, this function blocks the calling process at one end of the pipe until the data the calling process has written to the pipe has been successfully read at the other end of the pipe.

Determining Pipe Status

DosQueryNPHState and DosQueryNPipeInfo can be used to obtain information about named pipes.

DosQueryNPHState

A client process can read data from the pipe, write data to the pipe, or both, depending on the access mode specified when the pipe was created. To check the current access mode, the client process can call DosQueryNPHState.

The following code fragment shows how to use DosQueryNPHState to obtain information about a named pipe:

```
#define INCL_DOSNMPIPES    /* Named-pipe values */
#include <os2.h>
#include <stdio.h>

HPIPE    Handle;            /* Pipe handle        */
ULONG    PipeHandleState;   /* Pipe-handle state */
APIRET   rc;                /* Return code        */

rc = DosQueryNPHState(Handle, &PipeHandleState);

if (rc != 0) {
    printf("DosQueryNPHState error: return code = %ld", rc);
    return;
}
```

Figure 9-7. Getting Information about a Named Pipe

On successful return, *PipeHandleState* will contain information that describes the nature of the named pipe.

DosQueryNPHState returns the following information about the pipe handle and the attributes of the pipe:

- The end of the pipe that the handle is for (server or client end)
- The pipe type (byte pipe or message pipe)
- The instance count
- The blocking mode (blocking or nonblocking)
- The read mode (byte-read mode or message-read mode).

The values for pipe type and instance count cannot be changed, so they are always the same as those that were specified when the pipe was created with DosCreateNPipe. The information returned for blocking mode and read mode, however, can come from different sources:

- If the handle is for the server end of the pipe, then the blocking mode and the read mode were set with DosCreateNPipe, but could have been reset with DosSetNPHState.
- If the handle is for the client end of the pipe, then the blocking mode and the read mode were set to "blocking" and "byte-read" by the system when the client called DosOpen. However, again, they could have been reset with DosSetNPHState.

The pipe attributes are described in more detail in "Creating Named Pipes" on page 9-11.

An application can use DosSetNPHState to change the wait mode and the read mode. The pipe cannot be changed to no-wait mode when another thread is blocked on a read or write operation to the same end of the pipe.

DosQueryNPipeInfo
More detailed information about a named pipe can be obtained by using DosQueryNPipeInfo. This function returns information in a PIPEINFO data structure that includes the name of the pipe, the current and maximum instance counts (the current number of pipes and the maximum number of times the pipe can be created), the size of the input and output buffers for the pipe, and the pipe identifier of the client process.

The following code fragment shows how to use DosQueryNPipeInfo:

```
#define INCL_DOSNMPIPES    /* Named-pipe values */
#include <os2.h>
#include <stdio.h>

HPIPE    Handle;          /* Pipe handle                     */
ULONG    InfoLevel;       /* Pipe data required              */
PIPEINFO InfoBuf;         /* Pipe information data structure */
ULONG    InfoBufSize;     /* Pipe data-buffer size           */
APIRET   rc;              /* Return code                     */

InfoLevel = 1;                    /* Ask for standard level of pipe info */

InfoBufSize = sizeof(PIPEINFO);   /* Length of pipe info data structure  */

rc = DosQueryNPipeInfo(Handle, InfoLevel, &InfoBuf, InfoBufSize);

if (rc != 0) {
    printf("DosQueryNPipeInfo error: return code = %ld", rc);
    return;
}
```

Figure   9-8. Using DosQueryNPipeInfo to Get Information about a Pipe

On successful return, the pipe information data structure contains a set of information describing the nature and the current state of the named pipe.

DosQueryNPipeInfo returns level 1 or level 2 file information for the pipe. Level 1 information includes the following:

- The actual sizes of the in-buffer and out-buffer
- The maximum number of pipe instances permitted
- The current number of pipe instances
- The length of the pipe name
- The ASCIIZ name of the pipe, including *ComputerName* if the pipe is in a remote computer system.

  Level 2 information consists of a unique 2-byte identifier for each of the pipe's client processes.

Examining the Contents of Named Pipes

DosPeekNPipe examines the current contents of a named pipe. It is similar to DosRead, except that DosPeekNPipe does not remove data from the pipe. In addition, DosPeekNPipe never blocks, even if the pipe is in blocking mode; if the pipe cannot be accessed immediately, ERROR_PIPE_BUSY is returned.

Because DosPeekNPipe does not block, it returns only what is currently in the pipe. Thus, if a message pipe is being examined, only a portion of a message might be returned, even though the specified buffer length could accommodate the entire message.

DosPeekNPipe also returns the state of the pipe. A named pipe can be in any of the following states: Connected, Disconnected, Listening, Closing. For more on pipe states see Table 9-1 on page 9-5.

The following code fragment shows how to use DosPeekNPipe:

```
#define INCL_DOSNMPIPES   /* Named-pipe values */
#include <os2.h>
#include <stdio.h>

HPIPE             Handle;      /* Pipe handle                     */
UCHAR             Buffer[200]; /* Address of user buffer          */
ULONG             BufferLen;   /* Buffer length                   */
ULONG             BytesRead;   /* Bytes read (returned)           */
struct _AVAILDATA BytesAvail;  /* Bytes available (returned)      */
ULONG             PipeState;   /* Pipe state (returned)           */
APIRET            rc;          /* Return code                     */

BufferLen = 200;  /* Length of the read buffer */

rc = DosPeekNPipe(Handle, Buffer, BufferLen,
              &BytesRead, &BytesAvail, &PipeState);

if (rc != 0) {
    printf("DosPeekNPipe error: return code = %ld", rc);
    return;
}
```

Figure   9-9. Using DosPeekNPipe to Peek into a Named Pipe

On successful return, the input buffer *Buffer* will contain up to the first 200 bytes from the named pipe, *BytesRead* will contain the number of bytes read into *Buffer*, *BytesAvail* will contain the total number of bytes that were available in the pipe, and *PipeState* will contain a value indicating the state of the named pipe

Closing Named Pipes

DosClose closes the specified pipe handle. When all of the handles that access one end of a pipe have been closed, the pipe is referred to as a *broken pipe*.

If the client end of the pipe closes, no other process can reopen the pipe until the server calls DosDisConnectNPipe (to acknowledge the client's close) followed by DosConnectNPipe (to prepare the pipe for a new client). Until it calls DosDisConnectNPipe, the server will receive ERROR_EOF if it tries to read from the pipe, and ERROR_BROKEN_PIPE if it tries to write to it. Clients that attempt to open the pipe receive ERROR_PIPE_BUSY.

If the server end closes when the client end is already closed, the pipe is deallocated immediately; otherwise, the pipe is not deallocated until the last client handle is closed.

The following code fragment shows how to close a named pipe. Assume that a previous call to DosOpen provided the named pipe handle that is contained in *Handle*.

```
#define INCL_DOSNMPIPES    /* Named-pipe values */
#include <os2.h>
#include <stdio.h>

HPIPE   Handle;      /* Pipe handle */
APIRET  rc;          /* Return code */

rc = DosDisConnectNPipe(Handle);

if (rc != 0) {
    printf("DosDisConnectNPipe error: return code = %ld", rc);
    return;
}
```

Figure   9-10. Closing a Named Pipe

Summary

Following are the OS/2 functions and data structures used with pipes.

Table 9-2. Pipe Functions	
Named-Pipe Functions	
DosCallNPipe	Combines the functionality of DosTransactNPipe and DosClose for a duplex pipe. This action is called a procedure call.
DosConnectNPipe	Prepares a named pipe for a client process by placing the pipe into the listening state.
DosCreateNPipe	Creates a named pipe.
DosDisConnectNPipe	Acknowledges that a client process has closed a named pipe.
DosPeekNPipe	Examines the data in a named pipe without removing the data. Also returns information about the state of the pipe.
DosQueryNPHState	Returns information about a named pipe handle.
DosQueryNPipeInfo	Returns information about a named pipe.
DosQueryNPipeSemState	Returns information about local named pipes that are attached to a shared event or muxwait semaphore.
DosSetNPHState	Resets the blocking mode and the read mode of a named pipe.
DosSetNPipeSem	Attaches a shared event semaphore to a local named pipe.
DosTransactNPipe	Writes to a duplex message pipe, then reads from it.
DosWaitNPipe	Waits for an instance of a named pipe to become available.
Unnamed-Pipe Functions	
DosClose	Closes a file or pipe.
DosCreatePipe	Creates an unnamed (anonymous) pipe.
DosDupHandle	Returns a new file handle for an open file or pipe.
DosOpen	Opens a file or pipe for reading or writing.
DosRead	Reads from a file or pipe.
DosWrite	Writes to a file or pipe.

Table 9-3. Pipe Data Structures

Data Structure	Description
AVAILDATA	Used to return a count of the available items in a named pipe.
PIPEINFO	Used to return level 1 information about a named pipe.
PIPESEMSTATE	Used to return information about local named pipes attached to a semaphore.

Chapter 10. Queues

Communication between processes is valuable in a multitasking operating system to enable concurrent processes to work together. Queues are one of three forms of interprocess communication (IPC), the other forms of IPC being semaphores and pipes.

This chapter describes how to create and use queues. Queues enable one or more processes to transfer data to a specific target process.

Note: The queues used for interprocess communication should not to be confused with the message queues used for communication between Presentation Manager (PM) and PM applications, nor with the printer queues used by the print spooler in managing print jobs.

The following topics are related to the information in this chapter:

- Memory (Shared Memory)
- Program Execution and Control
- Semaphores
- Pipes.

About Queues

A *queue* is a named, ordered list of elements that is used to pass information between threads of the same (related) process or between different (unrelated) processes.

Processes pass information to a queue in the form of elements. An element is a 32-bit unit of information. Queue elements can be values, flags, pointers to shared memory regions, anything that can fit into 32 bits. The format of a queue element depends entirely on the process that creates the queue (the queue owner). Only the queue owner can read elements from the queue; other processes can only write to the queue. Reading an element automatically removes it from the queue.

The process that creates the queue is known as the *server process* of the queue. The other processes that access the queue are known as *client processes*.

A queue can be thought of as looking something like Figure 10-1 on page 10-2, with one or more client processes writing elements to the queue and one server process reading the queue.

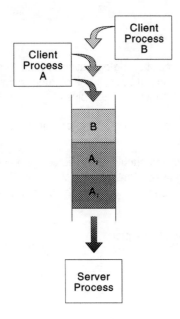

Figure 10-1. Queue with Server and Client Processes

The owner of the queue (the *server process*) can choose the order in which to read incoming information and can examine queue elements without removing them from the queue. Queue elements can be added and accessed in First-In-First-Out (FIFO), Last-In-First-Out (LIFO), or priority-based order.

Any process that has the name of a queue can open the queue and write to it. The processes writing elements to the queue must use the format determined by the queue owner.

Queues are very efficient. They pass only 32-bit sized elements, rather than large data structures. However, queues can be used only for one-way communication, because a client process can write to a queue but cannot read from one.

Typically, processes use queues to transfer information about the contents of a shared memory. The elements in the queue could contain the address and length of data areas in shared memory objects. The sending process allocates a shared memory object and gives access to the shared memory to the queue owner. The sending process can free the shared memory after writing the elements to the queue because the shared memory will not be deallocated until the queue owner frees it.

Any thread in the process that owns the queue can examine queue elements without removing them. This is called *peeking* at the queue.

The operating system supplies the process identifier of the process that writes an element to the queue, so that a process reading from or peeking at the queue can determine the origin of the element. The process identifier is returned as part of a REQUESTDATA data structure. Threads can use the ulData field of the REQUESTDATA data structure to pass additional information about the queue element.

If the queue is empty when a process attempts to read from it, the process can either wait for an element to become available or continue executing without reading from the queue. Semaphores can be used to indicate when an element is in the queue.

Queues and Semaphores

If a process manages only one queue, it typically waits for an element to become available. However, if a process manages several queues, waiting for one queue means that other queues cannot be read. To avoid wasting time while waiting, a process can supply an event semaphore when it calls DosReadQueue or DosPeekQueue. The process can then continue to execute without actually reading an element from the queue, because DosWriteQueue will post the semaphore only when an element is ready. The semaphore remains posted until someone resets it; usually the queue owner process resets the semaphore after it reads all the available information from the queue.

If a process uses a unique semaphore for each queue, it can use DosWaitMuxWaitSem to wait for the first queue to receive an element.

Only one semaphore is permitted per queue.

Queue Servers and Clients

The server process and its threads have certain queue-managing privileges. Only the server process and its threads can:

- Examine queue elements without removing them (DosPeekQueue)
- Remove elements from the queue (DosReadQueue)
- Purge all the elements in a queue (DosPurgeQueue)
- Write to the queue without opening it first (DosWriteQueue)
- Delete the queue (DosCloseQueue).

Both server and client processes can query the number of elements in the queue using DosQueryQueue.

Client processes can query the queue (DosQueryQueue) and add elements to it (DosWriteQueue), but they must first gain access to the queue by calling DosOpenQueue. When a client process is finished with a queue, it ends its access to the queue by calling DosCloseQueue. (Note that, unlike the server process and its threads, a client process cannot use DosCloseQueue to delete a queue.)

When a queue is opened by a client process, an access count is set to 1. Each client process has its own access count. The access count is incremented whenever a thread in a process opens the queue and decremented whenever a thread in the process closes the queue. Access to the queue by the client process ends when the access count for the process reaches 0. When the server process closes the queue, the queue is terminated and removed from the system.

Queue Element Order

DosReadQueue reads either a specified element or the first element in the queue. The first element in the queue depends on the queue type, which is specified when the queue is created. A queue can have FIFO, LIFO, or priority ordering.

Priority values range from 0 (lowest priority) through 15 (highest priority). The writing process assigns a priority to a queue element when the element is written to the queue. DosReadQueue reads elements from the queue in descending order of priority, regardless of the order in which DosWriteQueue placed the elements in the queue. Elements with equal priority are read in FIFO order.

Obtaining Information about Queues and Queue Elements

Any thread in the process that owns the queue can use DosPeekQueue to examine the elements in the queue to determine which one to actually read. Each call to DosPeekQueue returns the identifier of the next element in the queue, so the function can be called repeatedly to move through the queue. The identifier of the desired element can then be supplied to DosReadQueue.

Any process that has opened a queue can use DosQueryQueue to determine the number of elements in the queue. This function also returns an error value if the queue owner has closed the queue.

Using Queues

Queues are useful for a process to manage input from other processes. The examples in the following sections show how to create and use queues.

Note: In the example code fragments that follow, error checking was left out to conserve space. Applications should always check the return code that the functions return. Control Program functions return an APIRET value. A return code of 0 indicates success. If a non-zero value is returned, an error occurred.

Creating a Queue

A thread creates a queue by using DosCreateQueue and specifying a queue name and the queue type as arguments. The queue name must be unique and have the following form:

```
\QUEUES\QueName
```

The "\QUEUES\" is required, though it need not be uppercase. It is not a subdirectory.

The *QueName* parameter must conform to the rules for OS/2 file names, although no actual file is created for the queue.

The process that creates the queue is known as the *server process* of the queue. The other processes that access the queue are known as *client processes*.

The following code fragment creates a FIFO queue named \queues\sample.que:

```
#define INCL_DOSQUEUES    /* Queue values */
#include <os2.h>

HQUEUE hq;

DosCreateQueue(&hq, QUE_FIFO | QUE_CONVERT_ADDRESS,
               "\\queues\\sample.que");
```

Figure 10-2. Creating a Named FIFO Queue

When the server process creates the queue, it determines whether the ordering of queue elements is based on arrival (FIFO or LIFO) or priority. If the ordering is based on priority, then priority values must be assigned whenever data is added to the queue.

The server must also specify whether the operating system is to convert 16-bit addresses of elements placed in the queue by 16-bit processes to 32-bit addresses.

After a process has created a queue, any thread in that process can access the queue with equal authority.

Allocating Memory for Queue Data

When queues are used only to pass the addresses to data rather than the data itself, processes must allocate shared memory objects for storing queue data. The two most common methods of storing queue data are:

- Using a named shared memory object — for related processes
- Using unnamed shared memory objects — for unrelated processes.

Named Shared Memory Objects

Related processes generally use a single named shared memory object for storing queue data. The server process allocates the memory object by calling DosAllocSharedMem. Care must be taken to ensure that the memory object is large enough to meet application requirements.

The name of the shared memory object is established by agreement among the server and the client processes. For simplicity, the name can be the same as the queue name, except that the prefix \SHAREMEM\ must be used instead of \QUEUES\.

A client process accesses the named shared memory object by calling DosGetNamedSharedMem. It must then call DosOpenQueue to gain access to the queue of the server.

Before the server process ends, it releases the memory object by calling DosFreeMem.

Unnamed Shared Memory Objects

Unrelated processes generally use unnamed shared memory objects for storing queue data. This makes it possible for a client process to store data in a shared memory object without knowing its name. To use unnamed shared memory objects for storing queue data, the server process must take the following steps whenever it is called by a client:

1. Save the process identification (PID) of the client process.
2. Allocate an unnamed shared memory object for the data of the client process by calling DosAllocSharedMem.
3. Give the client process the capability of accessing the memory object by calling DosGiveSharedMem with the client's PID.

The client process must then call DosOpenQueue to gain access to the server's queue.

After each client completes its queue requests or ends, the server calls DosFreeMem to release the client's memory object.

Opening a Queue

Once the queue is created, the server process of the queue and the threads of the server process have immediate access to the queue and can proceed to access the queue. A client process must request access to a queue by calling DosOpenQueue. Once the queue is open, the client process can add an element to the queue with DosWriteQueue, and it can query the number of elements in the queue with DosQueryQueue.

DosOpenQueue retrieves the queue handle and the process identifier of the queue owner. The function also increments the queue's access count.

The following code fragment shows how another process would open the queue created with DosCreateQueue.

```
#define INCL_DOSQUEUES
#include<os2.h>

#define HF_STDOUT 1    /* Standard output handle */

HQUEUE  hq;
PID     pidOwner;
ULONG   cbWritten;
APIRET  rc;

rc = DosOpenQueue(&pidOwner, &hq, "\\queues\\sample.que");

if (rc) {
    DosWrite(HF_STDOUT, "\r\n Queue open failed. \r\n", 24, &cbWritten);
    DosExit(EXIT_PROCESS, 1);
}
else {
    DosWrite(HF_STDOUT, "\r\n Queue opened. \r\n", 19, &cbWritten);
}
```

Figure 10-3. Opening a Queue

When it is finished with the queue, a thread in the client process ends its access by calling DosCloseQueue. DosCloseQueue decrements the access count for the process each time it is called. When the access count reaches 0, the connection between the client process and the queue is terminated.

After a process has opened a queue, any thread in that process can access the queue with equal authority.

Note: If a queue was created by a call to the 16-bit DosCreateQueue, then it is not accessible to 32-bit DosOpenQueue requests, and ERROR_QUE_PROC_NO_ACCESS will be returned.

Writing to a Queue

The server process and any of its threads can add an element to a queue simply by calling DosWriteQueue. A client process, however, must first request access to the queue by calling DosOpenQueue.

Processes that communicate by passing the addresses of shared memory objects through the queue must have a shared memory object that they each have access to. Once a process opens the queue, it can allocate shared memory by using DosAllocMem with the OBJ_GIVEABLE attribute and then give the shared memory to the queue owner with DosGiveSharedMem.

A process that has opened a queue can write to the queue by using DosWriteQueue. The writing process must create elements in a form that the queue owner can read.

The following code fragment adds an element to a queue. Assume that the caller has placed the handle of the queue into *QueueHandle* already. Assume also that *DataBuffer* has been set to point to a data element in shared memory, and that *DataLength* has been set to contain the length of the data element in shared memory.

```
#define INCL_DOSQUEUES    /* Queue values */
#include <os2.h>
#include <stdio.h>

HQUEUE    QueueHandle;    /* Queue handle                          */
ULONG     Request;        /* Request-identification data           */
ULONG     DataLength;     /* Length of element being added         */
PVOID     DataBuffer;     /* Element being added                   */
ULONG     ElemPriority;   /* Priority of element being added       */
APIRET    rc;             /* Return code                           */

Request = 0;              /* Assume that no special data is being   */
                          /* sent along with this write request     */

ElemPriority = 0;         /* For priority-based queues: add the     */
                          /* new queue element at the logical end   */
                          /* of the queue                           */

rc = DosWriteQueue(QueueHandle, Request, DataLength,
                DataBuffer, ElemPriority);

if (rc != 0) {
    printf("DosWriteQueue error: return code = %ld", rc);
    return;
}
```

Figure 10-4. Adding an Element to a Queue

Once the process has written to the queue, it frees the shared memory. However, the memory will not be freed until the queue owner also frees it.

If the queue was created as a priority-based queue (as specified in the *QueueFlags* parameter of DosCreateQueue), then the priority of the element that is being added must be specified.

If the server process has ended, or if it has closed the queue before DosWriteQueue is called, then ERROR_QUE_INVALID_HANDLE is returned.

Reading from a Queue

The queue owner (server process) and its threads can read an element from the queue by using DosReadQueue. The owner can read the first element in the queue by specifying 0 as the element number. Alternatively, the owner can read a particular element in the queue by specifying an element code returned from DosPeekQueue. This function is not available to client processes.

DosReadQueue can either remove queue elements in the order that was specified when the queue was created (FIFO, LIFO, or priority), or it can use an element identifier from DosPeekQueue as input to remove a previously examined element.

The following code fragment reads an element from the queue. Assume that the caller has placed the handle of the queue into *QueueHandle* already and that the identifier of the process that owns the queue has been placed into *OwningPID* already.

```
#define INCL_DOSQUEUES    /* Queue values */
#include <os2.h>
#include <stdio.h>

HQUEUE        QueueHandle;   /* Queue handle                 */
REQUESTDATA   Request;       /* Request-identification data  */
ULONG         DataLength;    /* Length of element received   */
PULONG        DataAddress;   /* Address of element received  */
ULONG         ElementCode;   /* Request a particular element */
BOOL32        NoWait;        /* No wait if queue is empty    */
BYTE          ElemPriority;  /* Priority of element received */
HEV           SemHandle;     /* Semaphore handle             */
PID           OwningPID;     /* PID of queue owner           */
APIRET        rc;            /* Return code                  */

Request.pid = OwningPID;     /* Set request data block to indicate */
                             /* queue owner                        */

ElementCode = 0;             /* Indicate that the read should start */
                             /* at the front of the queue           */

NoWait = 0;                  /* Indicate that the read should wait */
                             /* if the queue is currently empty    */

SemHandle = 0;               /* Unused since this is a call that */
                             /* waits synchronously             */

rc = DosReadQueue(QueueHandle, &Request, &DataLength,
                  (PVOID *) &DataAddress, ElementCode, NoWait,
                  &ElemPriority, SemHandle);

if (rc != 0) {
    printf("DosReadQueue error: return code = %ld", rc);
    return;
}
```

Figure 10-5. Reading an Element from a Queue

On successful return, *DataLength* contains the size of the element on the queue that is pointed to by the pointer within *DataAddress*, *ElemPriority* has been updated to contain the priority of the queue element pointed to by *DataAddress*, and *Request.ulData* contains any special data that the DosWriteQueue caller placed into the queue.

If the queue is empty and *NoWait* is set to DCWW_WAIT (0), the calling thread waits until an element is placed in the queue. If the queue is empty and *NoWait* is set to DCWW_NOWAIT (1), DosReadQueue returns immediately with ERROR_QUE_EMPTY.

If *NoWait* is set to DCWW_NOWAIT, an event semaphore must be provided so that the calling thread can determine when an element has been placed in the queue. The semaphore is created by calling DosCreateEventSem, and its handle is supplied as a DosReadQueue parameter. The first time an event semaphore handle is supplied in a DosReadQueue or DosPeekQueue request for which DCWW_NOWAIT has been specified for a particular queue, the handle is saved by the system. The same handle must be supplied in all subsequent DosReadQueue and DosPeekQueue requests that are called for that queue; if a different handle is supplied, ERROR_INVALID_PARAMETER is returned.

When a client process adds an element to the queue, the system automatically opens the semaphore (if necessary) and posts it. The server can either call DosQueryEventSem periodically to determine whether the semaphore has been posted, or it can call DosWaitEventSem. DosWaitEventSem causes the calling thread to block until the semaphore is posted.

After the event semaphore has been posted, the calling thread must call DosReadQueue again to remove the newly added queue element.

If QUE_CONVERT_ADDRESS is specified in the call to DosCreateQueue, the operating system will automatically convert 16-bit addresses to 32-bit addresses.

Peeking at a Queue

The server process and its threads can examine a queue element by calling DosPeekQueue. This function is not available to client processes.

Unlike DosReadQueue, DosPeekQueue does not remove the element from the queue.

DosPeekQueue can either examine elements in the order that was specified when the queue was created (FIFO, LIFO, or priority), or it can examine the next element in the queue after a previous DosPeekQueue request has been called. By making multiple DosPeekQueue requests, the server process can search through a queue, examining each element in turn. When it locates the element it is searching for, the server process can remove the element from the queue by calling DosReadQueue.

If several threads are using the same queue, the process writing to the queue can use the ulData field of the REQUESTDATA data structure to indicate that an element is directed to a particular thread. The thread can peek at the queue whenever data is available and read any elements containing the appropriate value in the ulData field.

The following code fragment shows how a thread can use DosPeekQueue to examine the elements in a queue. Assume that a previous call to DosOpenQueue provided the queue handle that is contained in *QueueHandle*. Assume that the identifier of the process that owns the queue has been placed into *OwningPID* already.

```
#define INCL_DOSQUEUES      /* Queue values */
#include <os2.h>
#include <stdio.h>

HQUEUE        QueueHandle;    /* Queue handle                          */
REQUESTDATA   Request;        /* Request-identification data   */
ULONG         DataLength;     /* Length of examined element    */
PVOID         DataAddress;    /* Address of examined element   */
ULONG         ElementCode;    /* Indicator of examined element */
BOOL32        NoWait;         /* No wait if queue is empty     */
BYTE          ElemPriority;   /* Priority of examined element  */
HEV           SemHandle;      /* Semaphore handle              */
PID           OwningPID;      /* PID of queue owner            */
APIRET        rc;             /* Return code                   */

Request.pid = OwningPID;      /* Set request data block to indicate  */
                              /* queue owner                         */

ElementCode = 0;              /* Indicate that the peek should start */
                              /* at the front of the queue           */

NoWait = DCWW_WAIT            /* Indicate that the peek call should  */
                              /* wait if the queue is currently empty */

SemHandle = 0;                /* Unused since this is a call that    */
                              /* synchronously waits                 */

rc = DosPeekQueue(QueueHandle, &Request, &DataLength,
                  &DataAddress, &ElementCode, NoWait,
                  &ElemPriority, SemHandle);

if (rc != 0) {
    printf("DosPeekQueue error: return code = %ld", rc);
    return;
}
```

Figure 10-6. Peeking at the Elements of a Queue

On successful return, *DataLength* contains the size of the element on the queue that is pointed to by the pointer within *DataAddress*, *ElementCode* has been updated to indicate the next queue element, *ElemPriority* has been updated to contain the priority of the queue element pointed to by *DataAddress*, and *Request.ulData* contains any special data that the DosWriteQueue caller placed into the queue.

If the queue is empty and *NoWait* is set to DCWW_WAIT (0), the calling thread waits until an element is placed in the queue. If the queue is empty and *NoWait* is set to DCWW_NOWAIT (1), DosPeekQueue returns immediately with ERROR_QUE_EMPTY.

If *NoWait* is set to DCWW_NOWAIT, an event semaphore must be provided so that the calling thread can determine when an element has been placed in the queue. The semaphore is created by calling DosCreateEventSem, and its handle is supplied as a DosPeekQueue parameter. The first time an event semaphore handle is supplied in a DosPeekQueue or DosReadQueue request for which DCWW_NOWAIT has been specified for a particular queue, the handle is saved by the system. The same handle must be supplied in all subsequent DosPeekQueue and DosReadQueue requests that are called for that queue; if a different handle is supplied, ERROR_INVALID_PARAMETER is returned.

When a client process adds an element to the queue, the system automatically opens the semaphore (if necessary) and posts it. The server can either call DosQueryEventSem periodically to determine whether the semaphore has been posted, or it can call DosWaitEventSem. DosWaitEventSem causes the calling thread to block until the semaphore is posted.

After the event semaphore has been posted, the calling thread must call DosPeekQueue again to examine the newly added queue element.

If QUE_CONVERT_ADDRESS is specified in the call to DosCreateQueue, the operating system will automatically convert 16-bit addresses to 32-bit addresses.

Purging a Queue

The server process or any of its threads can empty a queue of all its elements by calling DosPurgeQueue. This function is not available to client processes.

Warning: This is an unconditional purge of all elements in the queue.

The following code fragment shows how the owner of a queue can empty the queue of all data elements. Assume that the owner of the queue has saved the queue's handle (obtained in a previous call to DosCreateQueue) in *QueueHandle*.

```
#define INCL_DOSQUEUES    /* Queue values */
#include <os2.h>
#include <stdio.h>

HQUEUE   QueueHandle;      /* Queue handle */
APIRET   rc;              /* Return code */

rc = DosPurgeQueue(QueueHandle);

if (rc != 0) {
    printf("DosPurgeQueue error: return code = %ld", rc);
    return;
}
```

Figure 10-7. Purging a Queue

Closing a Queue

DosCloseQueue can be used both to end access to a queue and to delete a queue. The action taken as a result of a DosCloseQueue request depends on:

- Whether the requesting process is the server process or a client process
- The value of the access count, which is maintained for each client process by the operating system. The access count for a client process is incremented whenever DosOpenQueue is called, and decremented whenever DosCloseQueue is called.

If the requesting process is a client, and the access count equals 0, DosCloseQueue ends the client's access to the queue, but the queue itself is not affected. If the access count does not equal 0, the count is decremented, but the process retains access to the queue.

If the requesting process is the server, DosCloseQueue purges any outstanding elements from the queue and deletes the queue regardless of the access count; client processes that still have the queue open receive ERROR_QUE_INVALID_HANDLE on their next request.

Summary

Following are the OS/2 functions and the data structures used with queues.

Table 10-1. Queue Functions

Function	Description
DosCloseQueue	Closes a queue.
DosCreateQueue	Creates a queue.
DosOpenQueue	Opens a queue for use.
DosPeekQueue	Examines a queue element without removing it from the queue. Also returns information about the element it peeked at.
DosPurgeQueue	Empties a queue of all its elements.
DosQueryQueue	Returns the number of elements in a queue.
DosReadQueue	Reads (and removes) an element from a queue. Also returns information about the element it read.
DosWriteQueue	Writes an element to a queue.

Table 10-2. Queue Data Structures

Data Structure	Description
REQUESTDATA	Used to return information about a queue element, and about the process that added the element to the queue, when the element is read or peeked at.

Chapter 11. Timers

This chapter describes how to create and use timers. Timers enable applications to time events by waiting for an interval to elapse or by waiting for a semaphore to be posted.

The following topics are related to the information in this chapter:

- Program Execution and Control
- Semaphores.

About Timers

Because the OS/2 operating system is a multitasking system, an application cannot predict when it will lose execution control or how much time will elapse before control returns. A *timer* enables an application to suspend operation for a specific length of time, to block a thread until an interval has elapsed, or to post an event semaphore at repeated intervals.

Timers are managed by the operating system. When an application requests a timer, the system monitors the system clock and notifies the application when the interval has elapsed.

The system clock counts the number of system-clock interrupts (clock ticks) that have occurred since the system was started. On most hardware, clock ticks occur approximately 32 times a second, so the length of a tick is approximately 31.25 milliseconds.

When an application specifies a timer interval, the system rounds up the interval to the next clock tick. For example, if an application requests a 10 millisecond interval, it will sleep for at least 31.25 milliseconds. If an application requests a 100 millisecond interval, the actual interval will be at least 125 milliseconds (4 ticks).

Because the OS/2 operating system is a preemptive operating system, there is no guarantee that a thread will resume immediately after the timer interval. If a higher priority process or thread is executing, the timed thread must wait.

Although timers are not absolutely accurate, they can be used where the inaccuracy can be ignored. In a real-time control application, for example, an event can be timed in seconds or minutes, so an error of a few milliseconds is unimportant. If an application requires as much accuracy as the system can provide, it can dedicate a thread to managing timer intervals and then elevate the priority of that thread.

Suspending Threads

An application can use DosSleep to suspend operation of a thread for a specified interval. The system waits the specified number of milliseconds (subject to the round-off error just discussed) before returning control to the application. Because a sleeping application yields execution control to the system, the system can execute other processes or threads while the application sleeps.

The following code fragment shows how to suspend the calling thread for one minute:

```
#define INCL_DOSPROCESS    /* Process and thread values */
#include <os2.h>
#include <stdio.h>

ULONG   TimeInterval;      /* Interval in milliseconds  */
APIRET  rc;                /* Return code               */

TimeInterval = 60000;

rc = DosSleep(TimeInterval);

if (rc != 0) {
    printf("DosSleep error: return code = %ld", rc);
    return;
}
```

Figure 11-1. Suspending a Thread

See "Suspending the Current Thread" on page 7-31 for more information on DosSleep.

Asynchronous Timers

DosSleep is useful for temporarily suspending a thread but is much less useful for timing. Typically, an application carries out part of its task and then waits an interval. If the execution time varies (as it will if the application runs on different hardware), the overall interval varies. In these situations, asynchronous timers provide greater precision than DosSleep.

The OS/2 operating system supports two types of asynchronous timers, single-interval (one-shot) and repeated. DosAsyncTimer starts a single-interval timer. During the timing interval, the application can carry out other tasks. The system posts an event semaphore when the timing interval elapses. The application can reset the semaphore with DosResetEventSem before starting the timer. DosAsyncTimer yields a more accurate timing interval than DosSleep because the interval is independent of the execution time.

DosStartTimer starts a repeated timer. The system posts an event semaphore each time the interval expires. The application can reset the semaphore before starting the timer and after each posting. When the application resets the semaphore with DosResetEventSem, it can check the *cPosts* value to determine how many times the semaphore has been posted. If the semaphore has been posted more than once, the application has missed a timer interval.

Using Timers

Applications frequently need to synchronize the execution of threads, to cause an event to occur after a specified interval, or to cause an event to occur at regular intervals. Timers are typically used to enable an application to pause before processing user input or to carry out a task at a given time.

The operating system provides the following timer functions:

- DosSleep suspends the execution of the calling thread, enabling other threads to run while the calling thread sleeps.

- DosAsyncTimer starts a single-interval timer.

- DosStartTimer starts a repeated-interval timer.

- DosStopTimer stops a single-interval or repeated-interval timer.

The system also provides two functions, DosGetDateTime and DosSetDateTime, for getting and setting the system date and time.

The timers that are started by DosAsyncTimer and DosStartTimer are asynchronous timers; that is, the timers run independently of the calling thread, enabling the calling thread to perform other operations while the timer is running. When an asynchronous timer interval expires, the system notifies the application by posting an event semaphore.

Time intervals for DosAsyncTimer, DosStartTimer, and DosSleep are specified in milliseconds; however, it is important to recognize that the actual duration of the specified time interval will be affected by two factors:

- First, the system clock keeps track of time in less precise units known as *clock ticks*. On most hardware, clock ticks occur approximately 32 times a second, so each tick interval lasts approximately 31.25 milliseconds. (To determine the duration of a clock tick on your computer, call DosQuerySysInfo and examine the timer-interval field.)

  Because clock ticks are less precise than millisecond values, any time interval that is specified in milliseconds will essentially be rounded up to the next clock tick.

- Second, because the OS/2 operating system is a priority-based, multitasking operating system, there is no guarantee that a thread will resume execution immediately after the timer interval expires. If a higher priority process or thread is running, or if a hardware interrupt occurs, the timed thread blocks. (To minimize delays caused by preemptive scheduling, an application can dedicate a thread to managing time-critical tasks, and then raise that thread to a higher priority.)

These factors usually cause the timer interval to be longer than requested; however, it will generally be within a few clock ticks.

Timers for Presentation Manager applications are provided through the message queue. Therefore, a Presentation Manager application will not use the timer functions unless it performs some real-time control task.

Note: In the example code fragments that follow, error checking was left out to conserve space. Applications should always check the return code that the functions return. Control Program functions return an APIRET value. A return code of 0 indicates success. If a non-zero value is returned, an error occurred.

Suspending the Current Thread

An application can suspend a thread by using DosSleep. DosSleep suspends the execution of the calling thread for a specified time interval.

DosSleep requires one argument—the amount of time (in milliseconds) to suspend the thread. This value is rounded up to the nearest clock tick. If a time interval of 0 is specified, the thread gives up the remainder of the current time slice, enabling other ready threads of equal or higher priority to run; the calling thread will run again during its next scheduled time slice. If there is no other ready thread of equal or higher priority, DosSleep returns immediately; it does not yield to a thread of lower priority.

If there is a round-off error or if other threads in the system have higher priority, a thread might not resume execution immediately after the sleep interval.

The following DosSleep call suspends a thread for at least 5 seconds:

```
DosSleep(5000);
```

Note that the specified time interval refers to execution time (accumulated scheduled time slices), not to elapsed real time. Elapsed real time will be longer and will vary, depending on the hardware and on the number and priorities of other threads running in the system. In addition, even though the calling thread is scheduled for execution as soon as the specified time interval has elapsed, its execution could be delayed if a higher priority thread is running or if a hardware interrupt occurs.

Because the above factors usually cause the sleep interval to be longer than requested (though generally within a few clock ticks), DosSleep should not be used as a substitute for a real-time clock.

Note:

1. Elapsed real time for the asynchronous timers (started by DosAsyncTimer and DosStartTimer) will be much closer to their specified time intervals because these timers run independent of the execution of the calling thread.

2. To ensure optimal performance, do not use DosSleep in a single-thread Presentation Manager application. (Use WinStartTimer.)

Timing a Single Interval

To carry out other tasks while the timer counts an interval, an application can use DosAsyncTimer. This function sets a single-interval timer without stopping the application—the timer runs asynchronously to the calling thread, enabling the thread to perform other operations while it is waiting for the specified time interval to expire. When the interval elapses, the operating system notifies the application of the expiration of the timer by posting an event semaphore. The application resets the semaphore before starting the timer and monitors the semaphore to determine when the time has elapsed. The application can use DosCreateEventSem with the initial state FALSE to create a reset semaphore. For more information on semaphores, see Chapter 8, "Semaphores" on page 8-1.

The following code fragment creates an event semaphore and then calls DosAsyncTimer to count an interval while the application performs other tasks:

```
#define INCL_DOSDATETIME    /* Date/Time and Timer Support */
#include<os2.h>

HEV hev;
HTIMER hTimer;

/* First create a private, reset, event semaphore. */

DosCreateEventSem((PSZ) NULL, &hev, 0, FALSE);

/* Start async (one-shot) timer; post semaphore in 10 seconds. */

DosAsyncTimer(10000,        /* Time in milliseconds (10 sec)      */
              (HSEM) &hev, /* Semaphore handle                   */
              &hTimer);    /* Timer handle (used to stop timer) */

   .
   .     /* Do other processing here, then wait for semaphore. */
   .

DosWaitEventSem(hev, SEM_INDEFINITE_WAIT);
```

Figure 11-2. Using a Single-Interval Timer with an Event Semaphore

Before starting the timer, the thread creates the event semaphore with DosCreateEventSem, specifying its initial state as reset. If the semaphore was previously created by the same process, the thread resets it by calling DosResetEventSem. If the semaphore was previously created by another process, then the thread must call DosOpenEventSem to gain access to the semaphore before calling DosResetEventSem.

Next, the thread calls DosAsyncTimer, specifying the handle of the event semaphore and the desired time interval. The thread can then perform other tasks. However, in order for the application to be notified of the expiration of the timer, one or more threads in the application must call DosWaitEventSem.

When the time interval expires, the system posts the semaphore, and any threads that were blocked on DosWaitEventSem requests can resume their execution. If another time interval is required, the semaphore is reset, and both DosAsyncTimer and DosWaitEventSem are called again. (To time regular repeated intervals, use DosStartTimer.)

The timer can be canceled before its time interval expires by calling DosStopTimer.

Timing Repeated Intervals

To count an interval repeatedly, an application can use DosStartTimer. This function starts a repeated-interval timer.

Unlike DosAsyncTimer, DosStartTimer does not stop after the first interval is counted. The timer runs asynchronously to the calling thread, enabling the thread to perform other operations while it is waiting for the specified time intervals to expire. The system notifies the application of the timer's expirations by posting an event semaphore.

The application resets the semaphore before starting the timer and whenever the system posts the semaphore. The application can use the value returned in the post-counting parameter by DosResetEventSem to assure the semaphore was posted only once before it was reset.

The following code fragment starts a timer and then waits on and resets the associated event semaphore. Assume that the handle of the targeted event semaphore has been placed into *SemHandle*.

```
#define INCL_DOSDATETIME    /* Date and time values */
#include <os2.h>
#include <stdio.h>

ULONG     TimeInterval; /* Interval (milliseconds) */
HSEM      SemHandle;    /* Event-semaphore handle  */
HTIMER    Handle;       /* Timer handle (returned) */
APIRET    rc;           /* Return code             */

TimeInterval = 30000;  /* Set the periodic time interval to */
                       /* elapse every 30 seconds           */

rc = DosStartTimer(TimeInterval, SemHandle, &Handle);

if (rc != 0) {
    printf("DosStartTimer error: return code = %ld", rc);
    return;
}
```

Figure 11-3. Using a Repeated-Interval Timer with an Event Semaphore

On successful return, *Handle* will contain the handle of this periodic timer. DosStopTimer can be used later to stop the periodic timer.

A repeated timer will continue to count the interval and post the semaphore until the application terminates or the application uses DosStopTimer to stop the timer explicitly. The following code fragment shows how to stop a periodic timer that has been started previously with DosStartTimer:

```
#define INCL_DOSDATETIME   /* Date and time values */
#include <os2.h>
#include <stdio.h>

HTIMER    Handle;    /* Handle of the timer */
APIRET    rc;        /* Return code         */

rc = DosStopTimer(Handle);

if (rc != 0) {
    printf("DosStopTimer error: return code = %ld", rc);
    return;
}
```

Figure 11-4. Stopping a Repeated-Interval Timer

Before starting the timer, the event semaphore must be reset. If the semaphore does not exist, the thread can create it with DosCreateEventSem, specifying its initial state as reset. If the semaphore was previously created by the same process, the thread resets it by calling DosResetEventSem. If the semaphore was previously created by another process, then the thread calls DosOpenEventSem to gain access to the semaphore before calling DosResetEventSem.

Next, the thread calls DosStartTimer, specifying the handle of the event semaphore and the desired time interval. The thread can then perform other tasks. However, in order for the application to be notified of the timer's expirations, one or more threads in the application must call DosWaitEventSem.

When the time interval expires, the system posts the semaphore, and any threads that were blocked on DosWaitEventSem requests can resume their execution. Each time the semaphore is posted, it must be reset with DosResetEventSem before the next timer expiration. DosWaitEventSem must also be called to wait for the semaphore to be posted again.

In addition to resetting the event semaphore, DosResetEventSem returns the semaphore's post count (the number of times the semaphore has been posted since the last time it was in the set state). An application can use the post count to ensure that it has not missed a timer interval; if the post count is greater than one, the application missed a timer interval.

Summary

Following are the OS/2 functions used with timers.

Table 11-1. Timer Functions	
Function	**Description**
DosAsyncTimer	Starts an asynchronous, single-interval timer.
DosSleep	Suspends the current thread for a specified time interval.
DosStartTimer	Starts an asynchronous, repeated-interval timer.
DosStopTimer	Stops an asynchronous, single-interval or repeated-interval timer.

Chapter 12. Error Management

Error checking and error handling is extremely important in a multitasking operating system. The conditions in which an application is executing can change at any time due to the activity of other programs executing concurrently with the application. This chapter describes the functions that an application can use to manage errors that occur during processing.

The following topic is related to the information in this chapter:

- Exception Management.

About Error Management

Successful completion of most Control Program functions is indicated by an error return code of 0. In the event of an error, Control Program functions usually return an error code that has a non-zero integer value. The non-zero value equates to a symbolic error identifier in the include file, BSEERR.H. The symbolic identifiers indicate the cause of the error. For example, a return code of 2 from DosOpen equates to the symbolic identifier ERROR_FILE_NOT_FOUND; the cause of the error is that the file being opened cannot be found.

DosErrClass and DosError are supplied to assist in error processing.

- DosErrClass takes as input a non-zero return value that was received from any control-program function. (Any return value other than 0 indicates that an error occurred.) The output is a classification of the error and a recommended action. Depending on the application, the recommended action could be followed, or a specific recovery action could be performed.

- DosError enables an application to prevent the operating system from displaying a default error message in a pop-up window when either a hard error or a software exception occurs.

Classifying Return Values

When a control-program function has been successfully completed, a return value of 0 is returned to the calling thread. A non-zero return value indicates that an error has occurred.

Each non-zero value corresponds to a symbolic error identifier that indicates the cause of the error. For example, a return value of 2 from DosOpen (indicating that the file was not found) corresponds to the symbolic identifier ERROR_FILE_NOT_FOUND.

DosErrClass helps applications deal with non-zero return values by taking a return value as input and returning both an error classification and a recommended action. Depending on the application, the recommended action could be followed, or a more specific recovery routine could be executed.

Disabling Error Notification

A hard error is typically an error (such as the opening of a disk-drive door while a diskette is being read, or any similar kind of device error) that cannot be resolved by software. When a hard error occurs, the system default action is to prompt for user input by displaying a message in a pop-up window.

DosError disables the default action, foregoing the displayed message and causing an appropriate return value to be returned to whichever control-program function was running when the hard error occurred. The application must determine the appropriate response by referring to the return value.

DosError also enables the application to disable end-user notification if either a program exception or an untrapped numeric-processor exception occurs. However, if one of these exceptions occurs while user notification is disabled, the application will still be ended.

As with hard errors, the system default is that user notification for these exceptions is enabled.

Using Error Management

The OS/2 operating system supplies DosErrClass and DosError for error processing. DosErrClass aids in determining the appropriate action that an application should take in response to an error. DosError enables applications to disable the pop-up windows used by the operating system to inform the user of a hard-error or an exception.

Note: In the example code fragments that follow, error checking was left out to conserve space. Applications should always check the return code that the functions return. Control Program functions return an APIRET value. A return code of 0 indicates success. If a non-zero value is returned, an error occurred.

Classifying Errors

DosErrClass receives a non-zero return value from another control-program function as input. It then classifies the return value, tells where in the system the error occurred, and recommends a corrective action.

In the following example, an attempt is made to delete a nonexistent file. The return value is then passed to DosErrClass so that more information about the error can be obtained, including any corrective actions that can be taken.

```
#define INCL_DOSQUEUES
#include <os2.h>

#define FILE_DELETE "JUNK.FIL"

ULONG   Error;
ULONG   Class;
ULONG   Action;
ULONG   Locus;
APIRET  rc;

Error = DosDelete(FILE_DELETE);     /* File name path                */

rc = DosErrClass(Error,             /* Return value to be analyzed   */
                 &Class,            /* Error classification          */
                 &Action,           /* Recommended corrective action */
                 &Locus);           /* Where the error occurred      */
```

Figure 12-1. Classifying File Errors

When called by a family-mode application, this function can return a valid error classification only for errors that have actually occurred. Also, the classifications of a given return value might not be the same for family-mode and OS/2-mode applications.

Disabling Hard-Error and Exception Messages

DosError disables or enables end-user notification of hard errors, program exceptions, or untrapped, numeric-processor exceptions.

In the following example, pop-up windows for hard errors and exceptions are disabled, then enabled again.

```
#define INCL_DOSMISC   /* Error and exception values */
#include <os2.h>

#define ENABLE_HARDERROR    1
#define DISABLE_HARDERROR   0
#define ENABLE_EXCEPTION    0
#define DISABLE_EXCEPTION   2
#define ENABLE_ERRORPOPUPS  ENABLE_EXCEPTION | ENABLE_HARDERROR
#define DISABLE_ERRORPOPUPS DISABLE_EXCEPTION | DISABLE_HARDERROR

APIRET rc;    /* Return code */

rc = DosError(DISABLE_ERRORPOPUPS);  /* Action flag for disable */
rc = DosError(ENABLE_ERRORPOPUPS);   /* Action flag for enable  */
```

Figure 12-2. Disabling and Enabling Hard-Error and Exception Messages

The action to take is encoded as a binary flag. The following table shows the bit-values and their meanings.

Table 12-1. Bit Values to Enable and Disable Hard-Error and Exception Pop-up Messages

Bit	Value	Meaning
0	1	Enables hard-error pop-up messages.
0	0	Disables hard-error pop-up messages.
1	0	Enables exception pop-up messages.
1	1	Disables exception pop-up messages.

If DosError is not called, user notification for hard errors and exceptions is enabled by default.

Summary

Following are the OS/2 functions used for error management.

Table 12-2. Error Management Functions

Function	Description
DosErrClass	Returns information on the classification of a non-zero return code, and a recommended corrective action.
DosError	Disables and enables hard-error and exception pop-up messages.

Chapter 13. Exception Management

An *exception* is an abnormal condition that can occur during program execution. Common causes of exceptions include:

- I/O errors
- Protection violations
- Math errors
- Intervention by the user or by another process.

Activities that can cause exceptions include:

- Trying to use memory that you do not have permission to access
- Dividing by 0
- The user pressing Ctrl+Break.

Exceptions include both unexpected errors (such as a memory protection violation) and expected errors (such as guard-page exceptions). Exceptions can be a *synchronous exception*, that is, caused by an action of the executing thread, or an *asynchronous exception*, caused by an event external to the executing thread (such as the user pressing Ctrl+Break). When an exception is caused by the user pressing Ctrl+Break or Ctrl+C, or by another process issuing DosKillProcess for your process, the exception is called a *signal exception*.

In most cases, the default action taken by the operating system when an exception occurs is to terminate the application that caused the exception. Rather than having the operating system default action occur, an application can register its own subroutine to handle exceptions. These routines are called *exception handlers*. Exception handlers enable an application to handle some errors itself, allowing the application to avoid termination (or at least to terminate gracefully).

When exception handlers are registered, they are added to an *exception handler chain*. The chain starts empty and each new handler is added to the head of the chain. Exceptions are passed to the exception handlers in the chain in Last-In-First-Out order, so the last exception handler to be registered is the first one to get an opportunity to handle each exception.

Exception handlers have the capability to complete critical code sections without being interrupted by other asynchronous exceptions; these critical code sections are called *must-complete* sections.

Exception handlers can be removed from the exception handler chains with DosUnsetExceptionHandler. Another way that exception handlers can be removed from the chain is with an *unwind* operation. When unwinding an exception handler, the exception handler is first called, then removed from the exception handler chain.

The following topics are related to the information in this chapter:

- Memory
- Program Execution and Control.

About Exception Management

A multitasking operating system must manage applications carefully. A serious error (such as an attempt to access protected memory) occurring in one application cannot be permitted to damage any other application in the system. To manage errors that might damage other applications, the OS/2 operating system defines a class of error conditions called exceptions and defines default actions for those errors.

When an exception occurs, the default action taken by the operating system is usually to terminate the application causing the exception (unless the application has registered its own exception handling routines). In some cases, when the exception can safely be ignored, execution is allowed to continue.

Rather than having the operating system default action occur, an application can register its own *exception handlers* routines. An exception handler routine could be written to correct certain error conditions—when these error conditions occur, the thread's exception handler gets the exception, corrects the condition, and the thread continues executing rather than being terminated immediately by the operating system. The operating system's default action is taken if there are no user-defined exception handling routines or if all user-defined routines return without handling the exception.

An application can use DosSetExceptionHandler to register an exception handling routine. DosSetExceptionHandler takes a pointer to an ExceptionRegistrationRecord data structure as its only argument. The first field in this data structure is a pointer to the previous exception handler in the chain. This field is maintained by the operating system and must never be modified by an application. The second field is a pointer to the exception handling routine that will be registered by the operating system.

A single exception handler can be used to handle all the exceptions that you choose to handle. It is not necessary to have a separate exception handler for each exception.

Once an exception handling routine is registered, the system will notify it when an exception occurs. The operating system sends synchronous exceptions only to the thread causing the exception. An application must register an exception handler for each thread that is handling exceptions. When the operating system terminates an application, however, a process-termination exception is sent to all threads used by the application to be terminated. When the user presses Ctrl+Break, an asynchronous signal exception is sent only to Thread 1, the main thread, of the executing process.

The exception handling routine is passed the following four parameters that provide exception-specific information:

ExceptionReportRecord
Describes the exception and its parameters. The first field of this data structure contains the number of the exception that occurred.

ExceptionRegistrationRecord
The ExceptionRegistrationRecord data structure used to initially register the exception handler. This is a microprocessor-specific value.

ContextRecord

Describes the machine state at the time the exception occurred.

DispatcherContext

Contains state information on nested exception and collided unwinds. This information must not be modified by the application.

Details of the parameters and data structures can be found in "Exception Handler Interface" on page 13-15.

The operating system places the exception handlers for each thread in an *exception handler chain*. Registering an exception handler adds it to the head of the chain.

When an application registers an exception handler, the exception handler is added to the head of the chain. If the application calls a routine in a dynamic link library (DLL), the DLL might register an exception handler in case there is an exception while its code is executing; the DLL deregisters the exception handler before returning control to the application. The DLL's exception handler would be ahead of the application's exception handler in the chain.

Exception handlers in the chain are notified of an exception in Last-In-First-Out (LIFO) order. Thus, if an exception occurs while your thread is executing, the exception handler for your thread is notified of the exception first. If your exception handler chooses to handle the exception, the earlier exception handlers in the chain never see the exception. If your exception handler chooses not to handle the exception, it is passed along to the next earlier exception handler in the chain. If no exception handler in the chain chooses to handle the exception, the operating system takes the default action for the exception.

If an exception happens while DLL code is executing, and if the DLL's exception handler chooses to handle the exception, your application's exception handlers will never be aware it.

System Exceptions

The operating system defines a class of error conditions called *system exceptions*, and specifies the default actions that are taken when these system exceptions occur. The default action taken by the operating system in most cases is to terminate the thread that caused the system exception.

System exceptions include both synchronous and asynchronous exceptions. *Synchronous exceptions* are caused by events that are internal to the execution of a thread. For example, synchronous exceptions could be caused by invalid parameters, or by the request of a thread to end its own execution.

Asynchronous exceptions are caused by events that are external to the execution of a thread. For example, an asynchronous exception can be caused by a user entering a Ctrl+C or Ctrl+Break key sequence, or by a process calling DosKillProcess to end the execution of another process.

The Ctrl+Break, Ctrl+C, and DosKillProcess-generated exceptions are also known as *signals*, or as *signal exceptions*.

The operating system delivers exceptions that occur in 16-bit as well as 32-bit code. The sequence or hierarchy for delivering exceptions is as follows:

- When an exception occurs in 32-bit code, the system gives control only to the 32-bit exception handlers registered for the current thread. If the thread has not registered any 32-bit handlers, the system default action occurs.

- When an exception occurs in 16-bit code, the system first gives control to the 32-bit exception handlers registered for the current thread. If the exception is not handled by one of these handlers, control is passed to the 16-bit handler, if one exists for the given exception. If there is no 16-bit handler for the exception, the system default action occurs.

Notification of an exception is usually sent only to the thread that caused the exception. However, if a thread uses DosExit to terminate all the threads in the process, notification of the process-termination exception is sent to every thread in the process. The thread that used DosExit gets a XCPT_PROCESS_TERMINATE exception, all the other threads in the process get a XCPT_ASYNC_PROCESS_TERMINATE exception.

Exit-list processing occurs on a per-process basis after a process-termination exception has been delivered to each thread in the process and each thread has finally ended except Thread 1 (the main thread). Therefore, any thread that handles a process-termination exception must eventually end its own execution voluntarily. Otherwise, the process-termination sequence will not conclude properly.

The following tables briefly list the possible exceptions. For more detailed information about the system exceptions, including default system action, parameters, and related trap numbers, see the *Control Program Programming Reference*.

Table 13-1. Non-Fatal, Software-Generated Exceptions

Exception Symbolic Constant	Description
XCPT_GUARD_PAGE_VIOLATION	A guard page has been accessed.
XCPT_UNABLE_TO_GROW_STACK	The system is unable to allocate the memory page directly below the guard page just accessed.

Table 13-2. Fatal, Software-Generated Exceptions

Exception Symbolic Constant	Description
XCPT_IN_PAGE_ERROR	An I/O error occurred while reading a memory page into memory.
XCPT_PROCESS_TERMINATE	The thread has terminated itself with DosExit.
XCPT_ASYNC_PROCESS_TERMINATE	Another thread in the process has caused the thread to terminate.
XCPT_NONCONTINUABLE_EXCEPTION	An exception handler has attempted to continue execution in response to a non-continuable exception.
XCPT_INVALID_DISPOSITION	An exception handler has returned an invalid value.

Table 13-3. Fatal, Hardware-Generated Exceptions

Exception Symbolic Constant	Description
XCPT_ACCESS_VIOLATION	An access violation or page fault has occurred.
XCPT_INTEGER_DIVIDE_BY_ZERO	An attempt to divide by 0 has occurred in an integer operation.
XCPT_FLOAT_DIVIDE_BY_ZERO	An attempt to divide by 0 has occurred in a floating point operation.
XCPT_FLOAT_INVALID_OPERATION	An invalid floating point operation was attempted.
XCPT_ILLEGAL_INSTRUCTION	An attempt was made to execute an instruction that is not defined on the host machine's architecture.
XCPT_PRIVILEGED_INSTRUCTION	An attempt was made to execute an instruction that is not permitted in the current machine mode or that the application does not have permission to execute.
XCPT_INTEGER_OVERFLOW	An integer operation generated a carry-out of the most significant bit.
XCPT_FLOAT_OVERFLOW	A floating point operation generated a resulting exponent that is greater than the magnitude permitted for the operands.
XCPT_FLOAT_UNDERFLOW	A floating point operation generated a resulting exponent that is less than the magnitude provided for the operands.
XCPT_FLOAT_DENORMAL_OPERAND	An attempt was made to perform an arithmetic operation on a denormal operand.
XCPT_FLOAT_INEXACT_RESULT	The result of an operation is not exactly representable in the target format.
XCPT_FLOAT_STACK_CHECK	An illegal stack operation was attempted by the floating point coprocessor.
XCPT_DATATYPE_MISALIGNMENT	An attempt was made to store a data in an address that is not naturally aligned on a hardware architecture that does not provide alignment hardware.
XCPT_BREAKPOINT	A breakpoint instruction was executed.
XCPT_SINGLE_STEP	One instruction has been executed in single-step mode.

Table 13-4. Fatal Exceptions

Exception Symbolic Constant	Description
XCPT_INVALID_LOCK_SEQUENCE	An invalid operation was attempted within an interlocked section of code.
XCPT_ARRAY_BOUNDS_EXCEEDED	An array index outside its upper and lower boundary was detected.

Table 13-5. Unwind Operation Exceptions

Exception Symbolic Constant	Description
XCPT_UNWIND	An unwind operation is in process.
XCPT_BAD_STACK	An ExceptionRegistrationRecord data structure was reached that is not properly aligned or that is not within the current stack boundaries.
XCPT_INVALID_UNWIND_TARGET	The address of the target ExceptionRegistrationRecord is below the current stack pointer or not in the exception handler chain.

Table 13-6. Fatal Signal Exceptions

Exception Symbolic Constant	Description
XCPT_SIGNAL	A signal was made to your process (usually to stop). All the signal exceptions (Ctrl+Break, Ctrl+C, and XCPT_SIGNAL_KILLPROC) come under this exception.

Signal Exceptions

Signal exceptions are special events sent to a thread when the user presses certain key sequences or when another thread or process explicitly initiates the exception. There are three types of signal exceptions:

XCPT_SIGNAL_BREAK
When the user presses Ctrl+Break
XCPT_SIGNAL_INTR
When the user presses Ctrl+C
XCPT_SIGNAL_KILLPROC
When another process uses DosKillProcess to send a XCPT_SIGNAL_KILLPROC exception to your process.

Signal exceptions are sent only to Thread 1 (the main thread) in the process receiving the exception. If an exception handler is registered on Thread 1, it must be prepared to receive signal exceptions. The thread 1 exception handler can always ignore the signal exception by returning XCPT_CONTINUE_SEARCH.

If the thread 1 exception handler is to receive signal exceptions, it must use DosSetSignalExceptionFocus to notify the operating system that it wants to receive the XCPT_SIGNAL_INTR (Ctrl+C) and XCPT_SIGNAL_BREAK (Ctrl+Break) signals. Otherwise, these exceptions are not passed to the exception handler and the default action—to terminate the process—is taken by the operating system. The thread will get XCPT_SIGNAL_KILLPROC signals whether it uses DosSetSignalExceptionFocus or not.

All three of these signals are delivered by a single exception—XCPT_SIGNAL—and the exception handler for Thread 1 can choose to handle none, some, or all of the signals. The signal being sent can be determined by examining the exception information in ExceptionReportRecord.

The following table provides information about each type of signal.

Table 13-7. Signal Exceptions		
Signal	**Symbolic Constant**	**Description**
Ctrl+Break	XCPT_SIGNAL_BREAK	This exception is sent to Thread 1 in the current keyboard-focus process when a Ctrl+Break key sequence is received from the keyboard. The default action taken by the operating system for this exception is forced process termination.
Ctrl+C	XCPT_SIGNAL_INTR	This exception is sent to Thread 1 in the current keyboard-focus process when a Ctrl+C key sequence is received from the keyboard. The default action taken by the operating system for this exception is forced process termination.
Kill Process Signal	XCPT_SIGNAL_KILLPROC	This exception is sent to Thread 1 in the process specified when an application uses DosKillProcess. The XCPT_SIGNAL_KILLPROC signal exception results from an action external to the process. The default action taken by the operating system for this exception is forced process termination.

Handling Signal Exceptions

To handle signal exceptions, a process must first call DosSetExceptionHandler to register a handler for the exceptions. Next, the process must call DosSetSignalExceptionFocus, with the *Flag* parameter set to ON, in order to receive signal exceptions.

After a process calls DosSetSignalExceptionFocus, it remains the signal focus for its screen group until it calls DosSetSignalExceptionFocus again with the *Flag* parameter set to OFF, or until another process in the screen group makes a call to the same function with *Flag* set to ON.

Each call to DosSetSignalExceptionFocus with *Flag* set to ON increments a counter in the per-task data area of the process. Each call with *Flag* set to OFF decrements the counter. When a signal exception occurs, the system checks to see whether the value of the counter is greater than 0. If it is, the signal is sent.

DosSetSignalExceptionFocus returns ERROR_NESTED_TOO_DEEP if the value of the counter exceeds 65535. If a thread tries to turn off the signal focus when the value of the counter is 0, ERROR_ALREADY_RESET is returned.

All 32-bit exception handlers that are attached to thread 1 of the process will be given an opportunity to handle the signal. If no 32-bit exception handler returns XCPT_CONTINUE_EXECUTION in response to the signal, then the 16-bit handler for the signal will be executed, if one exists; if none exists, then the process will be terminated.

In order to continue receiving signals, the process must either return XCPT_CONTINUE_EXECUTION from a 32-bit exception handler, or it must call the 16-bit DosSetSigHandler function, specifying SIG_ACKNOWLEDGE as the value of the *Action* parameter to acknowledge the signal, or call DosAcknowledgeSignalException.

The typematic facility of the keyboard could cause a Ctrl+C or Ctrl+Break signal exception to repeat. For this reason, the system holds these exceptions until an exception handler returns XCPT_CONTINUE_EXECUTION, or calls DosAcknowledgeSignalException. However, only one signal exception is actually held; they are not queued by the system.

See "Must-Complete Sections" on page 13-11 for information about how a process can defer the handling of signal exceptions.

Sending Signal Exceptions

A process can send the XCPT_SIGNAL signal exception to another process by calling DosSendSignalException.

In order for the specified process to receive the exception, it must have an exception handler registered for Thread 1, and it must designate itself as the signal focus for its screen group by calling DosSetSignalExceptionFocus.

Presentation Manager applications cannot request exception focus for Ctrl+C and Ctrl+Break. However, establishing an exception handler for Ctrl+C and Ctrl+Break is supported for Vio-Window and full-screen applications.

Raising Exceptions

Asynchronous exceptions that have been deferred in a must-complete section are dispatched automatically by the system when the thread exits the must-complete section. However, a synchronous exception that has been deferred must be raised by calling DosRaiseException.

DosRaiseException can also be used to simulate either an asynchronous or synchronous exception. For example, a floating point emulator (a program that emulates a numeric coprocessor) can use this function to simulate an NPX exception.

Raising a software exception captures the machine state of the current thread in a ContextRecord data structure. The ExceptionAddress field of ExceptionReportRecord is set to the return address of the caller, as are the corresponding fields of the ContextRecord data structure. The system then calls each exception handler on the list, passing each a pointer to ExceptionReportRecord and the created ContextRecord data structures. In the case of a continuable exception for which XCPT_CONTINUE_EXECUTION is returned, DosRaiseException restores the potentially modified context back into the machine before returning. Note that control cannot return to the caller of DosRaiseException if the instruction pointer in ContextRecord has been modified.

The caller of DosRaiseException can set the EH_NONCONTINUABLE bit in the flags field of the ExceptionReportRecord data structure. By doing so, the caller guarantees that it is never returned to after the call to DosRaiseException. Note that once set, the EH_NONCONTINUABLE bit cannot be modified by any exception handler. The system will enforce this.

Following are some possible scenarios that might occur after a call to DosRaiseException has been made:

- If one of the exception handlers returns from a continuable exception with a status of XCPT_CONTINUE_EXECUTION, DosRaiseException returns NO_ERROR to the caller, and the thread resumes execution.

- If one of the exception handlers returns from a noncontinuable exception with a status of XCPT_CONTINUE_EXECUTION, the process is terminated, because it is illegal to return XCPT_CONTINUE_EXECUTION from a noncontinuable exception.

- If none of the exception handlers in the thread's chain of handlers returns with a status of XCPT_CONTINUE_EXECUTION, then the action taken depends on the exception number:

  - If the exception number indicates a user-assigned exception or an unassigned system exception, the process is terminated.

  - If the exception number is assigned to a system exception, and CS:EIP points to 32-bit code, no 16-bit handlers are called and the system default action is taken. Depending on which system exception has been raised, the default action is either to terminate the process, or to continue execution of the thread with NO_ERROR returned to the caller.

  - If the exception number is assigned to a system exception that maps to a 16-bit exception and CS:EIP points to 16-bit code, a 16-bit exception handler is called, if one is registered. Otherwise the operating system takes the default action.

User-Defined Exceptions

Exceptions can also be defined by the application. These are called *user-defined exceptions* (as opposed to system-defined exceptions, which are those exceptions defined by the operating system). Applications can define an exception in the following fashion:

```
#define XCPT_YOUR_EXCEPTION 0xE004ABCD
```

The application then raises the exception, using DosRaiseException:

```
DosRaiseException(XCPT_YOUR_EXCEPTION);
```

The exception handlers in the exception handler chain that are ahead of the application's exception handler will see the exception, but they will not recognize it, so they will return XCPT_CONTINUE_SEARCH. Only the application's exception handler will recognize the exception.

The application's exception handler must return XCPT_CONTINUE_EXECUTION so that the exception will not continue to be passed down the exception handler chain.

Must-Complete Sections

A thread can defer the handling of *asynchronous* exceptions by creating a *must-complete section*. A must-complete section is a section of code that cannot be safely interrupted; it must be allowed to complete its execution even if an asynchronous exception occurs while within its boundaries. For example, a must-complete section can be used:

- When modifying shared-memory data structures that cannot be modified through an atomic operation
- Across database update operations
- During a remote communications operation.

Creating a must-complete section ensures that the execution of critical instructions will be completed and that resources will be cleaned up before the thread ends. When used in conjunction with a *mutual exclusion (mutex) semaphore*, a must-complete section also ensures that a thread will have exclusive access to a resource.

The boundaries of the must-complete section are defined by DosEnterMustComplete and DosExitMustComplete requests. While a thread is executing instructions in a must-complete section, the system will hold *asynchronous exceptions*, which include signal exceptions and asynchronous process terminations.

The system increments a counter each time DosEnterMustComplete is called, and decrements the counter when DosExitMustComplete is called. Any asynchronous exceptions that have been held are dispatched when the counter reaches 0. A count greater than 1 indicates the degree of nesting of the must-complete section. If DosExitMustComplete is called when the count is already 0, ERROR_ALREADY_RESET is returned.

The handling of *synchronous* system exceptions and user-defined exceptions is not deferred by the system. To defer the handling of these exceptions, a procedure typically registers an exception handler (by calling DosSetExceptionHandler) and initializes a local *Raise Exception* flag to 0 before entering the must-complete section. The flag is set to 1, and the information is stored, if the exception handler receives a synchronous exception that it wants to reraise later.

If the value of the *raise exception* flag is 0 after the thread exits from the must-complete section, then no exceptions occurred, and the thread continues its normal operation.

If the value of the flag is 1 after the must-complete section has been completed, then an exception occurred, and the thread must call DosRaiseException to raise the deferred exception for handling.

Note: A thread must not call a function that is outside the scope of the must-complete section (for example, a DLL routine), because an error in the called routine could cause the process to end without returning. Keep must-complete sections as short as possible.

Unwinding Exception Handlers

In addition to handling exceptions, exception handlers are used to clean up resources during the execution of a nonlocal GOTO instruction or during thread termination. (A nonlocal GOTO instruction jumps to a label outside the current procedure. The label is a procedure address or an address within a procedure that is on the stack, higher in the call frame chain.)

DosUnwindException calls and removes exception handlers from a thread's chain of registered exception handlers up to, but not including, a specified exception handler. This is known as an *unwind operation*. DosUnwindException can also be used to unwind all exception handlers from the thread's exception handler chain and to terminate the thread.

For example, with the C language setjmp() and longjmp() routines, the setjmp() would save the address of the current exception handler structure, along with any other information that is necessary to perform the longjmp() routine. (The address of the current exception handler structure is obtained from the head of the exception handler chain. A pointer to the head of the chain is located in the Thread Information Block.)

The longjmp() routine would initiate the unwind of procedure call frames by calling DosUnwindException and passing to it the saved address of the ExceptionRegistrationRecord data structure. If the address of the ExceptionRegistrationRecord data structure is not found in the chain, then the XCPT_INVALID_UNWIND_TARGET exception is raised, and the chain is not unwound.

The machine state at the time of the call to DosUnwindException is captured in ContextRecord. The EH_UNWINDING flag is set in the exception flags field of the ExceptionReportRecord data structure. The EH_EXIT_UNWIND flag is also set if the ExceptionRegistrationRecord parameter is set to 0 (if the application does not provide its own ExceptionReportRecord parameter the operating system will construct one). A backward walk through the procedure call frames is then performed to find the target of the unwind operation.

The first parameter to DosUnwindException is the address of an exception handler's EXCEPTIONREGISTRATIONRECORD. DosUnwindException will unwind exception handlers up to, but not including that exception handler. If a -1 is passed to

DosUnwindException for this parameter, DosUnwindException will unwind all the exception handlers on the chain. If a 0 is passed to DosUnwindException for this parameter, DosUnwindException will unwind all the exception handlers on the chain and exit.

There is no return from a call to DosUnwindException, unless the stack is invalid. Control is transferred to the specified instruction pointer address. If DosUnwindException encounters an error during its processing, it raises another exception rather than return control to the caller.

If the target call frame is reached and an exit unwind is not being performed (that is, an ExceptionRegistrationRecord is not 0), then the computed machine state is restored from ContextRecord and control is transferred to the address specified by the target-IP address parameter. Note that the stack pointer is not restored, making it possible to transfer information on the stack. It is the responsibility of the code at the target address to reset the stack pointer as necessary.

DosUnwindException is called with C language calling conventions, which permits the use of a variable number of arguments. Thus, the caller can pass any amount of information on the stack, to be picked up at the target-IP address.

If an exit unwind is being performed (the ExceptionRegistrationRecord parameter is 0 or -1), then all call frames are unwound until the base of the stack is reached.

If the ExceptionReportRecord parameter is specified, then each exception handler encountered during the unwind operation is called, using the specified record. If this parameter is not specified, then DosUnwindException constructs an ExceptionReportRecord that specifies the exception XCPT_UNWIND.

Colliding Unwinds

During an unwind operation, it is possible for one unwind to collide with a previous unwind. This occurs when the scope of the second unwind overlaps the scope of the first unwind. Following are two situations:

- The target frame of the second unwind is a frame that has already been unwound by the first unwind.

- The target frame of the second unwind is a valid frame that is positioned before or after the target frame of the first unwind.

Either of these situations could occur during the following scenarios:

- An unwind handler calls unwind, or

- An unwind handler hits an exception that has called unwind.

In the first scenario, the second unwind is attempting to unwind to an invalid target. This causes the exception XCPT_INVALID_UNWIND_TARGET to be raised.

In the second scenario, the first unwind is abandoned, and the second unwind continues to its target. The second scenario is far more likely.

Note: A user program that uses high level language exception mechanisms must never call DosUnwindException, because this could create conflicts with the runtime exception strategy of the high level language. Unwind operations in this case are performed through language-supported facilities such as the C language longjmp() routine.

Nested Exceptions

A *nested exception* is an exception that occurs while another exception is being handled.

The operating system supports nested exceptions because an unhandled exception that occurs in an exception handler should be handled at a higher level—that is, by an ancestor of the procedure that registered the offending handler.

When a nested exception occurs, the EH_NESTED_CALL flag is set in the exception structure to indicate that a nested function call is being made. The normal convention then is for the handler to return immediately without handling the exception if the EH_NESTED_CALL flag is set. Without this flag, it would be easy to create an infinitely recursive situation.

For example, suppose we have the following scenario:

1. Procedure main calls procedure PA, which establishes exception handler HA.
2. Procedure PA calls procedure PB, which establishes exception handler HB.
3. Procedure PB calls procedure PC, which establishes exception handler HC.
4. Procedure PC calls procedure PD.

The chain of exception handlers now looks like the following figure.

TIB (Thread Information Block)

Figure 13-1. Exception Handler Chain with Nested Exceptions

Now suppose that procedure PD causes an exception. The system refers to the current thread's chain of exception handlers.

Because procedure PD has no handler, the system calls HC, the handler for procedure PC, with the EH_NESTED_CALL flag clear. If handler HC returns CONTINUE_SEARCH, the system calls the next handler in the chain, handler HB, again with the EH_NESTED_CALL flag clear.

Now suppose that exception handler HB causes an exception while it is processing the original exception. The call frames for the procedures are arranged in the following order on the stack:

1. Procedure main
2. Procedure PA
3. Procedure PB

4. Procedure PC
5. Procedure PD
6. The operating system's exception dispatcher
7. Procedure HB, which is the exception handler procedure
8. The operating system's exception dispatcher

The system will now start traversing the exception handler chain again. Exception handler HB could have registered an exception handler, which would be the first handler in the chain. If it had registered a handler, it would be called with the EH_NESTED_CALL flag clear.

The range of the nested exception is exception handlers HC and HB. The end of this range can be determined by the fact that exception handler HB is the currently active handler.

These exception handlers have already been given a chance to handle the original exception. They are now about to be called again in a nested range. Therefore, when handlers HC and HB are called again, they will be called with the EH_NESTED_CALL flag set. If they do not handle the exception, then exception handler HA will be called with the EH_NESTED_CALL flag clear, because it is outside the nested range.

Process Exit Lists

A process executes any routines registered in its exit list (with DosExitList) after the Process Termination exception has been delivered to each thread in the process and after each thread except Thread 1 has finally been terminated. If a thread handles the process termination exception, it must eventually voluntarily terminate, or the exit-list sequence will not finish running properly. Threads must not use DosCreateThread, DosExecPgm, DosStartSession, or DosExit when they are delivered a process termination exception.

Error Pop-Up Screens

Some error conditions, such as general protection violations, cause the operating system to display a pop-up screen containing information about the error. An application can use DosError to disable error pop-up screens. Typically, a Presentation Manager application would disable error pop-up screens if it sets up its own routines to handle errors that would ordinarily generate pop-up screens.

DosError is also used to control and disable *hard errors*, which usually have to do with reading from and writing to disks.

Exception Handler Interface

Exception handlers are passed four parameters. The interface for writing a 32-bit exception handler is:

```
ExceptionHandler (ExceptionReportRecord,
                  ExceptionRegistrationRecord,
                  ContextRecord,
                  DispatcherContext);
```

Figure 13-2. Exception Handler Interface

The exception handler returns XCPT_CONTINUE_EXECUTION to indicate that the exception has been handled and is to be dismissed, or XCPT_CONTINUE_SEARCH to indicate that the exception has not been handled and is to be passed to the next exception handler on the chain.

Note that there are no invalid exception numbers; if a handler does not recognize an exception number, it simply returns XCPT_CONTINUE_SEARCH.

In addition to handling exceptions, exception handlers are used in *unwind operations*. An unwind operation simply calls and removes exception handlers from the exception handler chain of the thread. Unwind exceptions are not actually being delivered to the handlers, so the individual return codes are irrelevant, and they do not affect the unwind operation.

A single exception handler can be used to handle all the exceptions that you choose to handle. It is not necessary to have a separate exception handler for each exception.

A handler is not required to return to the system; it can handle the exception, and then continue thread execution directly. For example, when an application executes a longjmp(), the C language compiler adds code that essentially performs an unwind operation to clean up the stack. Execution then resumes at the point where the target setjmp() occurred.

For synchronous exceptions, an exception handler can alter the contents of the interrupted thread's context, except for the fields that cannot normally be altered during thread execution. For asynchronous exceptions (signal and termination) changes made to the context of the thread are ignored.

Some exceptions are *continuable*; if the thread's exception handler handles the exception, execution can continue. If the exception condition is such that execution cannot be continued safely, the exception is said to be *noncontinuable*. If an exception is noncontinuable the EH_NONCONTINUABLE bit is set in the exception structure, and it is an error to indicate the exception has been handled. Returning XCPT_CONTINUE_EXECUTION causes an XCPT_NONCONTINUABLE_EXCEPTION exception to be raised.

Generally, exception handlers can use any function while they are handling an exception. However, while handling a process-termination exception, an exception handler must not call DosCreateThread, DosExecPgm, or DosStartSession, because unpredictable results can occur. A handler also must not call DosExit while handling a process-termination exception, because this request will cause the exception to be dispatched as a nested exception to the current thread's entire chain of handlers.

Exception Handler Parameters

ExceptionReportRecord (EXCEPTIONREPORTRECORD) - input/output
A pointer to the exception report record, which describes the exception and its parameters.

ExceptionRegistrationRecord (EXCEPTIONREGISTRATIONRECORD) - input/output

This is a microprocessor-specific value. For the 80386 microprocessor, this is a pointer to the exception registration record data structure that was used to register the current exception handler.

ContextRecord (CONTEXTRECORD) - input/output

A pointer to a context record, which describes the machine state at the time the exception occurred.

DispatcherContext (DISPATCHERCONTEXT) - output

A pointer to a reserved field that receives state information on nested exceptions and collided unwinds. This field returns information to either the exception dispatcher (in the case of nested exceptions) or to the unwind routine (in the case of collided unwinds). User code must not modify the DispatcherContext field at any time.

When the system's exception handler is called (it is already registered by the exception dispatcher), the exception handler returns NESTED and fills in the DispatcherContext field with the address of the ExceptionRegistrationRecord corresponding to the exception handler most recently called by the exception dispatcher. This indicates how far the exception dispatcher progressed through the call chain before the nesting occurred. The EH_NESTED_CALL bit is set in the ExceptionReportRecord flags field for each exception handler that is called between handler of the exception dispatcher and the establisher of the most recently called handler.

In the case of a collided unwind, the exception handler registered by the unwind dispatcher will return COLLIDED_UNWIND and the DispatcherContext field will contain a pointer to the target frame of the current unwind.

Exception Management Data Structures

Applications use three data structures for exception management (the DispatcherContext parameter is for system use).

- ExceptionReportRecord data structure
- ExceptionRegistrationRecord data structure
- ContextRecord data structure.

An overview of each of these data structures is presented below.

ExceptionReportRecord Data Structure

The ExceptionReportRecord data structure describes an exception and any additional parameters associated with the exception. The data structure contains fields for the following information:

- Exception number
- Exception flags, describing exception attributes
- A pointer to a nested exception report record, if any
- The address where the exception occurred
- Information for any additional parameters.

For descriptions of the system exceptions see the *Control Program Programming Reference*.

Following are the flags that are set to indicate exception attributes. Only the
EH_NONCONTINUABLE flag can be set (but not cleared) by the user. All other flags are set
by the system.

EH_NONCONTINUABLE (0x1)

The exception is not continuable, and any attempt to continue causes the exception
XCPT_NONCONTINUABLE_EXCEPTION to be raised.

EH_UNWINDING (0x2)

The ExceptionReportRecord data structure describes an exception for which an unwind is
in progress.

EH_EXIT_UNWIND (0x4)

An exit unwind operation implies that call frames are being unwound until the base of the
stack is reached. Note that EH_UNWINDING is also set.

EH_STACK_INVALID (0x8)

Following are causes for this flag to be set:

- The user stack exceeds the limits specified by the Thread Information Block.
  Applications can get the Thread Information Block by calling DosGetInfoBlocks.

- A call frame exceeds the stack limits specified by the Thread Information Block.

- A call frame is not aligned on the stack.

This flag is set only when the ExceptionReportRecord is passed to an associated
debugger. It is not possible to build exception information on the user's stack when the
stack is invalid.

EH_NESTED_CALL (0x10)

ExceptionReportRecord describes an exception raised while the current exception
handler was active. That is, a nested exception is in progress, and the current handler
was also called to handle the previous exception.

ExceptionReportRecord data structures can be chained together to provide additional
information when nested exceptions are raised.

ExceptionRegistrationRecord Data Structure

The application is responsible for the creation and registration of the
ExceptionRegistrationRecord data structure. This is the data structure used by the
application when it established the exception handler on the chain.

The only restrictions are that each pointer in the linked list must either point directly to the
next pointer in the list or contain END_OF_CHAIN (-1), and the field immediately following
the pointer field must be the pointer to the exception handler code. No fields other than
these two will be examined by the operating system. The application can keep any state
information that it chooses in this data structure, as long as it does not alter either of the
fields used by the system.

When a procedure begins, it must create an ExceptionRegistrationRecord on the stack, fill in
the pointer to the exception handler routine, and link the data structure to the front of the
exception handler chain by calling DosSetExceptionHandler.

Similarly, when the procedure ends, it must remove ExceptionRegistrationRecord from the chain by calling DosUnsetExceptionHandler. This maintains the necessary frame-exception handler correspondence.

Notes:

1. For the benefit of assembly language programmers, the Thread Information Block (TIB) is located at FS:[0]. This speeds access to the TIB data structure.

2. Because the FS is used to point to the TIB, applications that use the FS register must restore the original value when they are finished. Exception handling depends on the FS register pointing to the TIB.

3. ExceptionRegistrationRecord data structure must be created on the stack of the application. That is, it must be a data structure that is local to the routine that registers the exception handler. It cannot be stored in the application's data segment. The reason for this is that the operating system must be able to determine the relative ordering of ExceptionRegistration records by examining their addresses.

ContextRecord Data Structure

The ContextRecord data structure describes the machine state at the time of an exception. This data structure is hardware dependent and is not portable. Therefore, as a rule, software should not use the information contained in this data structure. However, hardware dependent code, such as math libraries, can make use of this information to optimize certain operations.

For a hardware-initiated exception, ContextRecord contains the complete machine state at the time of the exception. For a software-initiated exception, ContextRecord contains the machine state at the time the software raised the exception.

The ContextRecord data structure consists of fields for the following:

- General purpose registers
- Segment registers
- The flags register
- The floating point environment and stack.

Note: With asynchronous exceptions (signal and termination exceptions), the context in ContextRecord is read-only. The exception handler can modify it, but the changes with be ignored.

With synchronous exceptions, changes to ContextRecord will be used when the context is restored.

Exception Handler Return Values

Exception handlers can return one of the following values:

XCPT_CONTINUE_SEARCH (0x00000000)

Indicates that the exception has not been handled. The system responds by passing the exception to the previously installed handler in the thread's chain of exception handlers.

XCPT_CONTINUE_EXECUTION (0xFFFFFFFF)
> Indicates that the exception has been handled. The operating system responds by dismissing the exception, restoring the context of the thread, and continuing the execution of the thread.

Using Exception Management

When an exception occurs, the system default action in most cases is to end the application that caused the exception. Instead of having the system default action occur, an application can register its own exception handling routines. Exception handlers can be written to take corrective action so that a thread can continue running rather than being terminated by the system.

If an exception is handled by the application's exception handler, the exception handler must return XCPT_CONTINUE_EXECUTION. If the application's exception handler does not handle the exception, the exception handler must return XCPT_CONTINUE_SEARCH. If all the exception handlers in the exception handler chain return XCPT_CONTINUE_SEARCH, the operating system takes the default action, which is usually to terminate the process that caused the exception.

Note: In the example code fragments that follow, error checking was left out to conserve space. Applications should always check the return code that the functions return. Control Program functions return an APIRET value. A return code of 0 indicates success. If a non-zero value is returned, an error occurred.

Example Exception Handler

This section of the chapter will present a simple exception handler. Because exception handlers are commonly used to handle memory faults, the example will show the exception handler working with a memory fault.

Memory exceptions can occur when an application attempts to access a guard page, attempts to use memory that has been allocated but not committed (a sparse memory object), or when an application attempts to write to memory that has read-only access. Without an application-registered exception handler, some of these exceptions might cause the application to terminate. If the application registers its own exception handler, it can correct the cause of the memory fault and continue to run.

If the application's exception handler handles the exception, it returns XCPT_CONTINUE_EXECUTION. If the routine does not handle the exception, it returns XCPT_CONTINUE_SEARCH so that the exception will be passed to the next handler in the chain.

The following code fragment shows an exception handling routine set up to deal with memory errors:

```
#define INCL_BASE
#define INCL_DOSEXCEPTIONS
#include <os2.h>

#define HF_STDERR 2      /* Standard error handle */

ULONG _cdecl myHandler(PEXCEPTIONREPORTRECORD pERepRec,
                       PEXCEPTIONREGISTRATIONRECORD pERegRec,
                       PCONTEXTRECORD pCtxRec,
                       PVOID p)
{
    ULONG   cbWritten, ulMemSize, flMemAttrs;
    APIRET  rc;

    /* Access violation at a known location */
    if (pERepRec->ExceptionNum == XCPT_ACCESS_VIOLATION &&
        pERepRec->ExceptionAddress != (PVOID) XCPT_DATA_UNKNOWN) {

        /* Page fault */
        if ((pERepRec->ExceptionInfo[0] == XCPT_READ_ACCESS ||
             pERepRec->ExceptionInfo[0] == XCPT_WRITE_ACCESS) &&
             pERepRec->ExceptionInfo[1] != XCPT_DATA_UNKNOWN) {

            DosWrite(HF_STDERR, "\r\nPage Fault\r\n", 15, &cbWritten);

            /* Now query the memory to find out why we faulted. */
            ulMemSize = 1;

            DosQueryMem((PVOID) pERepRec->pExceptionInfo[1],
                        &ulMemSize, &flMemAttrs);

            /* If the memory is free or committed, */
            /* we have some other problem.         */
            /* If it is not free or not committed, commit it. */
            if (!(flMemAttrs & (PAG_FREE | PAG_COMMIT))) {
                DosWrite(HF_STDERR,
                         "\r\nAttempt to access uncommitted memory\r\n",
                         40, &cbWritten);

                rc = DosSetMem((PVOID) pERepRec->ExceptionInfo[1],
                               4096, PAG_DEFAULT | PAG_COMMIT);

                if (rc) {
                    DosWrite(HF_STDERR, "\r\nError committing memory\r\n",
                             27, &cbWritten);

                    return (XCPT_CONTINUE_SEARCH);
                }
                else
                    return (XCPT_CONTINUE_EXECUTION);
            }
        }
    }
    return (XCPT_CONTINUE_SEARCH);
}
```

Figure 13-3. Exception Handler for Memory Errors

Registering an Exception Handler

An application uses DosSetExceptionHandler to register its own exception handling routines. More than one routine can be registered; the last routine registered will be called first.

One or more exception handlers can be registered for each thread in a process. Moreover, exception handlers can be specified not only for system exceptions, but also for user-defined exceptions that are anticipated for a particular thread.

Only Process Termination exceptions are sent to all threads in a process. Other exceptions (synchronous exceptions) are sent only to the exception handler registered for the thread where the exception occurred. The application must register an exception handler for each thread that is handling exceptions.

The following code fragment shows how an application registers an exception handling routine:

```
#define INCL_BASE
#define INCL_DOSEXCEPTIONS
#include <os2.h>

ULONG _cdecl myHandler(PEXCEPTIONREPORTRECORD,
                       PEXCEPTIONREGISTRATIONRECORD,
                       PCONTEXTRECORD,
                       PVOID);

VOID main(VOID)
{
    EXCEPTIONREGISTRATIONRECORD xcpthand = { 0, &myHandler };

    DosError(FERR_DISABLEEXCEPTION | FERR_DISABLEHARDERR);

    DosSetExceptionHandler(&xcpthand);

    /*
      .
      . Other processing occurs here; myHandler will handle the exceptions.
      .
    */

    DosUnsetExceptionHandler(&xcpthand);
}
```

Figure 13-4. Registering an Exception Handler

If a procedure registers an exception handler, it must deregister the handler by calling DosUnsetExceptionHandler before returning.

Notes:

1. A procedure must not call DosSetExceptionHandler if it performs language-specific exception or unwind handling. This restriction is not enforced, but unpredictable results could occur if it is violated.

2. DosSetExceptionHandler and DosUnsetExceptionHandler provide the portable means of implementing exception handlers. The non-portable approach is taken by directly manipulating the exception handler chain. High level languages generate code that abides by this restriction. Assembly language programmers must assume responsibility for verifying that handler registration and deregistration occur correctly.

3. ExceptionRegistrationRecord must be created on the application's stack. That is, it must be local to the routine that registers the exception handler, rather than a global variable. It cannot be stored in the data segment of the program.

   Note that in the code fragment above, the declaration

   ```
   EXCEPTIONREGISTRATIONRECORD xcpthand = { 0, &myHandler };
   ```

   is placed inside the braces. Therefore *xcpthand* is local to the *main()* routine and is stored on the program's stack.

Summary

Following are the OS/2 functions and data structures used for exception handling.

Table 13-8. Exception Handling Functions	
Exception Handling Functions	
DosRaiseException	Raises an exception.
DosSetExceptionHandler	Registers an exception handler.
DosUnsetExceptionHandler	Deregisters an exception handler (removes it from the exception handler chain).
DosUnwindException	Calls and removes exception handlers from a thread's chain of exception handlers.
Signal Exception Functions	
DosAcknowledgeSignalException	Acknowledges a signal exception.
DosSendSignalException	Sends a keyboard signal (Ctrl+C or Ctrl+Break) exception.
DosSetSignalExceptionFocus	Sets keyboard signal focus.
Must-Complete Functions	
DosEnterMustComplete	Enters a must-complete section of code.
DosExitMustComplete	Exits a must-complete section of code.

Table 13-9. Exception Handling Data Structures	
Data Structure	**Description**
CONTEXTRECORD	Contains information about the machine's context at the time of the exception.
EXCEPTIONREGISTRATIONRECORD	Contains information about the exception handler. Used in registering the exception handler.
EXCEPTIONREPORTRECORD	Contains information about the exception that occurred.

Chapter 14. Device I/O

Devices used with computers include the keyboard, video display, mouse, floppy and fixed disk drives, and external systems, such as modems and printers. This chapter describes the OS/2 functions used to access and control such devices.

The following topics are related to the information in this chapter:

- File Systems
- File Names
- File Management
- Semaphores.

About Device I/O

The OS/2 operating system uses devices to communicate with the real world. A device is a piece of hardware used for input and output. The keyboard and screen are devices, as are serial and parallel ports. The computer's speaker, which can be made to beep using DosBeep, is a device.

Accessing Devices

OS/2 applications usually communicate with devices through the operating system. Some devices, like the screen, have their own set of supporting functions. Most other devices can be accessed by using the standard OS/2 file system functions—DosOpen, DosRead, DosWrite, and DosClose. Using the file system functions, an application can open and access the device just as it would a disk file. Using the file system also enables applications to redirect the device's I/O stream.

Sometimes however, these higher-level approaches do not suffice. For these situations, the operating system provides several functions that interface with devices at a lower level. DosDevConfig is used to retrieve information about the devices available. DosPhysicalDisk can be used to retrieve information about a partitionable hard disk. DosDevIOCtl is used to send device-specific commands directly to a particular device driver.

Device Names

To open a device using DosOpen, the application must supply the reserved name for that device. For example, to open the console (both keyboard and screen), you must specify the name CON.

14-1

The following table shows some of the common reserved device names:

Table 14-1. Common Device Names	
Device Name	**Description**
CON	The system console. This device consists of both the keyboard and the screen. You can open CON for reading (from the keyboard), writing (to the screen), or both.
COM1	Serial port 1. You can open this device for reading, writing, or both. Other serial ports will have names in ascending sequence—COM2, COM3, and so on.
PRN	The default printer port. This device corresponds to one of the system's parallel ports, usually LPT1. You can open it for writing but not for reading.
LPT1	Parallel port 1. You can open this device for writing but not for reading. Other parallel ports will have names in ascending sequence—LPT2, LPT3, and so on.
NUL	The null device. This device provides a method of discarding output. If you open this device for writing, any data written to the file is discarded. If you open the device for reading, any attempt to read from the file returns an end-of-file mark.
SCREEN$	The screen. This device can be written to but not read from. Writing to the screen is similar to writing to the system console. Bytes are displayed as characters (unless the ANSI screen driver is loaded and the character represents an ANSI escape sequence).
KBD$	The keyboard. This device can be read from but not written to. Reading from the keyboard is similar to reading from the system console.

After an application uses a device, it should close it by using DosClose.

Device Drivers

The operating system communicates with devices through special programs called *device drivers*. A device driver acts as an interface between the operating system, together with its applications, and a physical device such as the keyboard, mouse, or printer. The device driver sends data to and receives data from a device, resolving device-independent requests from applications with the device-specific attributes of the device.

The primary method of communication between the operating system and a device driver is request packets. The operating system receives I/O requests from applications and sends data in the form of request packets to the device driver. The device driver communicates with the device either directly or through the BIOS and ABIOS interfaces. (Applications can communicate with device drivers also, by using DosDevIOCtl. See "IOCtl Interface" on page 14-3)

Devices work differently depending on the device driver installed. For example, if an application writes to the system console, each byte is interpreted as a character and is displayed on the screen. If, however, the ANSI display driver is loaded, some byte sequences direct the system to carry out certain actions on the screen, such as moving the cursor or clearing the screen. These byte sequences are called ANSI *escape sequences*.

Some devices are available to applications only if the appropriate device driver is installed. For example, an application cannot open a serial port unless a communications device driver, such as COM.SYS, has been loaded by using a DEVICE= command in CONFIG.SYS.

IOCtl Interface

Many devices have more than one operating mode. For example, a serial port typically can operate at a variety of bit rates (sometimes called baud rates). Because the modes are unique to each device, the operating system does not include specific functions to set or retrieve these modes. Instead the operating system provides an I/O Control (IOCtl) interface to enable applications to control devices by communicating directly with the device driver.

The IOCtl interface is a method that an application or subsystem can use to send device-specific control commands to a device driver. The IOCtl interface function for OS/2 applications is DosDevIOCtl.

DosDevIOCtl provides a generic, expandable IOCtl facility. Applications send commands and data to the device driver with DosDevIOCtl. The OS/2 kernel reformats the generic IOCtl packets into request packets then calls the device driver. The device driver then carries out the specified action. IOCtl commands can be sent to both block and character device drivers.

Before using DosDevIOCtl, the application or subsystem must first obtain the device handle by calling DosOpen for the device name. The opened device handle is used to specify the device the command is to go to.

Refer to the *Control Program Programming Reference* for details of DosDevIOCtl.

IOCtl Commands

DosDevIOCtl has many subfunctions. These are called generic IOCtl commands and typically are used to retrieve data from a device driver that is not available through standard OS/2 functions. For example, an application can use these functions to set the bit rate of a serial port or read input directly from a sector on a disk.

Category and Function Codes

Each IOCtl function has a category and a function code. The category defines the type of device to be accessed. The operating system has several predefined categories. In general, all codes in the range 0x0000 through 0x007F are reserved for predefined categories. A device driver can use additional categories, but they must be explicitly defined by the device and be in the range 0x0080 through 0x00FF.

In each category, a function code defines the action to carry out, such as reading from or writing to the device and retrieving or setting the device modes. The number and meaning of each function code depend on the device driver and the specified category.

There is a listing of the IOCtl control functions, by category and function, with parameter and data packet structures, in the Generic IOCtl Commands chapter in the *Physical Device Driver Reference*.

Parameter and Data Packets

DosDevIOCtl uses a parameter packet and a data packet to pass information to and from the device driver. The packets can vary in format and length, depending on the IOCtl function. Simple functions might use only a single variable, while more complex functions might require a more complex data structure for the parameter packet, the data packet, or both.

There is a listing of the IOCtl control functions, by category and function, with parameter and data packet structures, in the Generic IOCtl Commands chapter in the *Physical Device Driver Reference*.

Using the File System to Access Devices

An application can use the OS/2 file system functions—DosOpen, DosRead, DosWrite, and DosClose—with the standard (predefined) devices. The application simply specifies the name of the device in the call to DosOpen, then uses the returned handle to read from and write to the device. When the application has finished using the device, the application should close the device handle by using DosClose.

The following code fragment shows how an application can open the COM1 device (serial port 1) and write the contents of a disk file to the communications port:

```
#define INCL_DOSFILEMGR    /* File System values */
#define INCL_DOSDEVIOCTL   /* DosDevIOCtl values */
#include <os2.h>

BYTE abBuf[512];
HFILE hfCom, hfFile;
ULONG ulAction, cbRead, cbWritten;

DosOpen("COM1", &hfCom, &ulAction, 0, FILE_NORMAL, FILE_OPEN,
        OPEN_ACCESS_READWRITE | OPEN_SHARE_DENYNONE, (PEAOP2) NULL);

DosOpen("testfile", &hfFile, &ulAction, 0, FILE_NORMAL, FILE_OPEN,
        OPEN_ACCESS_READONLY | OPEN_SHARE_DENYWRITE, (PEAOP2) NULL);

do {
    DosRead(hfFile, abBuf, sizeof(abBuf), &cbRead);
    DosWrite(hfCom, abBuf, cbRead, &cbWritten);
} while(cbRead);

DosClose(hfCom);

DosClose(hfFile);
```

Figure 14-1. Writing the Contents of a Disk File to the COM1 Serial Port

Note: In this example code fragment and the ones that follow, error checking was left out to conserve space. Applications should always check the return code that the functions return. Control Program functions return an APIRET value. A return code of 0 indicates success. If a non-zero value is returned, an error occurred.

Using IOCtl Functions to Access Devices

Many OS/2 functions communicate with devices. Usually, this communication is transparent to the application (the application has no knowledge of how the communication actually occurs). At times, however, an application requires more direct access to a device. To accommodate this need, the operating system furnishes DosDevIOCtl. Applications can use DosDevIOCtl to send commands and data to a device driver; the device driver interprets these commands and sends the appropriate instructions to the physical device.

As an example, some devices have several operating modes. A communications port can operate at one of a number of bit rates and have several data-word formats. The actual commands to set these parameters might vary, depending on the communications hardware.

Named constants have been defined for the categories, functions, and commands that are passed to a device driver, to make it easier for application programmers to use DosDevIOCtl. These named constants are defined in the file BSEDEV.H. This file must be included in your application when you use the constants. This file also contains data structure definitions for the parameter and data packets commonly used with DosDevIOCtl. The following examples use the communications port to demonstrate how DosDevIOCtl works

Setting Communications-Port Parameters

You can use DosDevIOCtl to control the data parameters (bit rate, stop bits, parity, and data bits) of a communications port and to get the status of the COM port. The IOCTL_ASYNC category is used for communications-port control. The ASYNC_SETBAUDRATE function sets the COM port transmission rate. The ASYNC_GETCOMMSTATUS returns the COM port status-byte.

Setting the Data Rate

The ASYNC_SETBAUDRATE function sets the bit rate of a communications port.

The following code fragment sets the bit rate of COM1 to 9600 bits per second:

```
#define INCL_DOSFILEMGR      /* File System values */
#define INCL_DOSDEVIOCTL     /* DosDevIOCtl values */
#include <os2.h>

HFILE   hf;                   /* File handle for the device            */
USHORT  usBPS = 9600;         /* Bit rate to set the COM port to       */
ULONG   ulParmLen = 2;        /* Maximum size of the parameter packet */
ULONG   ulAction;             /* Action taken by DosOpen               */
APIRET  rc;                   /* Return code                           */

rc = DosOpen("COM1", &hf, &ulAction, 0, FILE_NORMAL, FILE_OPEN,
             OPEN_ACCESS_READWRITE | OPEN_SHARE_DENYNONE, (PEAOP2) NULL);

rc = DosDevIOCtl(hf,              /* Device handle                    */
             IOCTL_ASYNC,         /* Serial-device control            */
             ASYNC_SETBAUDRATE,   /* Sets bit rate                    */
             (PULONG) &usBPS,     /* Points at bit rate               */
             sizeof(usBPS),       /* Maximum size of parameter list   */
             &ulParmLen,          /* Size of parameter packet         */
             NULL,                /* No data packet                   */
             0,                   /* Maximum size of data packet      */
             NULL);               /* Size of data packet              */
.
.    /* Use the COM port here. */
.

rc = DosClose(hf);
```

Figure 14-2. Setting COM1 to 9600 Bits Per Second

Getting the COM Port Transmission Status

The ASYNC_GETCOMMSTATUS function get the transmission status of the specified COM port. This function has no parameter packet.

The following code fragment uses the ASYNC_GETCOMMSTATUS function to get the transmission status of COM1:

```
#define INCL_DOSFILEMGR    /* File System values */
#define INCL_DOSDEVIOCTL   /* DosDevIOCtl values */
#include <os2.h>

HFILE   hf;          /* File handle for the device       */
UCHAR   ucStatus;    /* The COM port status byte          */
ULONG   ulStatusLen; /* Length of status (the data packet) */
ULONG   ulAction;    /* Action taken by DosOpen            */
APIRET  rc;          /* Return code                        */

rc = DosOpen("COM1", &hf, &ulAction, 0, FILE_NORMAL, FILE_OPEN,
             OPEN_ACCESS_READWRITE | OPEN_SHARE_DENYNONE, (PEAOP2) NULL);

rc = DosDevIOCtl(hf,                    /* Device handle                    */
             IOCTL_ASYNC,               /* Serial-device control            */
             ASYNC_GETCOMMSTATUS,       /* Get the COM status byte          */
             NULL,                      /* No parameter packet              */
             0,                         /* Maximum size of parameter packet */
             NULL,                      /* Length of parameter packet       */
             (PULONG) &ucStatus,        /* Data packet                      */
             sizeof(ucStatus),          /* Maximum size of data packet      */
             &ulStatusLen);             /* Length of data packet            */
 .
 .   /* Use the COM port here. */
 .

rc = DosClose(hf);
```

Figure 14-3. Getting the Transmission Status of COM1

Summary

Following are the OS/2 functions and data structures used for device I/O.

Table 14-2. Device I/O Functions	
DosBeep	Generates sound from the speaker
DosDevConfig	Returns information about an attached device, such as a printer or a floppy disk drive.
DosDevIOCtl	Performs control functions on a device that is specified by an opened device handle
DosPhysicalDisk	Obtains information about partitionable disks
File System Functions Used to Perform I/O to Devices	
DosClose	Closes a file or device.
DosOpen	Opens a file or device for I/O.
DosRead	Reads from a file or device.
DosWrite	Writes to a file or device.

Table 14-3. Device I/O Data Structures	
Data Structure	**Description**
LINECONTROL	Used to set the line characteristics of a COM port through the IOCtl interface.
BIOSPARAMETERBLOCK	Used to return information about a logical disk through the IOCtl interface.
TRACKLAYOUT	Used for reading and writing disk sectors through the IOCtl interface.

Chapter 15. Message Management

This chapter describes the use of message files to hold an application's text messages to the user. Keeping messages in a message file simplifies changing those messages, for example when maintaining versions of the same application for different countries.

The following topic is related to the information in this chapter:

National Language Support.

About Message Management

For full-screen applications, text messages—used by an application to display information to the user—can be held in a *message file*.

To keep and maintain messages in a message file, create a separate message file for each national language you intend to support. Use the MKMSGF utility program to create a binary version of a message file, and the MSGBIND utility program to bind the binary file to the application's executable file. Binding the messages to an application's executable file inserts the messages into the .EXE file. This enables faster access (but, of course, a larger .EXE file).

The OS/2 operating system provides several functions to assist in message management. Applications can get messages from a message file, substitute variable information into the messages, and write messages to the screen or to a file.

Code Page Considerations
You can have versions of the message file for each code page you choose to support. When you use MKMSGF to create the message files, the utility will insert the code page information and link together the message files of the different versions.

When message files are linked together in this manner, DosGetMessage will search for the appropriate version of the message for the code page that is active at the time the function is called. If there is no version of the message for the current code page, the function will return the first version of the message, no matter which code page it is associated with.

Using Message Management

DosGetMessage retrieves a message from the specified system message file, and inserts variable information into the body of the message.

DosInsertMessage inserts variable text-string information into the body of the message, but does not retrieve the message.

DosPutMessage sends the message in a buffer, usually to a display screen. DosPutMessage formats the screen buffer to prevent words from being split at the end of a line.

DosQueryMessageCp retrieves the message file list of code pages and language identifiers.

Note: In the example code fragments that follow, error checking was left out to conserve space. Applications should always check the return code that the functions return. Control Program functions return an APIRET value. A return code of 0 indicates success. If a non-zero value is returned, an error occurred.

Message Retrieval and String Substitution

DosGetMessage retrieves a message from a system message file, and inserts variable text-string information into the message.

In the following code fragment, the message file is "D:\MESSAGE\AUTOMSG.MSG". The third message within the message file contains the string "%1 Error at Station %2". The application calls DosGetMessage to convert this message into the string "Automation Failure Error at Station 69B".

```
#define INCL_DOSMISC   /* Miscellaneous values */
#include <os2.h>
#include <stdio.h>

UCHAR    *IvTable[2];    /* Table of variables to insert       */
ULONG     IvCount;       /* Number of variables                */
UCHAR     DataArea[80];  /* Message buffer (returned)          */
ULONG     DataLength;    /* Length of buffer                   */
ULONG     MsgNumber;     /* Number of the message              */
UCHAR     FileName[40];  /* Message file path-name string      */
ULONG     MsgLength;     /* Length of message (returned)       */
UCHAR     Field1[20];    /* String to substitute into variable */
                         /* field %1 of the message            */
UCHAR     Field2[20];    /* String to substitute into variable */
                         /* field %2 of the message            */
APIRET    rc;            /* Return code                        */

strcpy(Field1,"Automation Failure");   /* Define the field with which to */
                                       /* perform the first substitution */

strcpy(Field2,"69B");         /* Define the field with which to  */
                              /* perform the second substitution */

IvTable[0] = Field1;          /* Set up the array of pointers to */
IvTable[1] = Field2;          /* substitute strings              */

IvCount = 2;                  /* Two variable message fields in message */

DataLength = 80;              /* Data buffer that will receive the  */
                             /* complete message is 80 bytes in size */

MsgNumber = 3;                /* Specify the third message in the */
                             /* message file                     */

strcpy(FileName,"D:\\MESSAGE\\AUTOMSG.MSG");   /* Path name of the */
                                               /* message file    */

rc = DosGetMessage(IvTable, IvCount, DataArea, DataLength,
               MsgNumber, FileName, &MsgLength);

if (rc != 0) {
    printf("DosGetMessage error: return code = %ld", rc);
    return;
}
```

Figure 15-1. Retrieving a Message and Substituting Text-Strings for Variables

On successful return, the *DataArea* buffer contains the complete message (with the two variable fields appropriately updated), and the *MsgLength* variable contains the length of the message that was placed into the *DataArea* buffer.

If an error occurs (that is, if the return code does not equal 0), a message that is related to the error will be placed in the message buffer. See the DosGetMessage API reference in *Control Program Programming Reference* for a description of the default messages that can be placed into the user's buffer if an error occurs during the processing of these requests.

Text String Substitution in Memory

DosInsertMessage inserts variable text-string information into a message that resides within program memory.

In the following code fragment, the message resides in a program string variable named *Message*. The message is the string "%1 Error at Station %2". The application calls DosInsertMessage to convert this message into the string "Automation Failure Error at Station 69B".

```
#define INCL_DOSMISC   /* Miscellaneous values */
#include <os2.h>
#include <stdio.h>

UCHAR   *IvTable[2];              /* Table of variables to insert    */
ULONG   IvCount;                  /* Number of variables             */
UCHAR   MsgInput[40] = "%1 Error at Station %2";    /* The input message */
ULONG   MsgInLength;              /* Length of input message         */
UCHAR   DataArea[80];             /* Message buffer (returned)       */
ULONG   DataLength;               /* Length of updated message buffer */
ULONG   MsgLength;                /* Length of updated message (returned) */
UCHAR   Field1[20];               /* String to substitute into variable */
                                  /* field %1 of the message         */
UCHAR   Field2[20];               /* String to substitute into variable */
                                  /* field %2 of the message         */
APIRET  rc;                       /* Return code                     */

strcpy(Field1,"Automation Failure");   /* Define the field with which to */
                                       /* perform the first substitution */

strcpy(Field2,"69B");             /* Define the field with which to  */
                                  /* perform the second substitution */

IvTable[0] = Field1;              /* Set up the array of pointers to */
IvTable[1] = Field2;              /* substitute strings              */

IvCount = 2;                      /* Two variable message fields in  */
                                  /* message                         */

MsgInLength = strlen(MsgInput);   /* Length of input message         */

DataLength = 80;                  /* Data buffer that will receive   */
                                  /* the complete message is 80      */
                                  /* bytes in size                   */

rc = DosInsertMessage(IvTable, IvCount, MsgInput, MsgInLength,
                  DataArea, DataLength, &MsgLength);

if (rc != 0) {
    printf("DosInsertMessage error: return code = %ld", rc);
    return;
}
```

Figure 15-2. Substituting Text-Strings for Variables in a String in Memory

On successful return, the *DataArea* buffer contains the complete message (with the two variable fields appropriately updated), and the *MsgLength* variable contains the length of the message that was placed into the *DataArea* buffer.

If an error occurs (that is, if the return code does not equal 0), a message that is related to the error will be placed in the message buffer. See the DosGetMessage API reference in *Control Program Programming Reference* for a description of the default messages that can be placed into the user's buffer if an error occurs during the processing of these requests.

Writing Messages

DosPutMessage is used to write the message to the screen or to a file on a disk.

The following code fragment writes the message string contained in *MessageBuffer* to the file specified by *FileHandle*. The message string has already been placed in *MessageBuffer* using either DosGetMessage or DosInsertMessage. *MsgLength* was set to the length of the message string by the same call that put the message into *MessageBuffer*.

```
#define INCL_DOSMISC   /* Miscellaneous values */
#include <os2.h>
#include <stdio.h>


HFILE   FileHandle;        /* Handle of output file or device */
ULONG   MsgLength;         /* Length of message buffer        */
UCHAR   MessageBuffer[80]; /* Message buffer                  */
APIRET  rc;                /* Return code                     */

rc = DosPutMessage(FileHandle, MsgLength, MessageBuffer);

if (rc != 0) {
    printf("DosPutMessage error: return code = %ld", rc);
    return;
}
```

Figure 15-3. Writing an Edited Message to a File

To write a message to the screen, use the standard output file handle.

Code Page Information Associated with Message Files

DosQueryMessageCp obtains a list of code page identifiers and language identifiers that are associated with a specified message file.

In the following code fragment code page and language identifiers associated with the message file "D:\MESSAGE\AUTOMSG.MSG" are retrieved.

```
#define INCL_DOSMISC    /* Miscellaneous values */
#include <os2.h>
#include <stdio.h>

UCHAR   BufferArea[20];  /* Buffer for the returned list */
ULONG   BufferLength;    /* Length of the buffer area     */
UCHAR   FileName[40];    /* Message file path-name string */
ULONG   DataLength;      /* Length of the returned data   */
APIRET  rc;              /* Return code                   */

strcpy(FileName, "D:\\MESSAGE\\AUTOMSG.MSG");  /* Path name of message file */

BufferLength = 20;                             /* Length of buffer area     */

rc = DosQueryMessageCp(BufferArea, BufferLength, FileName,
                       &DataLength);

if (rc != 0) {
    printf("DosQueryMessageCp error: return code = %ld", rc);
    return;
}
```

Figure 15-4. Getting Code Page and Language Identifiers Associated with a Message File

On successful return, the *BufferArea* buffer contains a set of information concerning the code page identifiers and language identifiers that are associated with the message file.

Summary

Following are the OS/2 functions for message management.

Table 15-1. Message Management Functions

Function	Description
DosGetMessage	Retrieves a message from the specified system message file, and inserts variable information into the body of the message.
DosInsertMessage	Inserts variable text-string information into the body of a message.
DosPutMessage	Sends a message to an output file or device.
DosQueryMessageCp	Retrieves a message file list of code pages and language identifiers.

Chapter 16. National Language Support

Many applications need to be independent of a particular language. Rather than being hard-coded in English, they want to support, for example, an English version of the application, and a French version, and a German version; preferably without having to change the program code for each version. Meeting this requirement is simplified through the use of such resources as string tables, menu templates, dialog templates, accelerator tables, and through the use of code pages.

This chapter describes the functions an application uses to be *NLS enabled*, or language independent.

The following topic is related to the information in this chapter:

- Message Management.

About National Language Support

The support of national languages by applications requires the following considerations:

- Displayed text must be translated into the appropriate language.

- Symbols or icons might not convey the same meaning in all countries. Alternative designs for different countries might be necessary.

- Translation changes the length of text strings.

- Different languages often have different text characters.

The use of national language resource files can help with the first three items, and the ability of the application to receive input and display output in any ASCII code page can help with the last item.

The use of ASCII code page 850 avoids many of the problems in this area, since it contains most of the characters required for Latin-1 languages, which include much of Western Europe and North and South America. However, older programs use code page 437 for U.S. English, and code pages 860, 863, and 865 for various languages. The code page applies to both input and output data.

Note: Code page 850 was used for translating Presentation Manager text. Use code page 850 whenever possible for all Presentation Manager applications that might require translation.

National Language Resource Files

When creating an application, define national language dependencies in resources that are held in resource files separate from the program code. That is:

- Keep pure text strings in string tables.
- Keep menus in menu templates.
- Keep dialog boxes in dialog templates.
- Keep accelerators in accelerator tables.

The language displayed by the application can then be changed by translating the resources, in most cases without changing the application.

However, when translating from one language to another, the length of a text string can change substantially. For example, when translating from English to German, the length of a text string can double in length. Table 16-1 furnishes a general idea of the amount of expansion that can be expected during translation.

Table 16-1. Translation Expansion	
For English Phrases	**Translation Expansion Factors**
Up to 10 characters	101 - 200%
11 - 20 characters	81 - 100%
21 - 30 characters	61 - 80%
31 - 50 characters	41 - 60%
51 - 70 characters	31 - 40%
Over 70 characters	30%

When designing your dialog boxes and text string messages, add white space to allow for the expansion that will occur when the text is translated. You might have to adapt the application program to allow for the change in the length of text strings after they are translated. For example, a change in the length of a text string can cause it to become misaligned with other displayed objects.

You can also use the Dialog Box Editor to adjust for misalignments, or to change the size of the dialog box. This would enable you to leave your application program unchanged.

Text strings explicitly displayed by the application program are more of a problem. You will have to include program code that can handle text strings of varying length and format them at runtime according to their size.

Language-Specific Versions of NLS-Enabled Applications

There are two methods of creating a specific national language version of a program designed to handle more than one national language. The choice of the method depends on the amount of available disk space and whether the user wants to change between different languages once the program is installed. The two methods are:

- Statically link the resources to the application's .EXE files. The executable files are then language-specific and cannot be changed to another national language. The specific .EXE files are then sent to the user.

- Place the resources into a language-specific, dynamic link library. Designate one library file for each national language. Selecting a particular library file for use with the application gives the desired version of the program. Using this method, all national languages can be shipped with the product; selection of the national language occurs during installation (for example, by naming a specific .DLL file). It is possible to change the national language setting while the program is operating.

About Code Page Management

A code page is a table that defines how the characters in a language or group of languages are encoded. A specific value is given to each character in the code page. For example, in code page 850 the letter "ñ" (lowercase) is encoded as hex A4 (decimal 164), and the letter "Ñ" (uppercase) is encoded as hex A5 (decimal 165).

Code page management enables a user to select a code page for keyboard input, and screen and printer output before starting an application, a system command, or a utility program in the OS/2 multitasking environment.

This means that a user in a particular country, such as England (code page 850), Norway (code page 865), or a language region such as Canadian French (code page 863) can use a code page that defines an ASCII-based character set containing characters used by that particular country or language.

Installable code page files include keyboard translate tables, display character sets, printer character sets, and country/language information for each code page supported.

The code page tables are shown in the *Presentation Manager Programming Reference*. Check the tables to ensure that the code page you plan to use contains the characters that your application needs.

Of particular interest are two code pages:

- Code Page 850
- Code Page 437

Code Page 850 (CP850)
Code Page 850 is also called the Latin-1, multilingual code page. This code page supports the alphabetic characters of the Latin-1-based languages. It contains characters required by 13 languages used in approximately 40 countries.

CP850 also provides the flexibility to develop new applications based on non-Latin-based or special industry-based code pages.

Code Page 850 supports countries using the following languages:

Belgian French	Canadian French
Danish	Dutch
Finnish	Flemish
French	German
Italian	Norwegian
Portuguese	Spanish
LAD Spanish	Swedish
Swiss French	Swiss German
U.K. English	U.S. English

Code Page 437 (CP437)

Code Page 437 is the standard personal computer code page.

The lower 128 characters are based on the 7-bit ASCII code. The upper 128 characters contain characters from several European languages (including part of the Greek alphabet) and various graphic characters. However, some of the accented characters, such as those used in the Nordic countries, are not represented. The missing characters are available in other code pages (code page 850 will usually contain the desired characters).

Note: Some of the 256 symbols that can be displayed are printer control characters, and are not printed.

ASCII and EBCDIC Code Page Support

The two leading character-coding systems are ASCII and EBCDIC. Presentation Manager applications can use an EBCDIC code page instead of an ASCII code page. Code pages based on both systems are supported by the OS/2 operating system. Lists of the code pages supported, and tables showing the contents of the code pages, are in the *Presentation Manager Programming Reference*.

Any code page that either is defined in the CONFIG.SYS file, or is one of the EBCDIC code pages supported, can be selected.

Code Page Preparation

During system initialization, the code pages specified in the CODEPAGE statement are prepared to enable run-time code page switching of the display, the keyboard, the printer, and the country information. The display, keyboard, and printer must be defined in a DEVINFO statement in order to be prepared. Country information is prepared for the system country code specified in the COUNTRY statement.

If a resource cannot be prepared for the selected code page during system initialization, it is prepared for a default code page. The following are the defaults:

- A keyboard layout defaults to the code page of the translate table designated as the default layout in the KEYBOARD.DCP file. The default layout is based on the national code page of its associated country. You must explicitly specify KEYBOARD.DCP in the DEVINFO statement for the keyboard in CONFIG.SYS.

- The display defaults to the code page of ROM_0 for the device.

   (ROM_0 means a device default code page that is the device native code page or the lowest addressed ROM code page.)

- The printer defaults to the code page of ROM_0 for the device.

   (ROM_0 means a device default code page that is the device native code page or the lowest addressed ROM code page.)

- The country information defaults to the code page of the first entry found in the COUNTRY.SYS file for the country code. Each entry is the same information for a given country code, but is encoded in a different code page. The first entry is based on the preferred country code page.

If country information cannot be prepared at system initialization because it is not found in the COUNTRY.SYS file, for a code page selected with the CODEPAGE statement, then it is prepared (maintained for run-time code page switching in memory) in the default code page. Similarly, a keyboard layout is prepared in its default code page if it cannot be prepared in the selected code page, because it is not found in the KEYBOARD.DCP file.

COUNTRY.SYS contains one default entry per country code, and KEYBOARD.DCP contains one default entry per keyboard layout based on these assignments:

Code Page Functions

At the system level, the operating system switches the code pages of supported displays and printers to agree with the code page of the process sending the output. At the application level, OS/2 functions enable a process to control code page assignments.

Using Code Pages

The OS/2 operating system provides applications with several functions to obtain information about and manipulate code pages. These functions enable applications to determine and set the current code page.

OS/2 code page management functions enable applications to read keyboard input and write display and printer output for multiple processes using ASCII-based data encoded in different code pages.

The system switches to the required code page, for a code-page-supported device, before input or output.

Note: In the example code fragments that follow, error checking was left out to conserve space. Applications should always check the return code that the functions return. Control Program functions return an APIRET value. A return code of 0 indicates success. If a non-zero value is returned, an error occurred.

Querying Code Page Support and the Current Code Page

DosQueryCp is used to determine the code page of the current process and the prepared system code pages. The following code fragment shows how to get the current code page, and then up to three other prepared pages:

```
#define INCL_DOSNLS    /* National Language Support values */
#include <os2.h>

ULONG  CpList[8];
ULONG  CpSize;
APIRET rc;    /* Return code */

rc = DosQueryCp(sizeof(CpList),    /* Length of list        */
                CpList,            /* List                  */
                &CpSize);          /* Length of returned list */
```

Figure 16-1. Obtaining the Current Code Page and Other Prepared Code Pages

The required code page is the current code page of the process at the time it opens a device, or a specific code page selected by the process with a set-code-page function. A character set can also be specified for some devices, for example, for some printers.

The country functions retrieve country- and language-dependent information in the current code page of the calling process, or in a code page selected by the process.

Setting the Code Page for Text Characters

Each process has a code page tag maintained by the operating system. A *code page tag* is the identifier of the current code page for the process.

A child process inherits the code page tag of its parent. The default code page for the first process in a session is the same as the session code page. The default code page for a new session is the primary code page specified in the CODEPAGE configuration statement.

To change the code page tag of a process, call DosSetProcessCp. This will not change the process code page tag of its parent or any child process.

Obtaining the Case Map String

DosMapCase performs case mapping on a string of binary values that represent ASCII characters.

The case map that is used is the one in the country file that corresponds to the system country code or selected country code, and to the process code page or selected code page. The default name of the country file is COUNTRY.SYS.

Obtaining the DBCS Environment Vector

DosQueryDBCSEnv obtains a double-byte character set (DBCS) environment vector that resides in the country file. The default name of the country file is COUNTRY.SYS.

The vector corresponds to the system country code or selected country code, and to the process code page or selected code page.

The following code fragment shows how to use DosQueryDBCSEnv:

```
#define INCL_DOSNLS    /* National Language Support values */
#include <os2.h>
#include <stdio.h>

ULONG        Length;              /* Length of data area provided        */
COUNTRYCODE  Structure;           /* Input data structure                */
UCHAR        MemoryBuffer[12];    /* DBCS environmental vector (returned) */
APIRET       rc;                  /* Return code                         */

Length = 12;                      /* A length of 12 bytes is sufficient  */
                                  /* to contain the DBCS data returned   */

Structure.country = 0;            /* Use the default system country code */

Structure.codepage = 0;           /* Return DBSC information for the      */
                                  /* caller's current process code page  */

rc = DosQueryDBCSEnv(Length, &Structure, MemoryBuffer);

if (rc != 0) {
    printf("DosQueryDBCSEnv error: return code = %ld", rc);
    return;
}
```

Figure 16-2. Obtaining a DBCS Environmental Vector

On successful return, the buffer *MemoryBuffer* will contain the country dependent information for the DBCS environmental vector.

Instead of the single-byte character set (SBCS) representation used for Latin text, some Asian countries use code pages that consist of double-byte character set characters, in which each character is represented by a two-byte code. The DBCS code pages enable single-byte data, double-byte data, or mixed (single-byte and double-byte) data.

Obtaining Formatting Information

DosQueryCtryInfo obtains country dependent formatting information that resides in the country file. The default name of the country file is COUNTRY.SYS.

The information corresponds to the system country code or selected country code, and to the process code page or selected code page.

Obtaining Collating Information for SORT

DosQueryCollate obtains a collating sequence table (for characters 00H through FFH) from the country file. The default name of the country file is COUNTRY.SYS. The SORT utility program uses this table to sort text according to the collating sequence.

The collating table returned corresponds to the system country code or selected country code, and to the process code page or selected code page.

National Language Support and Code Page Management Summary

Following are the OS/2 functions used in National Language Support and Code Page Management.

Table 16-2. Code Page Management Functions	
Code Page Functions	
DosQueryCp	Returns the current code page and the prepared system code pages.
DosSetProcessCp	Sets the code page of a process.
Country Dependent Functions	
DosMapCase	Performs case mapping on a string of binary values that represent ASCII characters.
DosQueryCollate	Obtains a collating sequence table (for characters 00H through FFH) that resides in the country file.
DosQueryCtryInfo	Obtains country-dependent formatting information that resides in the country file.
DosQueryDBCSEnv	Obtains a DBCS environment vector that resides in the country file.
DosQueryMessageCp	Retrieves a message file list of code pages and language identifiers.

Table 16-3. Code Page Management Data Structures	
Data Structure	**Description**
COUNTRYCODE	Contains the country and code page.
COUNTRYINFO	Contains more detailed, complete, information than COUNTRYCODE.

Chapter 17. Debugging

Debugging is the process of detecting, diagnosing, and eliminating errors in programs. A debugger application is designed to interact with and control the application that it is debugging. Because of the protected mode architecture of the OS/2 operating system, special steps must be taken to enable a debugger application to perform its functions in the application being debugged (for example, to examine and manipulate memory locations in the address space of another process).

The following topic is related to the information in this chapter:

Program Execution and Control.

About Debugging

DosDebug enables one application to control the execution of another application for debugging purposes.

An application is selected for debugging when it is started. DosExecPgm and DosStartSession both have flags that can be used to specify that the application being started is to be controlled by the starting application.

DosExecPgm starts an application within a new process. DosStartSession starts a new session within which one or more processes can be executing. See DosStartSession and DosExecPgm in the *Control Program Programming Reference* for details on how to start an application for debugging purposes. For information on processes and sessions, see Chapter 7, "Program Execution Control" on page 7-1 in this book.

Once a process has been selected for debugging, DosDebug is used to control its execution and to examine and manipulate its variables.

DosDebug provides a full set of debugging commands, including execution control commands—like single stepping and setting watchpoints—and commands to examine and manipulate the memory and registers of the process being debugged. The debugger process can access specific threads within a process being debugged and specific processes within a session being debugged.

DosDebug also has a rich set of notification messages to keep the debugger application informed of activities occurring during the execution of the application being debugged.

The debugger application can use the session and process control functions described in Chapter 7, "Program Execution Control" on page 7-1 to control the child process or session being debugged. For example, the debugger can use DosSelectSession to switch itself, or the session being debugged, to the foreground.

Using the Debugging Function

DosDebug provides a set of commands that permit one process to control another process for debugging.

In the following code fragment, the calling process uses DosDebug to modify a word in a controlled process. All the necessary steps have already been taken so that the calling process controls the second process—the process identifier of the controlled process has been placed into *PID*, the address of the word to be modified in the controlled process has been placed into *Addr*, and the value to be substituted in the controlled process has been placed into *Value*.

(Due to the size of the *debug_buffer* data structure, the code fragment has been divided into two figures. If you were actually entering this into a program, the information would be together as if it were all one figure.)

Note: In the example code fragments that follow, error checking was left out to conserve space. Applications should always check the return code that the functions return. Control Program functions return an APIRET value. A return code of 0 indicates success. If a non-zero value is returned, an error occurred.

```
#define INCL_DOSPROCESS    /* Process and thread values */
#include <os2.h>
#include <stdio.h>

struct debug_buffer {
    ULONG   Pid;         /* Debuggee Process ID        */
    ULONG   Tid;         /* Debuggee Thread ID         */
    LONG    Cmd;         /* Command or Notification    */
    LONG    Value;       /* Generic Data Value         */
    ULONG   Addr;        /* Debuggee Address           */
    ULONG   Buffer;      /* Debugger Buffer Address    */
    ULONG   Len;         /* Length of Range            */
    ULONG   Index;       /* Generic Identifier Index   */
    ULONG   MTE;         /* Module Table Entry Handle  */
    ULONG   EAX;         /* Register Set               */
    ULONG   ECX;
    ULONG   EDX;
    ULONG   EBX;
    ULONG   ESP;
    ULONG   EBP;
    ULONG   ESI;
    ULONG   EDI;
    ULONG   EFlags;
    ULONG   EIP;
    ULONG   CSLim;       /* Byte Granular Limits       */
    ULONG   CSBase;      /* Byte Granular Base         */
    UCHAR   CSAcc;       /* Access Bytes               */
    UCHAR   CSAtr;       /* Attribute Bytes            */
    USHORT  CS;
    ULONG   DSLim;
    ULONG   DSBase;
    UCHAR   DSAcc;
    UCHAR   DSAtr;
    USHORT  DS;
    ULONG   ESLim;
    ULONG   ESBase;
    UCHAR   ESAcc;
    UCHAR   ESAtr;
    USHORT  ES;
    ULONG   FSLim;
    ULONG   FSBase;
    UCHAR   FSAcc;
    UCHAR   FSAtr;
    USHORT  FS;
    ULONG   GSLim;
    ULONG   GSBase;
    UCHAR   GSAcc;
    UCHAR   GSAtr;
    USHORT  GS;
    ULONG   SSLim;
    ULONG   SSBase;
    UCHAR   SSAcc;
    UCHAR   SSAtr;
    USHORT  SS;
};
```

Figure 17-1. The debug_buffer Data Structure

```
                struct  debug_buffer  DbgBuf;    /* Debug buffer                      */
                ULONG   PID;                     /* Process ID of the controlled process */
                ULONG   Addr;                    /* Address in the controlled process */
                LONG    Value;                   /* Value to be substituted in the    */
                                                 /* controlled process                */
                APIRET  rc;                      /* Return code                       */

                DbgBuf.Cmd = DBG_C_WriteMem;     /* Indicate that a Write Word        */
                                                 /* command is requested              */

                DbgBuf.Pid = PID;                /* Place PID of controlled process   */
                                                 /* into the debug buffer             */

                DbgBuf.Addr = Addr;              /* Place the word address (within the */
                                                 /* controlled process) into the debug */
                                                 /* buffer                            */

                DbgBuf.Value = Value;            /* Place the value to be updated into */
                                                 /* the specified word of the controlled */
                                                 /* process                           */

                rc = DosDebug(&DbgBuf);

                if (rc != 0) {
                   printf("DosDebug error: return code = %ld", rc);
                   return;
                }

                /* Be sure to check DbgBuf.Cmd for the notification returned by DosDebug */
```

Figure 17-2. Modifying a WORD in a Process Being Debugged

The *Cmd* field in the debug buffer is used for two purposes. On input, the *Cmd* field is used to pass the commands that direct DosDebug's activities. On output, the *Cmd* field is used by DosDebug to return a notification indicating the events and activities that occurred during the call.

If DosDebug returns no error, a notification resides in the *Cmd* field of the debug buffer. The data returned with the notification varies, depending on the command passed in the *Cmd* field of the debug buffer data structure when DosDebug was called.

Not all fields in the debug buffer have to be defined on every DosDebug command. The same field can have a different meaning in different DosDebug commands.

Some notifications (such as DBG_N_ModuleLoad and DBG_N_NewProc) might require multiple returns to the debugger. These additional, pending notifications will be returned before the process being debugged is permitted to execute any more user code, and will be returned on the Go, Single Step, or Stop commands.

Additional notifications can be pending at any time, so a debugger must be ready to handle any notification any time a Go, Single Step, or Stop command is called.

Summary

Following are the OS/2 functions used for debugging.

Table 17-1. Debugging Functions	
Function	**Description**
DosDebug	Used by one process to control another for debugging purposes.

Index

Special Characters

Numerics

A

E

functions

  device I/O data structure list 14-8

  DosAcknowledgeSignalException 13-9, 13-24

  DosAddMuxWaitSem 8-25, 8-26, 8-28

  DosAllocMem 6-6, 6-9, 6-10, 6-12, 6-14, 6-22, 10-7

  DosAllocMem (in code) 6-10, 6-11, 6-12, 6-14, 6-15

  DosAllocSharedMem 6-19, 6-20, 6-22, 10-5, 10-6

  DosAllocSharedMem (in code) 6-19, 6-20

  DosAsyncTimer 11-2, 11-3, 11-4, 11-5, 11-8

  DosAsyncTimer (in code) 11-5

  DosBeep 14-1, 14-8

  DosBeep (in code) 7-29, 7-38

  DosCallNPipe 9-5, 9-6, 9-23

  DosClose 4-14, 4-15, 4-24, 9-9, 9-23, 14-1, 14-2, 14-8

  DosClose (in code) 4-12, 4-13, 4-14, 4-15, 9-10, 9-15, 14-4, 14-6, 14-7

  DosCloseEventSem 8-6, 8-7, 8-8, 8-28

  DosCloseEventSem (in code) 8-8

  DosCloseMutexSem 8-13, 8-16, 8-17, 8-20, 8-25, 8-27, 8-28

  DosCloseMutexSem (in code) 8-15, 8-17

  DosCloseMuxWaitSem 8-21, 8-22, 8-28

  DosCloseQueue 10-3, 10-6, 10-13

  DosConnectNPipe 9-3, 9-4, 9-5, 9-6, 9-12, 9-15, 9-21, 9-23

  DosCopy 3-6, 3-8, 4-4, 4-5, 4-24

  DosCreateDir 4-2, 4-25, 5-15

  DosCreateEventSem 8-5, 8-6, 8-28, 9-7, 10-10, 10-12, 11-4, 11-5, 11-7

  DosCreateEventSem (in code) 8-6, 8-19, 11-5

  DosCreateMutexSem 8-12, 8-13, 8-14, 8-28

  DosCreateMutexSem (in code) 8-13

  DosCreateMuxWaitSem 8-18, 8-19, 8-20, 8-23, 8-28, 9-7

  DosCreateMuxWaitSem (in code) 8-19

  DosCreateNPipe 4-11, 9-3, 9-5, 9-11, 9-14, 9-16, 9-17, 9-19, 9-23

  DosCreateNPipe (in code) 9-12

  DosCreatePipe 9-2, 9-8, 9-9, 9-10, 9-23

  DosCreatePipe (in code) 9-8, 9-10

  DosCreateQueue 10-4, 10-7, 10-8, 10-10, 10-13

  DosCreateQueue (in code) 10-5

  DosCreateThread 7-4, 7-11, 7-27, 7-28, 7-34, 7-43, 13-15, 13-16

  DosCreateThread (in code) 7-29, 7-34, 7-37

  DosDebug 17-1, 17-2, 17-4, 17-5

functions *(continued)*

  DosDebug (in code) 17-4

  DosDelete 4-2, 4-5, 4-24

  DosDelete (in code) 12-3

  DosDeleteDir 4-2, 4-25

  DosDeleteMuxWaitSem 8-20, 8-21, 8-25, 8-26, 8-27, 8-28

  DosDevConfig 14-1, 14-8

  DosDevIOCtl 2-12, 4-11, 14-1, 14-2, 14-3, 14-5, 14-6, 14-8

  DosDevIOCtl (in code) 14-6, 14-7

  DosDisConnectNPipe 9-4, 9-6, 9-12, 9-15, 9-21, 9-23

  DosDisConnectNPipe (in code) 9-22

  DosDupHandle 4-4, 4-15, 4-23, 4-24, 9-9, 9-10, 9-15, 9-23

  DosDupHandle (in code) 4-23, 9-10

  DosEditName 3-6, 3-7, 3-8, 4-24

  DosEnterCritSec 7-13, 7-32, 7-33, 7-43

  DosEnterCritSec (in code) 7-33

  DosEnterMustComplete 13-11, 13-24

  DosEnumAttribute 4-24, 5-16, 5-17

  DosErrClass 12-1, 12-2, 12-4

  DosErrClass (in code) 12-3

  DosError 12-1, 12-2, 12-3, 12-4, 13-15

  DosError (in code) 12-3, 13-22

  DosExecPgm 3-9, 4-5, 4-11, 7-5, 7-17, 7-18, 7-19, 7-20, 7-23, 7-24, 7-27, 7-43, 9-1, 9-8, 9-10, 13-15, 13-16, 17-1

  DosExecPgm (in code) 7-18, 7-19, 7-20, 7-21, 7-22, 7-25, 7-36, 9-10

  DosExit 7-5, 7-6, 7-23, 7-27, 7-35, 7-36, 7-43, 13-4, 13-15, 13-16

  DosExit (in code) 7-19, 7-23, 7-26, 7-29, 7-36, 7-38, 9-15, 10-6

  DosExitCritSec 7-13, 7-32, 7-33, 7-43

  DosExitCritSec (in code) 7-33

  DosExitList 7-5, 7-7, 7-25, 7-26, 7-27, 7-35, 7-43, 13-15

  DosExitList (in code) 7-26

  DosExitMustComplete 13-11, 13-24

  DosFindClose 4-6, 4-20, 4-25

  DosFindClose (in code) 4-19

  DosFindFirst 3-3, 3-4, 3-5, 3-6, 3-7, 3-8, 4-6, 4-18, 4-19, 4-25, 5-2, 5-16, 5-20

  DosFindFirst (in code) 4-19

  DosFindNext 3-5, 3-7, 3-8, 4-6, 4-18, 4-19, 4-25, 5-2

  DosFindNext (in code) 4-19

  DosFreeMem 6-7, 6-14, 6-16, 6-18, 6-22, 7-9, 10-5, 10-6

X